613

The World of Rob Donn

The Watch Hill near Tongue, after the painting by John More.

The World of Rob Donn

by
Ian Grimble

THE EDINA PRESS
EDINBURGH

THE EDINA PRESS LTD.
1 ALBYN PLACE, EDINBURGH EH2 4NG

First published 1979

ISBN 0 905695 08 9

Printed in Scotland by
Howie and Seath Ltd., Edinburgh

Contents

To the Clan Mackay Society
which has done me the honour
of electing me its Honorary Member

Acknowledgements

It is difficult for me to express adequately my debt to Professor Derick S. Thomson and to Dr Annie M. Mackenzie, for the help they have given me over the Gaelic texts of Rob Donn, without appearing to shift the blame for shortcomings in the English translations in this book. I can only say that without their guidance I could scarcely have approached the task in the first place.

I would like also to acknowledge the years of help and encouragement I have received from Dr John Lorne Campbell of Canna in the field of Gaelic studies. Throughout this period, it has been my privilege to hear James C. M. Campbell interpreting the songs of Rob Donn (as of many other bards) in a manner that might inspire anyone to seek a greater understanding of his art. And in the country of Rob Donn I enjoyed the help and society of living kinsfolk of the bard who were able to lead me towards the same goal by yet another path. Among these were George (Geordie Hamish) Mackay in Invernaver and Magnus (Bain) Mackay in Kirtomy, George Mackay in Portskerra, and others who have left us, though recordings of their voices remain. Among the living, I would like to thank particularly Mr and Mrs Joseph Mackay in Talmine and Mr and Mrs Robert Mackay in Bettyhill for the years of friendship no less than for the enthusiasm in which I have received such lasting happiness. I also owe a special debt to Mrs G. Lindsay Smith, grand-daughter of Dr Hew Morrison, whose edition of Rob Donn's poetry I have cited for the most part in this book. Hew Morrison appears to have been the last scholar to use the lost diaries of the Reverend Murdo Macdonald, and Mrs Smith has placed at my disposal her grandfather's transcripts, from which the many unpublished excerpts in my text are taken.

Finally I wish to express my gratitude to the University of Aberdeen for the bursary which helped me to pursue these studies, and to the Scottish Arts Council for the generous grant that enabled me to complete them. In addition, I am indebted to the governors of Catherine McCaig's Trust for their financial help with publication.

I. G.

CHAPTER ONE

Early Years

ON 1st August 1714 Queen Anne, the last sovereign of the house of Stewart to reign in the British Isles, died and was succeeded by George I, of the dynasty of Hanover that has occupied the throne ever since. The following winter there was born in the most distant corner of his kingdom a child who, like his monarch, did not speak the English language. On the other hand, his native tongue was one that had been spoken in the British Isles long long before English had been heard here, and during the Dark Ages it had been the speech of men who had brought Christian civilisation to the savage tribes of King George's native Germany. The child's name was Robert Mackay, known throughout his life and ever after as Rob Donn.

> *I was born in the winter*
> *Among the lowering mountains,*
> *And my first sight of the world*
> *Snow and wind about my ears.*[1]

In the Outer Hebrides, where it rains for some part of seven days out of nine, the wind sometimes blows with incredible force but the snow rarely lies long if it falls at all. This extreme Atlantic climate, softened by the Gulf Stream, also envelops the west coast of the northern Highlands in its blanket. Here lay the western extremity of Rob Donn's world, an expanse of country extending from Cape Wrath to the borders of Assynt and containing the township of Eddrachillis. Here scattered communities lived along a deeply indented coast between its many offshore islands and the chain of barren mountains whose principal peaks are Foinaven and Arkle. In that soft, autumnal climate the Atlantic palm grows in its most northerly latitude and many Alpine plants flourish, while to the north of them this seaboard ends in the storm-swept cliffs of Cape Wrath.

1

Between the chain of mountains and this peninsula a pass led to the limestone oasis of Durness on the north coast and thence to the huge region of mountain, strath and sea-loch which was the world of Rob Donn. On its coast the force of the wind can be as fierce as in the Hebrides, but among the mountains the snow may lie long and deep during the winter in valleys where those gales cannot penetrate.

> *Wealthy deer and cattle country*
> *And most rich in corn,*
> *Land protected from the tempest,*
> *Sheltered from the storm.*[2]

East of the Foinaven-Arkle range of hills lies the wilderness still known as the Reay forest, not because it contains more than a few stunted birches in the valley bottoms, but because it was the deer-forest of the Mackay Chief, Lord Reay. A small winding valley called Strath Beg curls through it, boggy with the rainfall of the bare surrounding hills, which it pours into the southern end of Loch Eriboll. Beyond the tumble of hills to the east a larger valley called Strathmore lies beneath the terraced cliffs of Ben Hope. It was here that one of the sub-tenants on the estate of Lord Reay gave birth to Rob Donn during the white, stormy winter following the accession of George I to the throne of the newly United Kingdom in 1714.

No Gaelic-speaking society in the British Isles had preserved its immemorial way of life, affected less by external influences, than the one into which he had been born. To some extent this was due to its remoteness, for the Mackay country was the most distant part of the mainland from the Scottish capital: and even farther distant from London, which had so recently become the capital of a United Kingdom under the Anglo-Scottish Treaty of 1707. But the reasons were also political, because the Mackays had played a prominent part in the Revolution of 1688 which had deprived the last Stewart King of his throne. General Hugh Mackay of Scourie, a cousin of the Chief, had been King William's Commander-in-Chief in Scotland during the conflict by which he secured his father-in-law's crown: and although Lord Reay was then too young to play an equally active part, he stepped forward as an active supporter of the Pro-testant Succession in the Jacobite uprising of 1715, and his territories were consequently unaffected by the misfortunes which befell those who had fought on the losing side during these upheavals.

2

These territories were indeed somewhat diminished since the time when his ancestor had married a daughter of the Lord of the Isles in 1415, and had been described as the leader of four thousand fighting men.[3] Then the Chief had been recognised in state documents as proprietor of the entire province of Strathnaver, a land which extended all the way from its western seaboard between Assynt and Cape Wrath to the Caithness frontier in the east. Its underbelly was a chain of mountains and high moorlands which separated it from the earldom of Sutherland to the south, and it took its name from the principal river which flowed up its centre from Loch Naver to the sea—a name in all probability surviving from a lost prehistoric tongue, though some reconciled it with a Gaelic word which would make of Strathnaver a Valley of Giants.

The name of the earldom beyond was, by contrast, clear in its meaning for it had been the Southland of the Vikings as they sailed down from Norway, past Orkney and the inhospitable coast of Caithness to its level pastures and sandy beaches at the entrance to the Moray Firth. Here a Sutherland Clan had evolved under its Chiefs of that name, until, early in the sixteenth century, their earldom passed to a branch of the Gordons of Huntly in Aberdeenshire. Two centuries later this family had adopted the surname of Sutherland and had also secured the ownership of the central valley from which the province of Strathnaver derived its name.

Although diminished in this manner, the country in the Mackay Chief's possession was still of vast extent, and it contained the challenging features of topography that had bred a mountain race during so many centuries. Mountains, headlands and an unpredictable ocean separated one pocket of inhabitable land from another so that travel between them was an adventure. Looking over the flat, lush green strath in which he had been born, Rob Donn could not see the high cattle pastures above the cliffs of Ben Hope on one hand nor the deer forest beyond the crags opposite. To the south the ground rose too steeply to enable him to glimpse the bare uplands that marked the frontiers of Lord Reay's territory, and twists in the valley hid Loch Hope from view. It was an enclosed, autonomous world in which the bard first saw the light of day. Yet it was intricately connected with all the other scattered townships of the Mackay country, and the binding link which dominated their fortunes was a genealogical one.

The very name Clan (the Gaelic word for children) presupposes that all its members descend from one or another of its Chiefs, but in each generation it was the sons of the reigning Chief who enjoyed

3

the most immediate access to any available leases of clan property. his daughters to a dowry paid out of his rents. The solvency of a chiefship might depend as much on the size of families in each successive generation as upon such accidents as the weather, the price of cattle or distant politics. When the first Lord Reay succeeded to the chiefship in 1614, both ends of Strathnaver had already passed to his father's brothers, never to be recovered by the senior line. Scourie in the far west had been alienated to the sept which gave William of Orange his Scottish general in the Revolution of 1688: had he not died in battle he would have been created Earl of Scourie.[4] On the Caithness border to the east, Strath Halladale was held by the branch that became known as the Mackays of Bighouse. Most curiously, this English word for the Tigh Mór had passed into Gaelic by Rob Donn's time, so that he referred to the Laird of Bighouse as Fear Bhiogais.

In the next generation, the first Lord's younger brother received the estate of Strathy immediately to the west of the Bighouse property, and one of the first Lord's sons was given the patrimony of Melness by the Kyle of Tongue, another the comparatively barren lands of Sandwood north of Scourie in the far west.[5] Thus the resources of the chiefship had shrunk considerably by the time the second Lord Reay followed his eldest son to the grave in 1680, leaving two others who supported themselves by military service abroad, four daughters for whom doweries would have to be found, and an infant grandson who would provide a much-needed respite while he grew up. This period coincided with the Revolution of 1688 and the Jacobite uprising of 1715, through which the Mackays passed unscathed, but it was over by the time Rob Donn was passing his childhood in Strathmore.

The third Lord Reay, Chief of Mackay during the greater part of Rob Donn's lifetime, enjoyed that office for no less than sixty-eight years and was remembered as Am Morair Mór, The Great Lord. He lived by the Kyle of Tongue, about twelve mountainous miles north-east of Rob Donn's native strath, in an unfortified mansion house that had been rebuilt in 1678 after it was destroyed during Oliver Cromwell's reign. It still stands beside the waters of the Kyle with the wing that the third Lord added at right-angles to the original building, though the contents associated with the Mackay chiefship have vanished from it long since. Nearby the church erected by the first Lord Reay still serves the parish of Tongue, and remains one of the most attractive post-Reformation churches on the north coast of Scotland although regrettably its fine seventeenth

4

century laird's loft has been removed. These elegant seats of religious and secular authority stand, as Rob Donn saw them, in one of the most spectacular settings of the Scottish Highlands. To the south the sheer precipice of Ben Loyal rises above the green farmlands of Ribigill and from here an escarpment runs into the Kyle with the ruined tower of Castle Bharraich on its northernmost outcrop above the water. It is of unknown antiquity and possesses no history. The former castle of the Chiefs stood on a promontory of Farr Point to the east until it was destroyed by the Gordons of Sutherland in 1554.[6] Beyond Castle Bharraich stood the home of the cadet branch of the Mackays of Melness, near to the narrows of the Kyle where the ferry crossed the shallow tidal water between Tongue and Melness. The little houses of the lesser folk were scattered along the widening shores until they curved out of sight and reached the cliffs against which the Atlantic waves pounded.

This huge amphitheatre was called Kintail Mackay, to distinguish it from Kintail Mackenzie in Wester Ross. Rob Donn pronounced it the jewel of the Mackay country when he declared that he nevertheless preferred the deep glen that wound into the Reay forest behind his home.

> *Even if I received for my delight*
> *Kintail Mackay,*
> *I would far rather dwell*
> *In Glengolly with its trees.*[7]

Second in magnificence to the seat of the Chief at Tongue stood his mansion in the far west, beside the white sands of Balnakil bay and the green pastures of Durness. This ancient manor farm had been inhabited by the second Lord Reay while Tongue house was being rebuilt, and it was used besides as a hunting lodge for expeditions to the Reay forest, as a granary for the Chief's western estates, and as the residence of his heir. Like Tongue house it remains exactly as Rob Donn saw it, though it has also lost all its eighteenth century furnishings. The church beside it, which was completed in 1619 and resembles that of Tongue, is a forlorn ruin beside the parabola of sand that runs out to the headland called Farout or the Fair Aird.

The third Lord Reay married a daughter of General Hugh Mackay of Scourie and their son Donald, Master of Reay, went to live at Balnakil after his own marriage in 1732. When his mother died, leaving him sole heir, the third Lord took as his second wife Janet

5

Sinclair from Ulbster in Caithness, so that his second son Hugh possessed a different family connection with the society to the east of Strathnaver where Gaelic was not spoken. The problem of Hugh's patrimony was solved for him in 1721 when the heir to the estate of Bighouse in Strath Halladale on the Caithness border died, leaving only two sisters as co-heiresses.[8]

The Great Lord immediately made approaches to their widowed mother Katherine, Dowager Lady Bighouse, who agreed to send Elizabeth, the elder of the little girls, to live in Tongue house until she should be old enough to marry the Chief's son Hugh. She also gave him custody of the title-deeds of Bighouse to which Hugh would become heir, under an arrangement that protected her own rights in her late husband's estate. It was a convenient one for her since it relieved her of much responsibility while she enjoyed a second affluent marriage with an advocate, Robert Sinclair of Giese in Caithness. But it gave scant protection to the rights of her younger daughter Janet, who presently found a champion. The Chief's son Hugh had already been married at the age of seventeen or eighteen to Elizabeth when his young cousin William Mackay of Melness, on the farther shore of the Kyle of Tongue, returned from military service in the Netherlands, wed Janet in 1727, and laid claim to her share of the inheritance.[9]

The fracas that followed was still the talk of the neighbourhood years later when Alexander Sage came to Tongue as the schoolmaster and heard it. William of Melness, a great-grandson of the first Lord Reay, demanded to see the title-deeds of Bighouse and was refused. 'Being a man of as much resolution as he was hot and choleric, he resolved not tamely to submit to the injustice. Having ascertained that his Chief was at home, Melness armed himself with his claymore, secured by a strong leathern belt round his loins, to which was added a pair of loaded pistols. Thus accoutred, Melness crossed the ferry below Tongue, and directed his course to the residence of his Chief." When he had been admitted to the parlour he locked the door and ordered Lord Reay to surrender the titles: Reay agreed to do so and left the room. "His lordship, however, had no sooner put a strong door doubly bolted and a double pair of stairs between himself and his kinsman, than he took other measures. Opening a window, he called to his footman . . . to request Mr Mackay of Melness, whom he would find in the parlour, to come out and speak to him. The message was delivered, and on Melness making his appearance in the close, Lord Reay called from the window, "William, go home and compose yourself; the papers you'll never handle." [10] And neither did he, although the dispute rumbled on throughout the lifetime of Rob Donn. The Chief's son Hugh lived and died Laird of Bighouse.

When Hugh's Sinclair mother died, Lord Reay entered into a third marriage in 1713 with Mary Dowell, the daughter of a Writer to the Signet in Edinburgh, and it proved an expensive one for his estate. Under the marriage contract he bound himself to pay her an annuity of £1,200 Scots out of the rents of the baronies of Tongue, West Moine and Durness and 30,000 merks for the children. Hitherto he had begotten only two sons and one daughter from two marriages, but this time his wife presented him with two sons and four daughters.[11] She died economically before her husband (who refrained from marrying a fourth time), but three of their daughters remained unmarried, and one of these lived until 1812.

Upon his third son George the Chief settled the property of Strathmore, in which Rob Donn had been born, by a form of long lease known as a wadset.[12] But his fourth son Alexander had to be content with the purchase of a commission in the army, of which he made such use however that he rose to be Commander-in-Chief of the forces in Scotland and Governor of Stirling Castle.[13]

As it happened, the three principal houses of the Mackay country were well able to bear their family burdens at the time when Rob Donn first cast his critical and perceptive eyes upon them. The Scourie branch was still supported by the emoluments of the Dutch military service: Bighouse had been left to young co-heiresses and a widow who was a shrewd and provident business-woman: the chief-ship had been nursed through a long minority by competent trustees. It was among the cadet families of the Chief's house that the pressure on local resources was most apparent, and particularly that of Sandwood between Cape Wrath and Scourie. Here lived one of the last two surviving grandsons of the first Lord Reay, Robert Mackay.

He was known as the Tutor of Farr, because his elder brother had obtained from the Earl of Sutherland a wadset of Farr, Swordly and Kirtomy in 1719 and then died, leaving Robert the curator of his three children.[14] Rob Donn referred always to Robert of Sandwood as The Tutor. He married twice and fathered sixteen children, and what is most remarkable is that all of his eight daughters found a husband although they could scarcely have been well-dowered. It is significant that four of his sons embraced army careers, while one became a planter in Jamaica and another a surgeon. Of the

7

remainder, the Tutor's eldest son died in his youth, to be commemorated in Rob Donn's earliest dateable elegy;[15] the other married the richest heiress in Strathnaver. While the attractions of his sisters can only be guessed, the assets of the Tutor's fortunate son were proclaimed by Rob Donn long before he won his prize.

> *I thought it no whim on my part*
> *To say that his step was handsome.*
> *Those who know him well said*
> *As he made his rounds in their presence,*
> *"He is without a woman to care for him—*
> *Heavens, what a great shame."*[16]

But there was another cadet of the Chief's house who married no heiress, inherited no patrimony, yet did not leave the country to seek his fortune. He descended from the first Lord Reay's brother John, who had been settled in Strathy, neighbouring Strath Halladale. John of Strathy's younger son John obtained a wadset of Skerray, a bowl of arable land surrounded by rocks between Tongue and the long bay of Torrisdale that runs to the mouth of the Naver river. John of Skerray's son Hector had a second son once again named John, whom Rob Donn designated always by the pedigree which was his sole inheritance—Iain Mac Eachainn 'Ic Iain.[17] But it was an asset of sorts to be the third cousin of Lord Reay, and Iain Mac Eachainn built upon it with the utmost energy and success.

The opportunity which launched him on his career was provided by the wadset of Strathmore that the Chief bestowed on his infant son George, in the barony of West Moine whose rents contributed to the annuity of the third Lady Reay under the terms of her marriage settlement. This barony possessed the rich salmon resources of the River Hope, while Strathmore lay between the immense deer preserves of the Reay forest and the high cattle pastures south of Ben Hope. In the early 1720s Iain Mac Eachainn went to live at Muisel in Strathmore as a manager of the cattle trade and of the deer hunts, though he does not appear to have been given any responsibility for the fishings.[18] As soon as the Chief's son Hugh was old enough to marry the heiress of Bighouse and to play a part in estate management, he was sent to join Iain Mac Eachainn in his activities; to serve an apprenticeship before he moved to his wife's property in Strath Halladale. Presently these two young men were joined by a third, when Iain Mac Eachainn heard of the precocious sub-tenant's son in Strathmore who had been expressing himself in witty verses since his infancy, and took Rob Donn into his household as a herd-boy.

It can only be presumed that Iain Mac Eachainn had already married by the time he settled at Muisel. His wife Catherine was the daughter of William Mackay who had once enjoyed the wadset of Strathan Melness, an inconsiderable property on the eastern side of the Moine headland that he had conveyed to his son John in 1719, who renounced it altogether in 1726.[19] The father was still living twenty years later,[20] and at some time after John had lost his title to Strathan Melness, Rob Donn addressed him in terms which suggest that he may have been dishonest as well as incompetent.

> John, son of William in Strathan,
> The end of your days may be bitter
> Although this weather is so calm
> That no one challenges you over the
>   price of the bull.
> People in favour have been ruined—
> All who were in office between Rispond
>   and Cape Wrath.
> The man who comes with great respect
> Will receive a hundred thousand curses
>   when he departs.[21]

This was not a sentiment likely to recommend Rob Donn to his master's wife at Muisel, but as he remarked on another occasion:

> The mere inducement of flattery
> Or caution through fear of danger
> Never was nor will be
> The basis for the opinions in my poetry.[22]

The ruins of a long-house beside the road through Strathmore at Muisel may be those of the household into which Rob Donn was received as a youth. Others of a similar structure can be seen in the ruined township of Rossal near Syre in the Naver valley, preserved as a historical monument. These long-houses were generally about a hundred feet long, with walls built to a height of about three feet above their foundations, the wooden joists that supported the roof embedded in them. The upper part of the walls, which might rise to a height of ten feet, was often of turf, and the roof was thatched with heather. At the upper end of the long-house was a room called the "chamber", with chimney and glazed window and a tent-bed in the partition that divided it from the next room. Here the family sat and also took their meals, while the bed was set aside for the use of guests.

The chamber opened into a second room in which the children slept, and this led to the bedroom of the parents. Beyond it lay the servants' hall, a room longer than the others that was called the *Ceàrn* in Gaelic. It possessed cross-lights in the form of small boarded windows on either side, and the fireplace often consisted of an old mill-stone in the centre of the room. The smoke from the peat fire that burned on it ascended to a hole in the roof through a funnel of wicker-work open at both ends, suspended from the ceiling. Here the youthful Rob Donn sat among the servants, joined often by Iain Mac Eachainn's young children and sometimes by their parents also. Only a slender partition divided them from the byre which occupied almost half of the total length of the long-house, a place that Rob Donn learned to detest, for he loved to be out in the hills with the cattle or taking part in the deer hunt.[23] "What torment I suffer all the year round in the byre," he complained.

> When the fodder is taken home
> And carried in for the cattle,
> Herself will be examining it
> At the first opportunity.
> If there should be a sheaf unthreshed
> What a rage she will fly into,
> And I will be for it
> If the bolls do not increase in number.
>
> If a grain of it is destroyed,
> Even what a small mouse would take
>   into a wattle-wall,
> She says angrily
> That some of her corn is missing.
> I and my captain will be
> Bickering bitterly,
> And though I only got a furlough
> I would gladly leave her.

When she makes an inventory
Of all the plough reins and tethers
It's up to me to remember
To look after all those ropes.
When she launched an attack on me
As I was sitting in a chair
I was filled with alarm
And I fled from her din.

But if autumn would come
I would not be wielding the flail.
There would be no concern about commerce,
Even if there weren't a bannock in the land.
There would not be a step between the Grey Hill:
And the waterfall in Dougall's Corrie
That I wouldn't be at liberty to follow . . .[24]

Not for Rob Donn the indoor occupations of the womenfolk: and
he developed a touching affection for Iain Mac Eachainn's daughter
Isabel, who shared his delight in the high Sàl pastures that lay to the
south of Ben Hope and in the wonders of nature amongst its
terraced cliffs. Once he depicted her, defending this environment
against her sister Mary, who had returned from her school at Thurso
in Caithness with some superior notions about rustic life in Strathmore. Rob Donn's poem opens with Mary's complaints.

Anyone doing as I have done
Would be eternally the worse for it,
Going to the mountain against my will
To the ruin of my health.
Part of my grievance is the Merkin Byre,
It is a place without a market
But spoons and coppers and open byre
And grain chaff on the floor.

It appears that there was a sort of mart here, which did not compare favourably with those of Thurso. The remains of Merkin wood
can still be seen about three miles north of the ruins of Iain Mac
Eachainn's house at Muisel, and there are a Merkin Craig and stream
about half-way along the eastern shore of Loch Hope. Isabel's
defence against her sister's attack on these surroundings makes a

11

pun of the word cairn and of the name for the servants' hall in their home, the smoky and convivial Ceàrn.

> The King of Britain has no chamber
> More delightful than the Cairn is to me
> For it is private for young girls
> And there are sounds there when you desire them;
> Grass and trees, blossom and leaf,
> And many hues upon them,
> And birds and echo like harp strings
> Playing the loveliest airs.

Rob Donn has given the word *echo* in English, not to the disdainful Mary from English-speaking Thurso, but to Isabel; as if to show that although she defends the simple life of his strath, she is just as well-educated as her sister. There are few English words in Rob Donn's poetry, since he never learned to speak that language, but he made what use he could of those that came his way. Mary he represented as clinging inflexibly to an attitude that was in fact generally held throughout metropolitan Britain at this time. The Romantic Movement had not yet promoted the notion that Rob Donn's world was Sublime, and it was more commonly dismissed as Horrid.

> It was not a congenial place for me on Sunday
> To be in a cave or a cairn,
> For unless there was a badger in it
>   during the year
> There was never anything better.
> Sounds of the mountain and gloom of the glen—
> The din is hateful to us.
> O torment of my heart, raging flood
> In the place where the grass is thickest!

Isabel protests:

> What reason have you for your antipathy
> To the high slopes?
> Do you not see how useful they are
> When the cattle arrive with their young?
> It is no hardship to sit in a spot
> In the roar of the full flood
> Hurtling in its course opposite you,
> Its favourite grass growing.

12

Mary's case is strongest when she refers to the long winter of those northern latitudes, and the lad who had come into a world of snow and wind did not duck this issue.

> *What is true in your song*
> *For as long as the warmth of summer lasts*
> *Will fade at Halloween,*
> *And winter will come to extinguish it.*
> *The foliage of the tree-tops*
> *Has turned to russet*
> *And the face of the strath has lost its hue*
> *With the onset of ground-drift.*

Isabel could not have heard anyone ask the question "When winter comes, can spring be far behind?" But according to the youthful Rob Donn, she had given the matter some thought.

> *The land will bide until summer;*
> *It is hibernating now.*
> *Birch and hazel on the day of Beltane*
> *Will be the harbingers of growth.*
> *There will be curds and churning in the straths*
> *And melting of the snow-drifts,*
> *And how sweet the spectacle, beautiful*
> * the increase*
> *Of calves and milk and cream.*

It is typical of Rob Donn's art that he should have given Mary the last word, with scarcely a hint that her attitude was detestable in his eyes, particularly her contempt for that centre of his social and cultural life, the *ceàrn* of the tacksman's long-house.

> *It is my own opinion that you have a deficit*
> *In your cheese-making.*
> *If your hills were left without sowing,*
> * without harrowing,*
> *Then there would be no produce.*
> *The Lowlands are manifestly preferable*
> *To the company of a rabble*
> *With the smoke of the fire blinding me*
> *Beside a divot wall.*[25]

Whatever the nature of Rob Donn's feelings for Isabel, the cattleman could never have courted the tacksman's daughter. It was in other directions that he cast his roving eyes, as a poem describes which he composed during one of the droving expeditions on which he accompanied Iain Mac Eachainn and Hugh of Bighouse to the cattle fair at Crieff in Perthshire. Remaining in the tacksman's employment as he grew to manhood, this became another of his tasks, and almost as enjoyable a one as playing a part in the great deer hunts, taking him to distant places and into every variety of company. A Lowland landlord, James Ramsay of Ochtertyre, who was twenty years younger than Rob Donn, described the driving of the cattle to the southern sales as he witnessed this central activity of the northern economy. "Fairs may be classed among Highland diversions, being formerly attended by people of every rank. Though business was transacted at them, and every article bought which the country did not afford, yet pleasure and the hopes of meeting their friends and acquaintances were the true errands of most of the company."[26] But the youthful drover was disturbed by night thoughts of the girl he had left at home, and of the other young men who might be trying to court her: and anon his mind filled with the rival delights of the deer forest.

> Although my bed is comfortable
> Sleep does not come my way.
> Often my thoughts steal
> On the wind towards the northern
> Highlands.
> How much better I should prefer to
> be beside you
> In the glens of the calves
> Than to be counting the Sàl cattle
> In the parks of Crieff.

Rob Donn had heard the excellent air known as *Logie of Buchan*, and had set his jumbled thoughts, so characteristic of a mind half-awake, to its melody.

> Dear to me is the path to the deer forests
> Although I am in the woods on a bare board
> Between sheep thickets
> And heather slopes
> And the brindled stags
> In the spring of the year when they are young;
> And beneath the peaks of the crags—
> Freely I made my bed there.

14

Deep are my feelings for the lass
Who lives beyond the bard,
Who is to be found of an evening in the fold
When the cattle return from every airt.
Indeed I had no aversion for you,
Far distant though I am from you now.
Often I lost my sleep on account of you
And great was the reward of your kiss.

Son of the Williamsons, since that time
You had plenty of privacy
And you close to the girl
While she was reaping hay—
Though you were caught in her company
I wouldn't worry about you,
Since you've become so polite
That you wouldn't have uttered a word.
Young stalwart on your way home
Without any regret over my absence,
Even if I were to remain in this town
Until ploughing-time comes,
Young Angus of the Alasdairs,
Keep your distance
And don't put any hindrance on our association
After all the promises between us.[27]

At the time when Rob Donn was assessing the prowess of his
rivals in this way, he had grown into a young man whom a contemporary remembered as "brown-haired, brown-eyed, rather pale-
complexioned, clear-skinned and I would say good-looking. When
he entered a room his eye caught the whole at a glance, and the
expression of his countenance always indicated much animation and
energy. In figure he was rather below middle size, stout and well-
formed according to his size."[28] Another observer disagreed as to
whether he was handsome, generally a matter of somewhat personal
taste. "He was of low stature and by no means a good-looking man,
though remarkable for a lively and expressive countenance, and

15

great activity."[29]   Rob Donn referred at least twice to his low stature.

> *Do you not see the effect of the cattle on Rob Donn?*
> *He was a moderately upstanding man before he came*
>   *here.*
> *Do not you see him now?   He is no taller than a kid.*
> *The ashes of the hearth-stone have matted his hair.*[30]

On another occasion he demonstrated his gift for packing two meanings into a single succinct phrase as he commented on how little he stood to lose if he were to be prosecuted by the law. "It is not far from my chin to the ground."   Such was the intelligent, extrovert, thick-set youth with the penetrating glance whom Iain Mac Eachainn had nurtured to manhood in his home, introduced to the gentry of his clan, and taken into the larger world beyond the barony of West Moine.   He was attractive enough to the women who naturally filled his thoughts at this age, for he understood them and there was vitality in his desire for them, and women appreciate these qualities better than a handsome face.   But there was one gift that he lacked, and it proved fatal when he fell deeply in love and offered marriage.   He belonged to the bottom rung of the social and economic hierarchy of Clan Mackay, and he was not the kind of man to remedy this as he possessed such a golden opportunity of doing, through his access to men of position and his association with the cattle trade.   He would achieve a somewhat different goal, that of a bard unique in the annals of Scotland, but he had not achieved it by the time Ann Morrison jilted him in favour of a man who followed the more substantial calling of a carpenter.   In doing so she gained the best of both worlds, for she became the Laura to Strathnaver's Petrarch, and is immortalised in the earliest poem that exhibits the range of Rob Donn's talent in its full originality and intricacy.

Poetry inevitably loses much in translation and this is especially true of the poems of Rob Donn.   He expressed himself with an economy of language that sometimes amounted almost to short-hand, yet it often contained ideas of great complexity and double meanings which frequently depended on the alternative meanings of a Gaelic word.   For instance, in his poem on Ann Morrison he exploited the fact that the word for a carpenter, *saor*, also means "free": an accident of the language which cannot be conveyed into English.   Then there is the spectrum of meanings that have become attached to the Gaelic word *ceann*, a head, whose idiomatic range is expanded from verse to verse.   *Cul chinn*, the back of the head, also

16

denoted the common grazing of a Highland township, beyond the dyke which ran behind its crofts. *Air mo chinn* may mean "behind my croft", denoting the grazing area, but it may also mean "near me" or "awaiting me". Such was the exercise in which Rob Donn sought to disentangle himself from the unattainable Ann Morrison, and although he has presented such a puzzle to the translator, a literal English version at least reveals the bard's unromantic modernity, his life-like range of moods, his candid phallic imagery, the bantering tone of his farewell.

> *The shieling is a sad place for me, when the present company*
>   *in it—*
> *Rather than the company who used to be there—*
>   *are near to me—*
> *Anna of the passionate breast, finely-arched brows,*
>   *shining hair, style;*
> *And honey-mouthed Isabel, melodious, sweet.*
> *Alas for things as they were at the back of my croft—*
> *I have grown so bereft, there is no point in talking about it.*
>
> *I wandered across the fold and up into the woods*
> *And everywhere I used to caress my love.*
> *When I saw that fair fellow courting his wife*
> *I wish I had not come near them or beside them.*
> *That's how it was behind my croft*
> *To make me so dispirited—though it's shameful to sing*
>   *about it.*
>
> *"Fair Anna, Donald's daughter, if you knew my condition,*
> *It is unrequited love for you that deprived me of my reason.*
> *It remains as lively with me as in your presence,*
> *Teasing and provoking, wounding me to the heart.*
> *All through the day I am in turmoil,*
> *Trying to quench it, while it grows in me like a tree."*
>
> *But she spoke very disdainfully, superciliously to me,*
> *"You don't deserve to be beside me, stroking my head.*
> *Six men have been seeking me since the year of your courtship*
> *And the others would hardly expect you to surpass them.*
> *Ha! Ha! Ha! Are you deranged?*
> *If it's love that will cause your death, you are going to*
>   *pay for it."*

c

"But how can I hate you, even though you have grown so
   cold to me?
Whenever I disparage your name behind your back
Your image floats with its fascination as an embodiment
   of my dreams
So that I will conceive love to be that which will never alter,
And this is proved as it wells up again
And it grows then as high as a tower.

Since it was rumoured that you would forsake me for the
   carpenter
My sleep is disturbed with dreams of love.
Of the affection that was between us I cannot break free:
When I am not beside you, love is like a bailiff to me.
But if I am to be without you
It would do me good to get a kiss from you before you
   leave the district."[31]

But Laura had not jilted this earthy, satirical Petrarch with
impunity. He had placed in her mouth the boast that six other men
had been courting her, a boast that was not necessarily damaging
to her reputation on the face of it. However, he relieved his feelings
in a simpler song in which he had more to say about these six rivals
to John Murray the carpenter and himself. For the longer poem
he had himself composed a melody of such distinction that it has
helped to preserve *'S trom leam an àiridh* among Scotland's favourite
love songs: he set his lampoon on the rival lovers to the air *Tibbie
Fowler in the Glen.* Some of his victims were easily identifiable,
others were introduced by a conundrum into which he inserted the
English word *two* for a reason no longer discernible, and also a
Greek word which would be more surprising if it were not the term
poly gamos—which had already passed into the English language and
has been found apt to describe this propensity in other races besides.

There is a certain maiden up in the shieling—
Many have given love to her; alas for him who does
   not get close to her.

At the beginning of the year a crowd were seeking her,
Three of them coming and three of them leaving.

A broad, short man, a middle-sized man,
A black-haired man, brown man, bent man, straight man.

18

The Gunn fellow is amiable, enterprising, friendly,
Active, prosperous, robust and handy.

Robert Abrach is clever, gallant,
Possesses horses, clumsy-legged, rich in cattle.

Some of the people to be named in this context
Are a miller, turner, husbandman and grieve.

The letters of the alphabet are not more numerous
Than the number of young men who have been seeking
    her lately.
There were I, N, D; there was E, two of Angus,
U, R, O, all polygamous.[32]

Ann Morrison was not necessarily upset by these slanders. They belonged to a currency of humour that has survived in the Mackay country to this day, and Rob Donn saw no objection to dictating the poem for preservation years later, when his own family had acquired a personal interest in Ann's reputation. For in 1773, five years before his death, he witnessed the marriage of his own daughter Christine to Ann's son Hugh Murray and in the following year he had the satisfaction of composing a poem on the birth of a baby boy who was Ann's grandson and his own.[33]

His poetry does not depict a man who would have pined for long over his disappointment, however deeply he felt it at the time. Presently he courted Janet, daughter of Thomas Mackay in Strathmore, and after their marriage the couple went to live at Bad na h-achlais, a short distance north of Muisel near the shore of Loch Hope. A member of their parish paid this tribute to Rob Donn's wife after both she and her husband were dead, "Janet Mackay was a remarkably sensible woman, and so active in her habits that she kept their concerns at home in order when Robert was absent." Another asset she possessed that must have been especially precious to the bard. "She was a fine singer, and it was delightful to hear them in the winter evenings sing together."[34]

But for Janet there were to be no passionate poems, only the dry, disparaging references which remain to this day the conventional way in which an inhabitant of the Mackay country speaks of the woman who has succeeded in trapping him in marriage. For conjugal love is held to be so private that husband and wife are rarely seen to this day to touch one another, or to pay each other any compliment. At least, this was so until the present transformation of manners that is at present sweeping through the Highlands. "A thrall in Janet's house," Rob Donn once called himself [35]—not an unexpressive phrase for a man to use who was as much a prey to feminine attraction as any could be, yet spent the remainder of his life in what appears to have been a willing thralldom.

REFERENCES FOR CHAPTER ONE

1. *Songs and Poems in the Gaelic language by Rob Donn*, ed. H. Morrison, Edinburgh 1899 (later referred to as *Rob Donn*), 36, lines 1-4.
2. *Ibid.* 315, lines 1-4.
3. *Scotichronicon*, Edinburgh 1759, II, 489.
4. A. Mackay, *The Book of Mackay*, Edinburgh 1906 (later referred to as *Book of Mackay*), 172.
5. *Ibid.*, 302-4, 310, 321, 329.
6. R. Gordon, *A Genealogical History of the Earldom of Sutherland*, Edinburgh 1813, 135.
7. *Rob Donn*, 314, verse 3.
8. *Book of Mackay*, 306, gives 1722 as the date of the father's death and none for that of the son. Bighouse MS. (b) 20 in the Scottish Record Office Edinburgh (later referred to as SRO.), gives January 1710 as the date of the father's death, 1721 as that of the son, Bighouse MS. (b) 10 shows the Dowager Lady Bighouse in a business transaction with "Hugh Mackay of Bighouse my son-in-law" in 1737.
9. *Ibid.*
10. D. Sage, *Memorabilia Domestica*, Wick 1889, 35-6.
11. Reay MS. 28/2c, SRO, Edinburgh.
12. Reay MS. 33/24 (30).
13. *Book of Mackay*, 194.
14. *Ibid.*, 329. cf. Reay MS. 19 series.
15. *Rob Donn*, 11-13.
16. *Ibid.*, 158, lines 19-24.
17. *Book of Mackay*, 310-15.
18. This date is estimated from the tradition that Rob Donn entered the service of Iain Mac Eachainn at an early age. cf. *Rob Donn*, xvii.
19. Reay MS. 25/4, 25/7.
20. i.e. in 1747 when Iseabail Nic Aoidh married and he was mentioned in a poem composed on that occasion, *Rob Donn*, 152, third stanza.
21. *Rob Donn*, 111, last stanza.
22. *Ibid.*, 20-21, first 4 lines of second stanza.
23. *Memorabilia Domestica*, 13-14.
24. *Rob Donn*, 237-8, lines 1-2; 9-39. While these lines were not considered by the bard's editors to refer to Iain Mac Eachainn's wife, they are consistent with everything else he had to say about her, her brother and her father. It is also noteworthy that he never paid any compliment to the wife of his patron. Besides, there is no other known candidate.

25. *Ibid.*, pages 119-21 in their entirety.
26. J. Ramsay, *Scotland and Scotsmen in the 18th Century*, Edinburgh 1888, II, 405.
27. *Rob Donn*, 145-7, lines 1-8, 25-56.
28. *Ibid.*, lviii.
29. D. Beaton, "The Reverend Alexander Pope, Reay, Caitnness" in *Old Lore Miscellany*, Wick 1911, IV, 50.
30. *Rob Donn*, 454, lines 9-12, reading *lic-theallaich* as *leac an teallaich* in line 12.
31. *Ibid.*, 148-50 in their entirety.
32. *Ibid.*, 396-7 in their entirety.
33. *Ibid.*, 424.
34. *Ibid.*, xlix.
35. *Ibid.*, 436, lines 11-12.

CHAPTER TWO

Influences

LONG before Rob Donn entered the service of Iain Mac Eachainn at Muisel he must have heard the traditional tales that were still a staple entertainment throughout the Scottish Highlands. His father Donald Donn enjoyed no particular reputation as a singer or a story-teller, but his mother was noted among those who could fill the long winter evenings with the inexhaustible folklore of the Celtic Fingalians, of the Norse invaders of a later century with whom popular fancy locked them in combat, and of the more recent strife in which the Mackays had preserved their precarious independence from the Earls of Sutherland. Like the legends out of which the ancient Greeks composed such incomparable dramas, or the tales of the west which inspired so many American films of a later age, the folk-songs and tales of the Gael contained the usual measure of strife and bloodshed together with much tenderness and piety. By fortunate chance the Reverend Alexander Pope, "a hopeful young man, having the Irish language", came as minister to the parish of Reay in 1734, and he set about collecting the Gaelic ballads of the area at about the time of Rob Donn's marriage, thus preserving the very repertoire which the youthful poet must have heard at his mother's knee.[1] It belongs to the same corpus of balladry that the Dean of Lismore in Argyll had preserved in writing two centuries earlier.

Place names gave a local habitation to legendary heroes within the Mackay country. Dominating the Kyle of Tongue stood that wonder of natural sculpture, Ben Loyal, its western flank supported by buttresses like a mediaeval cathedral, its summit crowned by a rock outcrop resembling a shark's fin in the distance, though it possesses a flat top about the size of a tennis court. The mountain's northern precipice contains indentations known as the Screes of the Tusks, for it was told that the Fingalian leader Finn, father of Ossian, had killed the wild boar that menaced the country upon this mountain and dragged it down the north face. In fact the tale relates to pre-Christian Ireland, and contains a Homeric element.

Originally it was the handsome Diarmaid who performed the feat at the request of Finn, who wished to be revenged on him because Diarmaid had eloped with Finn's wife. When Diarmaid was not killed by the boar, Finn asked him to measure the dead beast with his feet, and one of its bristles penetrated the only part of Diarmaid's body that was vulnerable—his Achilles heel. As Diarmaid bled to death, he begged Finn for a drink of his healing cup, and Finn refused it.

> *Diarmaid, son of generous Ua Duibhne,*
> *Alas for his death through jealousy!*
> *Brighter than the sun was his breast,*
> *Redder than the blossom of clusters was his lip.*[2]

In the lands in which Dean MacGregor of Lismore recorded this ballad version of the story, the Campbells actually called themselves Clan Diarmaid, as the supposed descendants of the Fingalian hero. But it was a common belief that all Gaels descended from these giant ancestors, and the hopeful young minister of Reay, the Reverend Alexander Pope, received evidence of it when a man came to his manse (which is still preserved) to chant a ballad of Diarmaid. "There is an old fellow in this parish that very gravely takes off his bonnet as often as he sings *Duan Dearmot* (The Lay of Diarmaid). I was extremely fond to try if the case was so, and getting him to my house I gave him a bottle of ale, and begged the favour of him to sing *Duan Dearmot*. After some nicety he told me that to oblige his parish minister he would do so, but to my surprise he took off his bonnet. I caused him to stop, and would put on his bonnet; he made some excuses; however, as soon as he began, he took off his bonnet; I rose and put it on. At last he was like to swear most horribly; he would sing none unless I allowed him to be uncovered; I gave him this freedom, and so he sung with great spirit. I then asked him his reason; he told me it was out of regard to the memory of that Hero. I asked him if he thought that the spirit of that Hero was present; he said not, but he thought it well became them who descended from him to honour his memory."[3]

Amongst the most remarkable of the Gaelic ballads are those which represent Ossian as having outlived the Fingalians and survived into the Christian era. In conversation with Saint Patrick, the two men discuss the relative merits of the old pagan values and those of the new religion. The minister of Reay's own surname stems from those times for it stands for a Father of the Celtic Church, and in the Orkney islands which he could see from his parish, it has been given to certain isles in which they carried out their missionary activities—Papa Westray and Papa Stronsay.

Other Gaelic ballads represent the Fingalian heroes as the defenders of Scotland against the Viking invaders, so little concern does oral tradition show for dating. Rob Donn's native Strathmore possessed the alternative Norse name of Urradale in memory of a legendary Norseman who was said to have penetrated here on a plundering expedition; and there were shielings, hills and corries named after him—Airidh Uaraidh, Beinn Uaraidh and Coire Uaraidh. Later tradition suggested that he had been one of the captains of the great Norwegian King Haakon the Fourth, last Norse sovereign of the Hebrides until his defeat at the battle of Largs in 1263 and his death in Orkney on the journey home. Near the Kyle of Tongue a little loch was named after King Haakon, just as the narrows in the sound of Sleat through which he had led his fleet are still known as Kyleakin.

To such ancient themes as these there is no reference in Rob Donn's poetry; but that is not because he was ignorant of them, for they were on the lips of all his folk. He received no formal schooling, but had he done so it would have taught him the names of English Kings and Queens, not those of Ossian or Haakon. Rob Donn ignored these because his fascination lay in the world of living people around him, not in a dead classical past. The racy ballad style of much of his verse reveals how deeply imbued he was with its cadences, while his recorded conversation between Iain Mac Eachainn's daughters recalls those of Ossian and Saint Patrick.

Another poetic influence that enveloped Rob Donn from his earliest years was provided by the Reformed Christian religion. After the abolition of the Roman Catholic Church by Act of Parliament in 1560, the promotion of the Reformed faith had been largely the achievement of the local gentry. A powerful catalyst had been the zeal of Robert Bruce, son of the baron of Airth castle, where he was born, and descended on his mother's side from the royal Stewarts. After he had succeeded John Knox in the pulpit of St Giles', he alarmed King James the Sixth so severely with his extreme claims for the new theocracy that he found himself exiled to Inverness. Here it was natural that he should have consorted with the Munros of Easter Ross, since it is unlikely that any Bruce of Airth in Fife had ever been a Gaelic speaker, while the bilingual Munroes were early promotors of the new Protestant order in the north. The influence of this outstanding preacher with the social background

24

of a courtier and the aptitudes of a stateman fell upon Alexander Munro, who carried it into Strathnaver.

By this time the Book of Common Order had been published in Gaelic with an introduction that roundly condemned the profane entertainments represented by the Ossianic tales and ballads. More recently the Catechism of John Calvin had been printed in Gaelic also: while the Bible, which it had been a fundamental principle of the Reformation to make available in the vernacular, remained in a language as incomprehensible to Gaels as the Latin Vulgate version. The Reverend Alexander Munro's solution to this was to compose Gaelic hymns that told the Bible stories and preached their lessons in a form in which they could easily be memorised. One of his surviving poems contains fifteen quatrains in which Noah, Joseph, Susanna, Menasses and Cyrus contribute to the exposition of God's purposes. The other hymn's twelve quatrains are devoted to the Saviour.[4] Their poetic quality is very different from that of the metrical psalms which were being composed during the same period by Rous the Cornishman, and which were introduced into Lowland Scotland during Alexander Munro's lifetime. It was not until long after Rob Donn's death that the religious feelings or literary taste of Gaelic speakers in the Mackay country were affected by the most degenerate corpus of verse ever composed in the English language.

At the time of Rob Donn's birth the mantle of Munro had fallen upon a Mackay who received on 10th February 1736 "the third part of the town and lands of Mudale" in the form of a tack.[5] Mudale is a green basin lying some five miles south-east of Strathmore in the moorlands not far distant from the frontier heights and the pyramid of Ben Klibreck; and John Mackay of Mudale thus lived within a short distance of the lands in which his ancestors, the earliest sept of Clan Mackay, had dwelt since time immemorial. They were known as the Abrachs after the daughter of Macdonald of Keppoch in Lochaber, who had borne a son to the Mackay Chief who married Elizabeth of the Isles in 1415. Whether she had become a second wife to the Chief, or whether the child was illegitimate, is not clear, but the Abrachs received for their patrimony the largest valley in the Mackay country, in which the river Naver runs from its loch to the sea through the parish of Farr.

After the Gordons had obtained possession of the earldom of Sutherland they pounced upon this prize, and by the time Rob Donn was born the strath from which the Mackay province took its name was theirs. Originally the chieftains of the Abrachs lived at Achness at the end of Loch Naver, where the ruins of their dwelling and of a

25

little church are still to be seen above a huge stone-walled sheep pen: and when Alexander Munro began his ministry in Strathnaver, William Mackay of Achness, the last of them to retain that property, still maintained himself there.[6] His son was called Neil Williamson, the name of a whole tribe of dispossessed people of that area. Rob Donn mentioned a Williamson among his rivals in the poem he composed at Crieff, and he also mentioned an Abrach among the suitors for Ann Morrison. John Mackay of Mudale was a grandson of Neil Williamson—whose first cousin had married the daughter of the Reverend Alexander Munro. So there were family reasons why John of Mudale should have been influenced by the religious poetry of the Munro preacher.

Similarly, there were family reasons why Rob Donn should have met John of Mudale before he encountered any other living poet, for Mudale (as he was generally called in a land filled with John Mackays) was married to Iain Mac Eachainn's first cousin, besides being a near neighbour whose home was visible from the high Sàl pastures on the southern flank of Ben Hope. And he could hardly have failed to influence the young bard, he whose poems gave so much edification throughout the Protestant Highlands for another two centuries despite the fact that they were not committed to print until 1835.[7] The most famous of them tells the story of the Christian redemption against a historical background, while others handle the Old Testament themes of Adam and Eve and the flood. Rob Donn never became a religious poet in any way comparable to Alexander Munro or John of Mudale. But their hymns are likely to have exercised a powerful influence on his youthful mind.

Beyond Strathnaver to the south-east, the valley of Kildonan runs through the Sutherland earldom to the sea at Helmsdale, beside the high cliffs of the Caithness border. In Kildonan lived another religious poet named Donald Matheson, whose compositions were to retain a degree of popularity equal to those of John of Mudale and ultimately to be published with them. Matheson had been born five years after Rob Donn, who consequently could not have heard his poems during the impressionable years of his youth; and who had reservations about their quality if a tradition speaks true. It was said that Matheson once asked him for his judgment and Rob Donn observed: "there is more piety in your poetry and more poetry in mine."[8]

It is hard to re-enter a literary environment so different from today's, in which poetry still played a central part in people's lives and circulated by oral transmission alone as fast as the contents of any book in a public library. One may read in print the Ossianic tales and ballads and the religious poems to which Rob Donn listened as a child beside the peat fire. One can only surmise when and where he heard the compositions of the secular bards who were his contemporaries in other parts of Scotland.

In earlier times the most remarkable dynasty of these had been the MacMhuirichs, who had kept alive a bardic literary tradition with ancient roots in Ireland since the Middle Ages. When Rob Donn was growing up, this family was represented by Donald Mac-Mhuirich, living on the ancestral property of Stadhlaigearraidh in South Uist.[9] He had travelled to Ireland for a part of his training and consequently could write in the old Irish script and compose in the ancient bardic metres, and it is just possible that Rob Donn came within sight of this spring of his country's ancient learning at the time when it was running dry at last.

For there is a tradition, supported by an allusion in his poetry, that Rob Donn paid a visit to Skye and there met the Reverend John Macpherson, who came as minister to Sleat in 1742.[10] If the bard did this, then it must have been soon after that date, since his poem tells that he was induced to make the journey by Hugh of Bighouse who had asked for the services of Rob Donn's wife in the Chief's house at Tongue where he still lived. By 1744 at the latest Hugh of Bighouse had departed to live on his wife's property in Strath Halladale, when he received sasine of the estate. The bard did not take kindly to being parted from his wife.

> *I will go to Tongue, however inconvenient,*
> *And give a sharp knock at the room where she's sleeping.*
> *Sweet is the drink from the cup that is stolen.*

He threatened the Chief's son not to make a cuckold of him as King David had done with the wife of Uriah the Hittite.

> *He's driving me off to the land of the Skyemen*
> *And the thought of David gives me distaste for the journey;*
> *I've the fear of death that he'll make a Uriah.*[11]

If Rob Donn did visit Macpherson, the minister left no mention of their encounter, although he was a man of literary tastes who took the trouble to record his acquaintance with Donald MacMhuirich in that bard's old age. But Rob Donn had not yet composed any of the serious poetry on which his fame so largely rests and the minister

27

might forgiveably have failed to appreciate that '*S trom leam an airidh* (The shieling is a sad place for me) would rank among the great love-songs of Scotland. His own interests were somewhat academic. Decades later Samuel Johnson examined some Latin verses of his composition during his visit to Skye and told Boswell, "He has a great deal of Latin and very good Latin."[12] The fact that Macpherson left no allusion to Rob Donn which survives cannot be taken as evidence that so curious a tradition is without foundation: and if it is true, then it is likely enough that the scholarly minister spoke to the bard of the MacMhuirichs and their bardic poetry.

There was a particular respect in which the Gaelic literary tradition differed from the English one, and this was in its treatment of nature. The Gaelic poet of the fifteenth century extolled "all the wonders to be found beneath the banks of each swift stream." Another of the same century exulted:

> *Cows yield sweet milk in milking folds;*
> *The fallow land is most rich in grass;*
> *Under its smooth demesne and mountain*
> *It is a lovely land under its heavy crop.*[13]

This love and respect for the natural world extended back through the centuries to the utterances of the saints of the Celtic Church, and it lived on in the new Protestant religious poetry. Early in the seventeenth century Alexander Munro exclaimed:

> *The wonder of the works of the Creator*
> *Made by him at the beginning of time,*
> *This is an epistle each man may read,*
> *The might of God, written in the Universe.*[14]

In 1726 the Lowland Scottish poet James Thomson had published the first of the four poems which were ultimately printed together as *The Seasons*, and this proved to be a portent for the Romantic Movement in English poetry. But William Wordsworth was not born until eight years before Rob Donn's death, and throughout the greater part of the eighteenth century the English (or Scots) and Gaelic poets differed most in their attitude to the natural world.

In 1724 there was born a bard who expressed this immemorial love and respect for his natural surroundings in a torrent of words that has scarcely been equalled. Duncan Bàn Macintyre belonged to a small clan which had for centuries provided foresters to the Lords of

Lorne. They had also supplied families of hereditary pipers to the Menzies and Macdonald Chiefs, and claimed that their forbears had played the bagpipe at Bannockburn: which may have been the case although Barbour's epic poem makes no mention of the instrument in its description of that battle. Duncan Bàn himself spent much of his life as a gamekeeper among the hills of Glenorchy, and it was to these hills and to the life of man the hunter that he paid his eloquent tribute. He possessed neither Rob Donn's intellectual capacity nor his gift for disciplined, incisive composition. Duncan Bàn's poems are a cataract of images: where Rob Donn observed people, he noted the plants and animals that surrounded him during his solitary tramps among the mountains.[15]

Duncan Bàn went to Edinburgh where he served in the city guard and enjoyed the rare distinction of seeing his poetry published during his own lifetime. He had composed poems on request for which his patrons were grateful, though some of them expose his intellectual limitations to a degree that is painful to his admirers. Never in his life did Rob Donn misuse his talent in this way.

But although the two poets were in essential respects so different they were united in their love for the deer forest and this was enough to ensure a convivial evening when they met, as they did on at least one occasion (according to tradition) during Rob Donn's droving expeditions. He only once piled on the adjectives as though in parody of Duncan Bàn, and that was in a poem of the sea. His rather exceptional poem in praise of Gleanna Golaidh appears by comparison with Duncan Bàn's immortal eulogy of the Misty Corrie to be both lean and reticent. If the two bards had travelled with Chaucer's pilgrims to Canterbury, it is Rob Donn who would have recorded the tales: Duncan Bàn would have left a detailed picture of the country through which they passed.

Spanning the worlds of the bardic MacMhuirichs and of the illiterate Duncan Bàn and Rob Donn stood the colossus Alexander Macdonald, known as Alasdair Mac Mhaighstir Alasdair. He may have been as much as twenty years older than Rob Donn although the exact date of his birth is uncertain. He belonged to the Macdonald gentry of the Isles which could trace its descent from the royal Stewarts, and his father was the minister of Islandfinnan, where he himself had become the schoolmaster by the time Rob Donn was growing up at Muisel. Macdonald could read classical Irish literature and write in its beautiful script: he was besides fully bilingual and wrote competently in English. Yet he did not have the appearance of the tidy, genteel scholar. "In person," an observer recorded,

"Macdonald was large and ill-favoured. His features were coarse and irregular. His clothes were very sluggishly put on, and generally very dirty. His mouth was continually fringed with a stream of tobacco-juice, of which he chewed a very great quantity."[16] He had become a convert to the Roman Catholic faith before Prince Charles Edward landed in Scotland and was thus inspired to become the supreme Jacobite poet. Amongst his compositions are those which have been judged the finest in modern Scottish Gaelic poetry.

There is no evidence that Rob Donn ever met him and little likelihood of it. But it is apparent that Alasdair Mac Mhaighstir Alasdair's poems reached his ears and influenced him profoundly. Macdonald had been able to read James Thomson's poems on winter and summer, published in 1726 and 1727, and he composed Gaelic poems on the same themes. Rob Donn not only followed his example, but he also emulated the erudite Macdonald's practice of introducing classical terms so far as he was able by referring to the sun as *Phoebus* in the stanzas he composed on winter. By the time he composed his songs in dispraise of Ann Morrison it is extremely probable that he had already heard Macdonald's bawdy poem in dispraise of Morag. Rob Donn would have found it hard to imitate the chiselled style of the elder poet, even if he had tried to do so. But while he used instead a confident manner of expression that was uniquely his own, the booming voice of Macdonald penetrated his thought and helped to form his art.

Another of the compositions which reveals this is the pibroch song that he composed for Iain Mac Eachainn's daughter Isabel. The art of pibroch itself had reached the Mackay country with its inventor Donald Mór MacCrimmon, who had left Skye to become piper to the Chief of Mackay sometime before the year 1612. So well did Donald Mór teach his art there that he left a family of distinguished Mackay pipers and composers behind him. One of these left Strathnaver to enter the service of Mackenzie of Gairloch, and by the time Rob Donn was growing up, the Gairloch school was represented by the blind piper John Mackay, known as Iain Dall, a musician not only celebrated for his composition of pibroch, but also as a composer of songs.

It was natural that the pipers, the supreme musicians of their age in the Highlands, should also have turned their talents on occasion to composing words that might be sung to an air related to a pibroch of their own composition. Donald Mór's son, Patrick Mór Mac-Crimmon, did so in 1626 when he made the elegy *Tog Orm mo Phiob* for the Macleod Chief, Ruaraidh Mór, to be sung to an air related to his pibroch lament on the same theme. His grandson Donald Bàn MacCrimmon did the same in the equally famous song he composed at the time of the Forty-Five, known as *The MacCrimmon Lamont*. This was when Rob Donn composed his pibroch song for Isabel, as we know because he set it to the Jacobite pipe-tune *Welcome to the Prince* and he must have done this before Isabel's marriage in 1747, since the words describe a single girl.

What was new in this was that a bard who was not a piper should set words to the ground or one of the other musical movements (or both) of a pibroch, and it was Alasdair Mac Mhaighstir Alasdair who pioneered this difficult art. Duncan Bàn followed his example, to which we owe his masterpiece, *The Praise of Ben Dorain*, while Rob Donn, equally characteristically, planted his favourite Isabel in his favourite surroundings.

Do you not see Mackay's daughter	*Nach faic thu Nic Aoidh*
Tending the calves	*Aig a'chrodh laoigh*
By the edge of the deer forest	*Am bonnaibh na frith'*
All by herself?	*'S i na h-aonar?*[17]

To fit the syllables of a stressed language into the strait-jacket of this kind of music was an exercise that one would have expected to appeal more to a MacMhuirich than to Rob Donn, and he neither attempted it often, nor with the same skill or care that Macdonald devoted to it. But as in his poem on winter, it could have been a spirit of emulation that spurred him to try his hand at it.

As it happened, there was another poet writing in English at this time whose art resembled Rob Donn's a great deal more closely than that of James Thomson, author of *The Seasons*. Curiously, he possessed the same Highland name as the minister of Reay, although his family had settled long before his birth in England. In the very year of Rob Donn's birth Alexander Pope had reached the summit of his fame with the publication of his mock-heroic epic *The Rape of the Lock*. Pope's axiom "the proper study of mankind is man" was one that Rob Donn would pursue throughout his life, and to it both men brought comparable qualities—an incisive judgment, a gift for exact and economical expression, a delight in ridiculing all that was pretentious and pompous, a flair for laying down pithy maxims, a satirist's eye for human frailties.

The outward circumstances of the two men were by contrast as different as could be. Pope was a sophisticated and highly literate townsman, and a Roman Catholic: Rob Donn an unlettered peasant in one of the most rural and culturally isolated corners of Britain, a Calvinist reared in an entirely different social and linguistic tradition. Each might have been expected to have lived out his life without ever hearing of the other, and certainly each developed the characteristics they possessed so early, so independently of the tastes of the societies that surrounded them, that it would have been unnecessary for either to have exercised any influence on the other.

Yet, by a curious chance, the English poet did probably hear of Rob Donn, because he learnt about his namesake in Reay and invited him to visit Twickenham, an invitation that the minister accepted. The Reverend Alexander Pope admired Rob Donn's talents sufficiently to compose a Latin epitaph for him at his death: it is inscribed on the bard's memorial in Durness cemetery: and it would have been surprising if he had not been asked in Twickenham whether there were any poets in his own country.

It happened also that in Rob Donn's twelfth year there came to the parish of Durness, in which the barony of West Moine lay, a minister who admired the work of the English Roman Catholic poet, and translated passages from it into Gaelic for the benefit of his flock. The all-important questions, which passages he translated, and how many of these Rob Donn heard in Strathmore, cannot be answered. Consequently it is fruitless to speculate whether Rob Donn would have composed poetry any different if he had never heard of Alexander Pope. His sole reference, in the remark that the beauty of one of Hugh of Bighouse's daughters was worthy of the pen of Pope, reveals scant insight into the colour of ink that pen used. We are left with the phenomenon of two poets so essentially alike, the one writing his poems for the palaces of a rich metropolis, the other composing them in his head in the Reay country in the broad dialect of a language which even the Scottish capital could not understand, and of the minister of Durness who formed the bridge between them.

His name was Murdo Macdonald, and he obtained his degree at St Andrews in 1722 when he was twenty-six years old. As soon as he had been licensed to preach by the presbytery there in September 1725, he set off for the north coast, where he took the post of tutor in the family of a cadet of the Bighouse Mackays at Rhenevie, a property that overlooks the sands of Naver mouth less than two miles from the church of Farr.[18] He was thus poised to begin his life-long ministry in the Mackay country at exactly the moment when a belated and radical reorganisation of its parishes was being carried out.

In the old days of Episcopacy the province of Strathnaver had belonged with the earldom of Sutherland to the diocese of Caithness, whose cathedral had stood at Dornoch, to this day the capital of Sutherland county. In 1707, when the Church of Scotland was protected as the Established Church of the nation under the terms of the Union with England, the presbytery of Tongue was still connected to that of Caithness based at Thurso, although this town was separated from the church of Tongue by over forty-five miles of difficult terrain while Gaelic was the language of one place, English of the other. More serious still, the parish of Tongue itself extended west over the great barrier of the Moine to include Durness and the scattered communities of the inaccessible world between. It was even supposed to minister to the coastal lands beyond, as far as the Assynt border. In 1707 the Reverend John Mackay was presented to Durness, and he stipulated that Durness and Edderachillis on the west coast should be erected into separated parishes, detached from distant Tongue.

The Reverend John Mackay belonged to the family of General Mackay of Scourie who had played such an important part in securing the Protestant Revolution of 1688: and he was the second cousin of the Chief to whom he made his demand for the erection of new parishes. He was characteristic, in fact, of the pious gentry which had played such a dominant role in planting the Reformed church in the Lowlands and Highlands alike. But the estate of the third Lord Reay was then too poor to meet such an expense, and not even the powerful personality of the Reverend John nor his social rank could secure the change. In 1713 he moved to Lairg in the Sutherland earldom, where his ministry became legendary for the strong-arm methods he employed to transform his flock into a God-fearing community. Some of his sermon-notes survive and they constitute the only body of contemporary Gaelic prose in the dialect spoken by Rob Donn.[19]

To Durness there came in his place the Reverend George Brodie, while the General Assembly in Edinburgh appointed a collection to raise the funds necessary to carry out the Reverend John Mackay's wishes for the erection of new parishes in the far north-west. In 1724 Lord Reay himself contributed to the fund and made gifts of sites for new churches, for which he received the formal thanks of the Assembly.[20] In the same year George Brodie moved to become the first minister of the new parish of Edderachillis, and in 1726 Murdo Macdonald left Rhenevie to begin his lifelong ministry in Durness. In 1727 the presbytery of Tongue, consisting now of the

33

parishes of Edderachillis, Durness, Tongue and Farr, was at last detached from Caithness.

Macdonald discovered on his arrival that there were no elders in the two parishes of the west to constitute kirk sessions. After making the acquaintance of his flock as quickly as he could, he forwarded a list of persons whom he considered fit for the office to the presbytery in August 1727. From this body he received a recommendation to catechists in his parish "to employ the most of their time in teaching the Shorter Catechism" and in explaining its meaning. Forty-eight copies of the Confession of Faith in Gaelic had just arrived for distribution throughout the Mackay country.[21] Aeneas Mackay was catechist in Durness and he was able to report to the presbytery in Tongue on 10th April 1729 that two hundred and fifty of his parishioners were able to repeat all the questions in the Shorter Catechism: which compared creditably to three hundred in the parish of Tongue and only two hundred in the parish of Farr beyond. The parish of Durness had been described in 1724, when it still comprehended Edderachillis, as containing "about 2,400 catechis-able people". The separated parish of Durness was estimated in 1755 to possess a thousand souls, while in 1790 the number in it was given as 1,182, of whom 509 were inhabitants of the barony of West Moine in which Rob Donn lived.[22]

By the time Aeneas Mackay made his report on the numbers of people who had mastered the Shorter Catechism, the bard was fifteen years old. Whether or not he was already one of the star performers, he must have felt the stimulus of the religious activity that had followed the arrival of the new minister.

In December 1737 Macdonald confided to his diary: "I have been at more than ordinary pains in public and private with the people to incline them to consider their ways, and particularly because very few of them can read, I have been endeavouring to shame and frighten them out of their unaccountable neglect of getting the questions, wherein the principles of the Protestant religion are most accurately and summarily set down, and my pains to this purpose for some seasons past have not been altogether useless."[23] The poetry of Rob Donn contains the most eloquent testimony in support of the minister's claim. From the age of thirteen, when other youths are at school and university, this unlettered herd-boy and cattleman was being subjected to an intellectual discipline capable of sharpening the mind as effectively as a course in philosophy or law, as his own quality of thought would reveal.

The Reverend Murdo Macdonald was a tough adherent of the old

34

Evangelical school which placed its doctrinal emphasis on free grace, and condemned as a fallacy the belief that man may achieve salvation by leading a blameless life or doing good works rather than by pinning his faith in the Redemption alone. At the fellowship meetings in which he discussed these grave issues, there can be little doubt of the level of argument he maintained. "It is ordinary in such conventions," he once observed severely, "to start questions either frivolous or ill-stated, and to allow ignorant people to harangue on them at random." Clearly such people would soon have been called to order by the minister of Durness.

In the end Rob Donn would describe Macdonald as the most important influence on his life, in what is judged by some to be his most impressive poem.

> *. . . If it could be a tribute or service to you*
> *To raise your fame on high for you,*
> *Who should do it more than I*
> *And who could deserve it more than you?*[24]

What is so remarkable is that in the face of this formidable influence, Rob Donn should have succeeded in retaining his independence of belief over one of the most important differences that divide Christians. He never permitted the Calvinist doctrine of justification by faith alone, upon which his minister placed such a strong emphasis, to undermine his belief in the saving power of good works. Some have found his poetry lacking in spiritual depth, although given to moralising, and it is true that his theme was Man not God. But in so far as the criticism is intended to imply that he was doctrinally slipshod or soft it is merely a back-handed testimony to his independence of mind.

At the time when the Reverend Murdo Macdonald came to Durness the Highlanders were evolving the so-called "long tunes" out of airs to which the metrical psalms were sung, which had reached them from the Lowlands. The precenter would introduce a line of the Gaelic metrical psalm, to be taken up in unison by the congregation, but with such a slow surge of individual ornamentation as to build up a spell-binding pattern of harmony and discord. This was another field in which Macdonald exercised a wonderful influence in his parish, for he was a powerful and melodious singer with a love of music that was to bear fruit in the achievements of his sons and of Rob Donn. Despite the bard's lack of any formal musical education, he was to compose more of his own original airs than any other Scottish Gaelic poet of his century: and their excellence—perhaps even the fact that he was able to do this at all—is one of the most precious gifts he received from his parish minister. In the circumstances he may be excused the fulsomeness with which he expressed his gratitude.

> The one to compare with you
> For voice and ear
> Has never been seen nor heard of
> And in my opinion he will not be heard of.
> Although rich in piety
> You showed appreciation for every talent,
> And well did you understand the songs
> And the one who composed the verses.[25]

The minister's visits to Rob Donn's corner of the parish were regulated by a presbytery instruction that he should preach on four successive Sundays in Durness and on the fifth in West Moine. "They further recommend him to have one discourse in English at least each Sabbath at Durness." This would be a religious service for guests in the mansion at Balnakil, all the more necessary after 1732 when the Master of Reay married and brought his wife to live in Durness. For she was a daughter of Sir Robert Dalrymple of Castleton in Angus and grand-daughter of a President of the Court of Session who hailed from North Berwick, a family that could never have spoken Gaelic.

Macdonald's diary reveals his wide taste for literature, and particularly for contemporary English writers, and this alone might have induced him to cultivate the society of the Master's household and the company of people as cultivated as himself. But he noted more than once that the conviviality of the nearby mansion was disturbing to him, and his duties of attendance there burdensome. In February 1740 he wrote that Saturday night merrymakers had interrupted his thoughts while he was trying to compose his sermon for the morrow. "Yesterday preparing for this, having besides my personal indisposing infirmities, interruptions from the foolish conduct of some neighbours of whom better things might have been expected" had spoilt his meditations. But he conceded: "I have in the meantime grounds of thankfulness that such disturbances are so rare and that I am helped to manage them with so little vexation to

36

myself and offence to others." Later in 1740 Marion Dalrymple died, after giving birth to two sons who would succeed one another in the chiefship during Rob Donn's lifetime.

Tolerant yet steadfast, the minister preferred communion with God and with the children of God committed to his charge to social entertainment. "Just now returned from the public work of thanksgiving." he had noted on 16th January 1740, "for which this day was set apart in testimony of our gratitude to God for a new year, and his goodness in the old. There was a collection of £4-16 sterling, which was added to the fund for pious uses in this parish, amounting now to above £60 sterling including the interest: is engrossed in the sum for which we have the security of the person of greatest distinction in the place, in whose hands we have lodged the money. Lord, it is thy goodness that the poor people in this parish have inclinations for such pious deeds, considering the deepness of their poverty which notwithstanding seems to abound to the riches of their liberality." The minister's stipend amounted to little more than £44 sterling a year, which helps to account for his admiration for the generosity of those poorer than himself.

Among those whose habits pleased him less was a parishioner of the name of MacCormack who had been threatened with exile to the plantations for the crime of adultery before Macdonald came to Durness. He was described as "an habitual sinner in this kind" and in due course paid the penalty of excommunication. In a land in which there were no Sunday newspapers to publish the details of such delinquencies, the pulpit of the minister and the songs of the bard supplied both the facts and the editorial comment. It will never be known whether the judgments of Rob Donn influenced his minister, since Macdonald never referred to him on paper although he commented freely on such writers as Fielding the novelist and Pope the poet. The bard, by contrast, left a succinct analysis of the minister's combination of severity and compassion, qualities that became deeply embedded in his own more ribald nature.

> *You were gentle to those in need,*
> *You were generous with reasonable people,*
> *You were shrewd of aspect, hard*
> *As stone towards the miscreant.*
> *You were bountiful in giving,*
> *You were a diligent preacher,*
> *You gave timely advice*
> *And in the end your hostility turned to love.*[26]

1. Beaton, *op. cit.*, 97: *Leabhar na Feinne*, ed. J. F. Campbell, London 1872.
2. N. Ross, *Heroic Poetry from the Book of the Dean of Lismore*, Edinburgh 1939, 75.
3. F. Collinson, *The Traditional and National Music of Scotland*, London 1966, 49.
4. M. MacFarlane, *A Handful of Lays . . . 1688*, Dundee 1923, 34-41.
5. Reay MS. 19.
6. *Register of the Privy Council of Scotland*, ed. D. Masson, Edinburgh 1896, xiii, 510.
7. *Dain Spiordail*, Inverness 1835, 9-31: J. Rose, *Baird na Gaidhealtachd mu Thuath*, Inverness 1851, 109, 131-2.
8. *Baird na Gaidhealtachd mu Thuath*, 245-84.
9. D. S. Thomson, "The MacMhuirich Bardic Family," in *Transactions of the Gaelic Society of Inverness*, 1963, xliii 276-304.
10. *Fasti Ecclesiae Scoticae*, ed. H. Scott, Edinburgh, 1915-61, vii, 175.
11. *Rob Donn*, 260, ll. 13-15: 261, lines 5-7.
12. S. Johnson and J. Boswell, *Tour of the Hebrides*, ed. R. W. Chapman, Oxford 1951, 339.
13. W. Watson, *Scottish Verse from the Book of the Dean of Lismore*, Edinburgh 1937, 29, verse 13: 37, verse 10.
14. J. Macinnes, *The Evangelical Movement in the Highlands of Scotland*, Aberdeen 1951, 268.
15. A. Macleod, *The Songs of Duncan Ban Macintyre*, Edinburgh 1952: D. Thomson, *An Introduction to Gaelic Poetry*, London 1974, 181-91.
16. J. Reid, *Bibliotheca Scoto-Celtica*, Glasgow 1832, 82: Thomson, *op. cit.*, 157-80.
17. *Rob Donn*, 183, lines 5-8.
18. *Book of Mackay*, 308.
19. *Scottish Gaelic Studies*, ix, 176-202; xi, 100.
20. Reay MS. 29/12.
21. D. Beaton, "Notes from the Tongue Presbytery Records," in *Old Lore Miscellany*, Wick 1914, VII, 41.
22. H. Morrison, "Notices . . . from the Diary of the Reverend Murdoch Macdonald" in *Transactions of the Gaelic Society of Inverness*, 1885, xi, 298. Sir John Sinclair, *The Statistical Account of Scotland* (later referred to as *Statistical Account*), III, 1792, 581.
23. Morrison, *op. cit.*, 2971 Unless otherwise stated, quotations from the Reverend Murdo Macdonald's lost diary are taken from transcripts copied into school notebooks in different hands, perhaps by children, and edited by the author.
24. *Rob Donn*, 21, lines 3-6.
25. *Ibid.*, 24, lines 9-16. The 1829 edition gives *cluasan* for *cluasaibh* in line 10. Airs to Rob Donn's songs are published in A. Gunn and M. MacFarlane, *Songs and Poems by Rob Donn Mackay*, Glasgow 1899.
26. *Rob Donn*, 22, lines 1-8.

CHAPTER THREE

Candid Commentator

THE seat of the Chief, the Earl of Sutherland's valley of the Naver to the east of it and the estate of Hugh of Bighouse on the border of Caithness beyond were divided from western Strathnaver by a high barren ridge, five miles in width, called the Moine (which means Peat in Gaelic.) The jagged cliffs of its headland extended far into the Atlantic, and owing to its width and height it was often mantled with snow when the land on either hand was dark, so that it was known as Whiten Head. To traverse the broken ground of the Moine, even in the driest weather, could be exceedingly wearisome: in winter it became hazardous when the snow, driven by strong winds, filled its black gullies and altered its contours entirely. The Reverend Murdo Macdonald scarcely ever failed to grumble into his diary about the discomforts of the Moine, when he was forced to cross it to attend presbytery meetings in Tongue, and there were occasions when he preferred the no less treacherous ocean.

One of these occurred in April 1737 when he planned to visit Thurso in order to attend the funeral of the Reverend William Innes, taking with him his wife, who was pregnant, and their children of eight and six years. The party set off from Balnakil for the little creek of Smoo about a mile from the manse. Here yawns the entrance to the cave that Sir Walter Scott was to make famous when he visited it, beyond a shingle beach on which boats could be hauled to safety. "The day was gloomy and foggy, as indeed it was to me in several respects and there was a gentle north-east breeze which made the heaving sea very unfavourable to our purpose, so that when we came to the place my wife durst not try it, but choosed to continue on horseback till she came to Rispond where she stayed the night." Here, after a day's travel, they had not yet crossed Loch Eriboll to reach the barony of West Moine.

"The bairnies went by sea from Smoo to Rispond and got the first handsell of seasickness. Next day being Thursday, there was a pretty brisk gale of south-easterly wind which was almost ahead of

39

us, but the crew thinking to make it by rowing and coasting close by shore, which they expected would shelter them, they set out with us towards the White Head as they call it. But as we were advanced half-way to turn the Head, the wind increased to such a height and contrariety to us that by the unanimous voice of the crew it was best to turn back, which we accordingly did, and in the afternoon came on shore at Badilhavish in West Moine: where I intended to stay, it being one of the preaching places of my parish." They had failed to pass the Moine after two days' travel, and were forced to remain where they were for another two days.

"On the Thursday we were in our boat off the Head, we observed just coming after us into Loch Eriboll two ships which were directed from their easterly course by the same cross-wind. This might alleviate our part of the calamity when great vessels must yield to the weather, nay, when God with east wind breaks the strong ships of Tarshish. It came in my head that we might in that case have the convenience of a passage in them just come to our hand. When therefore they came to anchor I went in the evening against a boisterous gale to see, but found none of them was bound for the south further than Peterhead. Thus God's ways are not ours, nor his thoughts ours always." Macdonald's own thoughts are obscure enough, since these ships could easily have carried his family to Thurso on their way to Peterhead, unless they intended to sail round the Orkney islands rather than face the dangers of the Pentland Firth. What is noteworthy is that despite his wife's fear of the sea, he made no attempt to transport her over the Moine but waited instead for a boat to make the journey.

When Rob Donn travelled to Tongue he may have preferred to avoid the Moine by passing round the southern flanks of the massif of Ben Hope, over the high Sàl pastures and down to the headwaters of the Kyle at Kinloch. Such an expedition he made while his wife was away serving the household of Hugh of Bighouse in the Chief's mansion, and in his poem on the subject he reported the complaints of other married men and women, separated for different reasons.

> *We are sorrowful, observing one another.*
> *I am sleeping and let me not be wakened.*
> *Neil is in the tavern, waiting for the fairs.*
> *I am sleeping and let me not be wakened.*
> *Neil is at the fair and Katy is uneasy;*
> *I am far from well and my wife away nursing*

And although we keep silent this situation galls me.
I am sleeping and let me not be wakened.

He did not keep altogether silent, according to his own confession,
but took a trip to Tongue for a drink from the stolen cup, and to
enquire whether Hugh of Bighouse "would keep me all the year
frustrated." This was when an attempt was made to mollify him
with the proposal that he should visit Skye, which reminded him
ominously of the biblical story of David and Uriah's wife.

James MacCulloch, don't you pity my predicament?
I am sleeping and let me not be wakened.
Without good food beside me, and sleeping solitary?
I am sleeping and let me not be wakened.
Don't you think I'm filled with the spirit of forgiveness
If ever I make peace with the wife who abandoned me?
Dash me if I don't remind her, when she's back,
*   how she treated me.*
I am sleeping and let me not be wakened.

Then said James: "Oh shame on your jealousy."
I am sleeping and let me not be wakened.
"She hasn't let you down as often as my wife."
I am sleeping and let me not be wakened.
"She has gone off frequently, brazen with excuses,
"And to tell you the truth I'm ready to forgive her—
"I wish with all my heart the woman were in heaven."
I am sleeping and let me not be wakened.

I went on my way to the home of John of the Donalds.
I am sleeping and let me not be wakened.
And he asked me briskly whether I'd seen Janet.
I am sleeping and let me not be wakened.
"Though she stays away a year, it's not worth lamenting
"So long as she comes home well-disposed and good-natured
"And has a civil tongue for the girl in your company."
I am sleeping and let me not be wakened.

Next we reach the earliest dateable reference to John Sutherland,
the schoolmaster at Tongue whom Rob Donn invariably addressed
as Iain Tapaidh—Clever John—and showered with ridicule. Sutherland himself composed poetry, whose quality can only be assessed

41

by the fact that not a line of it has been preserved in the Mackay country. Here his wife comments on his absence.

> *Then I had a word with David's daughter Isobel.*
> *I am sleeping and let me not be wakened.*
> *"How can one like you take pleasure in that fellow?"*
> *I am sleeping and let me not be wakened.*
> *"Tell me the truth and be frank in your speech:*
> *"Is your nature getting worse, or your good sense affected?*
> *"And how are you faring since Iain Tapaidh left you?"*
> *I am sleeping and let me not be wakened.*
>
> *Then Isobel said: "I am very peace-loving."*
> *I am sleeping and let me not be wakened.*
> *"I would take his explanation at the very Kirk Session."*
> *I am sleeping and let me not be wakened.*
> *"Although they were telling me his absence was shameful,*
> *"I've a troublesome brood from only two confinements,*
> *"Joseph and Barbara, Walter and Annabell."*
> *I am sleeping and let me not be wakened.*

This poem reveals the freedom of speech and movement that women enjoyed in a society in which private morals were closely supervised by the ministry. Its tenth verse shows that Neil Macleod's deserted wife Kate was not sitting tamely in Durness, waiting for her husband to return, but was going the rounds with Rob Donn as he discussed matrimonial difficulties in the parish of Tongue. When she decided to return to the west, she stopped at the sheriff-substitute's house of Ribigill to invite the comments of his wife, the Tutor's sharp-tongued daughter, before travelling back by way of Muisel in Strathmore.

> *Said Katy, returning and folding up her clothes—*
> *I am sleeping and let me not be wakened—*
> *"I'm off now to Muisel to tell my whole story."*
> *I am sleeping and let me not be wakened.*
> *"For there's a woman there who understands my grievances.*
> *"I'll tell her the whole truth about all that befell me*
> *"And she will give me sympathy although she cannot help me."*
> *I am sleeping and let me not be wakened.*
>
> *She went on her way past the wife of Donald Forbes—*
> *I am sleeping and let me not be wakened—*

Who answered artfully (for a quick retort was like her)—
I am sleeping and let me not be wakened—
"They leave us for three months, then they only stay a week
     with us,
"So it's hardly surprising if we wish they were home again.
"The day the court's held he can look to get a reprimand."
I am sleeping and let me not be wakened.

Katy went tearing off, putting on her coat—
I am sleeping and let me not be wakened—
And complained to the wife of Donald, son of George.
I am sleeping and let me not be wakened.
"Katy, be quiet, your grumbling's disgraceful.
"Supposing your husband were eight weeks at the fair,
"A good-natured person wouldn't say a word about it."
I am sleeping and let me not be wakened.

In his final verse Rob Donn quoted the advice of no less an authority than the elderly, twice-married Tutor of Farr; only to dismiss his male chauvinism with comments that must have made the bard popular among the womenfolk.

Did you hear the judgment given by the Tutor—
I am sleeping and let me not be wakened—
That always staying at home, and kindness, are fatal?
I am sleeping and let me not be wakened.
I'll tell you the habit you'ld best try to cultivate.
Don't stay away too long or be surly in your house.
Continual flogging's useless and blows achieve nothing.
I am sleeping and let me not be wakened.[1]

Rob Donn composed another portrait gallery of the parish of Tongue, this time examining local reactions to a man who ran about in a state of indecent exposure. It is probably the earliest streak-poem of the British Isles, and it was said to have been occasioned by the arrival in the Kyle of Tongue of a boat containing contraband liquor for that upholder of the law Donald Forbes, the sheriff substitute. It is not clear why one of the boat's crew found himself trouserless ashore, but perhaps he had been compelled to make his escape from one of the houses in embarrassing circumstances. Evidently he was stranded on the west shore because he went first to Melness house where the junior heiress of Bighouse lived with her disappointed husband.

43

He went yonder along the shore's ridge
Seeking a favour from the Laird of Melness,
Who said to him, "you ugly devil,
"Not a stitch will you get on your tail."

The Lady of Melness spoke courteously:
"I shall hide his thighs
"Though I don't know whether he is a man of God.
"He deserves something since he is destitute."

But this dedicated streaker took off without accepting the garment that was offered to him, and so arrived at Ribigill.

He went to the house of Donald Forbes
For it was right to seek out the guilty one.
Haughtily he threw the warp at him
When he learned of the row over his clothing.

The wife of Forbes does not appear to have been at home, otherwise a quick retort might have been more like her than ever. On went the delinquent until he reached the church farm of Tongue, which still bears its Norse name in a Scottish form.

To Kirkibol he hurried
To visit Margaret and Uisdean.
Said the latter with a scowl,
"Let a clout be thrown over him, bad though he is."

Today the only Scrabster on that coast is the port of Thurso in Caithness, but there used to be a small township of the same Norse name in this neighbourhood also.

It was to Scrabster he went then
To visit Donald and Barbara,
Who said: "It would be better for you
"To earn it like any other servant."

On he went until he reached the manse of Tongue, in which the Reverend Walter Ross had lived since 1730 with a wife who suffered the considerable disability of being unable to converse in Gaelic.

He went to the house of the Reverend Walter,
Since charity befits the man of religion.
As he stood in his downstairs room,
Great was the fright his wife received.

> The Minister said, speaking very smoothly,
> "What shall we do with the fine fellow?
> She replied in the tongue she knew,
> "Weel-a-wat, I canna tell ye."

Beyond the Kyle of Tongue a headland extends to the remarkable island of conglomerate basalt, called Eilean nan Ron because of the numbers of grey Atlantic seals that inhabit its rocks, and on its eastern flank lay the estate of Skerray in which Iain Mac Eachainn had been reared.

> He went round the edge of the Kyle,
> To see the Laird of Skerray about some clothing.
> The latter said in disgust,
> "What kind of madness has seized that fellow?"
> Margaret said he had hallucinations:
> James said it would be better he were clothed,
> And she answered sportively,
> "Let a cloak be thrown over the devil's penis."

But the streaker doubled on his tracks to regain his boat, whose skipper proved to be another English-speaker.

> Now he went running off as fast as he could
> In search of the skipper who was there in the boat,
> To see whether he would look into
> His loss of clothing.

> "You who gave instructions to come ashore
> "In an evil time that mustn't be talked about;"
> Observed Captain Hill as he turned his head,
> "What the devil means the fellow?"[2]

There are relatively few allusions in Rob Donn's poetry to the social world beyond Skerray to the east, where the parish of Farr belonged to the presbytery of Tongue but the administration to the earldom of Sutherland with its centre far to the south at Dunrobin castle. Within the orbit of his personal acquaintance, however, the bard delineated that society graphically and impartially, Walter Ross the minister, James MacCulloch the weaver, John Sutherland the schoolmaster, Donald Forbes the sheriff-substitute, no less than the head men of his clan and all those humble members of it who live only in his references to them. None could hope to be spared from his humour or his censure, not even Iain Mac Eachainn nor Hugh of

Bighouse, as they discovered when he considered them to have been guilty of sharp-practice in the course of their cattle dealings.

> *The Laird of Bighouse and Iain Mac Eachainn,*
> *The two people with mouths not to be shunned*
> *Though they robbed you the night before—*
> *Surely their conscience is stifled*
> *When they are selling cattle to the Lowlanders.*
> *But God will cut away with the blade of Justice*
> *Those riches from their children.*[3]

Westwards Rob Donn cast his net to the limits of the Mackay country, where the Reverend George Brodie ministered to the new parish of Edderachillis that bordered the ancient Macleod territory of Assynt. In February 1740 Murdo Macdonald noted: "baptised two children who were brought from another parish, whose minister Mr Brodie is indisposed for some weeks past . . . Lord, be gracious to that distressed brother and prepare him for life or death, and let his concerns learn submission to the divine will. That family had been for some time past flourishing, but Oh, how soon may they wither." Later in the same year George Brodie died, and in 1742 his widow Barbara was granted a tack of the small-holding of Achovarisaid.[4] So it was at some time before this date, while the minister's daughters were still living in the manse at Badcall south of Scourie, that Iain Mac Eachainn's elder son Hugh was courting Christine, the youngest of the three Brodie sisters, before he left to seek his fortune in Jamaica: because Rob Donn remarked that she was there in the poem of farewell that he placed in the mouth of Hugh.

> *My journey lies to Jamaica*
> *Many miles from this land,*
> *And my thoughts are returning*
> *To the shores of the Kyle.*
> *I look forward to steering*
> *Towards the goal of my travels*
> *Beyond the Fair Aird*
> *Between the heathery islands.*
>
> *Accept my explanation, Christine,*
> *And take courage for us both.*
> *It is honour that summons:*
> *How could I not listen, whatever the price?*

46

Without winning it through hardship
I certainly would not deserve your love,
And if I lose your favour
I am poorer than I thought.

But if I depart, lass,
On such a sure path,
And if it be my destiny to be so fortunate
Or so prosperous as to return,
I shall retain your attachment as it used to be
Or increase it two-fold,
And never again shall I leave you
On the plain of Badcall.[5]

The address that Rob Donn composed in Hugh's name contains
three stanzas, each of sixteen short lines. Their theme recalls the
Ulysses, not of Homer, but of the European renaissance: of Dante's
Divine Comedy and of the sixteenth century French sonnet *Heureux
qui, comme Ulysse . . .* As there is not the slightest evidence that
Murdo Macdonald would have been capable of translating either
for Rob Donn's benefit, it is natural to wonder whether his translations from the English poet Pope influenced him either. The bard
permitted Hugh to end with the protestation:

. . . If you would believe my words
Until the day when I see you again,
Having gained your love through such difficulties,
It will be my entire reward.[6]

After Hugh had departed on his travels, Rob Donn envisaged
Christine Brodie sitting like Penelope at her loom, and composed a
charming little song for her to sing at it, with the lilting refrain:

It's terrible what happened last year to me,
Last year, last year, last year to me:
It's terrible what happened last year to me—
Last year my lad went away from me.
  No sooner had you left
  Than it was reported up the country
  And although your love was like a fire within me,
  Others would not see me weeping on that account.

What made me mention that
Was fear lest my reputation should suffer from it:

47

And even if I let out a cry that you could hear,
Others would see that you did not come back.

Now, since you went away from the land
Your people are as my own kindred.
It is your love that is closest to me
And your reputation amongst others that is
*   sweetest to me.*

I am praying that you will come back
Before the sun harms you,
Before you take food that makes you ill,
And before you see a girl who seduces you.[7]

Was Rob Donn showing his own knowledge of Hugh's character when he placed that ominous thought in Christine's mind? Evidently he had come to Badcall on the west coast to present these poems to her, because her grandson later recorded how he composed another on the very next morning, after he had asked her what she had dreamt about the night before, and she had refused to tell him.

What you saw in a dream
You discreetly kept a secret;
You made excuses next day
So we are none the wiser.

Though the vision is without substance,
You keep its image in your heart.
You will be happier by far asleep
Than when you are awake.

As though she has hardly heard him, Christine is represented in this poem as interrupting the bard to address her absent lover. To understand her reference to cows, it must be remembered that in this cattle economy the very word was a synonym for a girl's dowry or for wealth.

Though there were seven nights before each day,
I would remain ever faithful to you.
I would rather than a pair of cows
That I had your heir upon my knee.

48

Rob Donn concludes this exchange with the reassurance:

> *His manliness is his asset*
> *And your modesty invests your reputation,*
> *And although the ocean separates you*
> *His influence is visible all around.*[8]

Hugh did prosper in Jamaica. He became a planter and also rose to the army rank of Colonel in that island in circumstances that remain obscure. But one of the remarks that Rob Donn had placed in the mouth of Christine was to prove prophetic. In Jamaica Hugh so far forgot Christine as to marry Frances de la Rue, and although she died in the West Indies, Hugh ultimately returned with their daughter, to marry another in Strathnaver.[9]

There is no evidence as to whether the Tutor of Farr's fifth son Rupert emigrated to Jamaica to become a planter at the same time as Iain Mac Eachainn's son. Rupert had already taken a wife from among the Gordons who had been settling in the Naver valley since it became the property of the earls of Sutherland, and Rob Donn composed a charming song of good wishes to him at his departure.[10]

Rupert's handsome brother George, who would soon become the Tutor's heir through the death of their elder brother, was the only one of this enormous family who did not adopt a profession that took him out of the country. He received for his portion the spectacular island of Handa just north of Scourie bay, about twelve miles south of Sandwood. Its perpendicular cliffs, rising to a height of about six hundred feet, were a nesting-place for innumerable fulmars and kittiwakes, but it also possessed sandy beaches, machair, moor and lochans. Rob Donn depicted George as a working farmer.

> *The Laird of Handa at the plough*
> *Advanced sedately, unerringly,*
> *On the lea-field of the glen, without township,*
> *without cairns,*
> *None leading the horse save a lassie.*[11]

In earlier times a Macleod of Assynt had maintained a twelve-oared galley on Handa, and George continued this tradition when he sailed to Lewis across the Minch with a Macleod crew in what Rob Donn described (though he may have been exaggerating deliberately) as a *birlinn*, or galley.

> *We travelling with George*
> *By sea to Stornoway,*

49

E

We sailing the whole night
Yonder towards the Point of Stoer,
Provisioned with food and drink, that galley,
Loaded with cargo, watertight, swift,
With helm, masts and rigging,
With pulleys and stitched sails.

We sailing closely round the Point
In the darkness of the night,
We continued towards Lochinver,
Rowing without a flicker of light.
The east wind began to blow on us
As day rose out of night,
And she could not be steered to any port
Between Puitig and Lochalsh.

In this poem the master of the terse, salient phrase also employs the flood of adjectives more characteristic of Duncan Macintyre's descriptive poetry.

In the morning we were obliged,
When the wind rose to a gale,
To turn our backs to the land
And our faces directly towards the sea,
Subjected to the drenchings and the beatings
Of the furious great waves,
Mountainous, foamy, stormy, deep-valleyed,
Sucking, thick-lipped, blue.

As she made headway
Forwards on her course,
The Macleods were unerring and expert
About the sheets of the sails.
Watchful, mindful, powerful
Was Patrick at the helm,
And George Roy of Tarbet was there
Doing the work of three.

That crew alternated
With fortitude and fear.
They were to be seen smiling
Though they had left rock and mountain behind,
With unfainting courage,

50

Without timidity in their actions
Though not a man out of the five of them
Had ever set foot in Lewis.

But the divine helmsman looked mercifully
On our plight in time,
When it was impossible to boast
Of sailor or of carpenter.
From the back of the great-troughed sea
And the water rushing forward in a torrent
And from the summit of the whirling waves
She struck her prow against land.

The somewhat shaken party had reached safety at Gress, a few miles north of the Eye peninsula.

When we came to that place
The people made us welcome.
We got our share of lodgings,
Such as had none to surpass them,
With high walls, lime and slates,
With upper floors, well-protected, neat,
With a generous Laird of the MacIvers
And the daughter of the Lord of Kildun.

Our Captain in that place
Was someone to boast of.
Not a glass came to the board there
But it was his health that was drunk,
While old women exclaimed
They had never seen anyone so handsome
And maidens whispered the question,
"Goodness, is he married?"[12]

George of Handa once gave Rob Donn a horse, and none could say that he had not earned it.[13]

But the central figure in Rob Donn's social world, the only Chief whom he would commemorate out of the four who succeeded one another during his lifetime, was the Master of Reay who lived in the mansion at Balnakil. Rob Donn called him:

The apex of society and of entertainment,
Of the men of poetry and of music.[14]

51

He praised the Master's good nature, simplicity and extreme generosity; and the minister did the same, though he had no taste for the Master's convivial habits. The man who would succeed as the fourth Lord Reay possessed another quality, however, which fitted him ill for that office. His own heir described him as "an easy facile man, and altogether ignorant of business," while his grand-daughter recalled that "though possessing a good plain understanding, graced with all the accomplishments of a gentleman, derived from liberal education and foreign travel, [he] was yet totally unacquainted with the business of ordinary life; and being, from an openness of disposition, perfectly artless and unsuspecting."[15]

After the death of his wife, the Master remarried in December 1741, and this time his bride Christine Sutherland came, not from the English-speaking Lowlands, but from Pronsy in Sutherland. She was an Episcopalian however who, to the distress of the Reverend Murdo Macdonald, declined to alter her religious beliefs. He described the effect of this on prayer meetings in the mansion at Balnakil after her husband had succeeded to the peerage. "Her aversion to his devotion had influence on the other domestics who therefore dwindled away one by one, till the peer had few or none to attend the diets of worship, which were at last quite superceded." This was the context in which the minister described the Master's shortcomings. "Were he not shackled by certain persons to whom his own weakness had given the ascendant over him, there would have been much more good done by him. There was indeed a good deal." Indeed, as Rob Donn would celebrate in one of his most impressive elegies.

It is hard to discover any genetic cause for the contrast between the amiable Master of Reay and his energetic half-brothers Hugh of Bighouse, George the advocate and Alexander the soldier. There is no discernable weakness to be discovered in his mother's stock though, had there been, he would have inherited a double strain of it since she was General Hugh Mackay of Scourie's daughter, while the second Lord Reay had married the General's sister. But he was content to leave the management of the Durness estate largely in the hands of Kenneth Sutherland of Keoldale, less than two miles south of Balnakil on the Kyle of Durness. Despite his name, Kenneth of Keoldale was closely related to the house of the Mackay chiefs, a great-grandson of the first Lord Reay, son of the Tutor's sister Margaret, and also married to the Tutor's daughter Catherine.[16] According to Rob Donn he was as just and generous as the Master, and although Macdonald sometimes shuddered over the state of his soul, he confirmed the bard's verdict on Sutherland's exercise of his executive powers.[17]

So long as Hugh of Bighouse lived at Tongue and took part in the droving trade with Iain Mac Eachainn, he was also a frequent visitor to Durness. But the activity which took him to the far west was that combination of business and pleasure, the deer hunt. When Hugh moved to Strath Halladale, he was no longer able to enjoy its delights so frequently according to Rob Donn, and it appears that he took up residence at Bighouse sometime between 1742 and 1744. He had already agreed with the Dowager Lady Bighouse "that he should free and relieve me yearly of all public burdens that then affected or might in time coming affect my jointure lands of Halladale" in return for possession of them in 1737, when she was the wife of Robert Sinclair of Giese.[18] But there were complications when she was widowed for the second time in 1742 and tried to hold on to her husband's property in Caithness. Her Sinclair son reported: "The cows and labouring cattle that were upon the Mains of Giese at Mr Robert's death are there still, and no title has been made to them, neither has the lady shewn the disposition she says she has from Mr Robert to them. And though it's very probable she may have such a disposition, yet it's proper it be seen . . . In case the lady (when the memorialist should happen at any time to be from home) should take it in her head to go away to Halladale and to lock the doors of the house of Giese in order to keep the memorialist out of the possession, may the memorialist in this case break open the doors?"[19]

Clearly this was not the kind of mother-in-law with whom it was safe to do business at a distance, especially as it transpired that she had obtained the disposition from her second husband in return for a promise to hand over all her property in Strath Halladale to the exclusion of the children of her first marriage. The time had come for Hugh of Bighouse to take personal possession of his wife's inheritance, especially when it was also contested by William of Melness.

After he had departed, Rob Donn expressed Hugh's love (and his own) for the world he had left.

> *Take my farewell and good wishes*
> *To the other end of the country*
> *Where I used to be joyful*
> *Between Tongue and Cape Wrath*
> *At the time when I climbed the brae—*
> *Though someone would exclaim "Ochoin"—*

And I would be well pleased
To be in the heights of the rugged hills
Where the tawny ones could be seen
Running lithely through the defiles
And the deer hounds in full chase
Jumping playfully at their hair
After hearing the burst of fire.
What a part of my happiness that was—
The offspring of the hind lying dead.

Oh Master of Reay,
What happiness it brings to your mind
What with the excellence of your people
And the mountain near to you—
From the door of your room
Right before your eyes
Where it lies between An Dunan
And the knoll of Meall a' Chuirn.
I think each morning
Of the time when we used to be there.
It was going so far away from you
That made me nostalgic.
I would like to see
A hart being beset
And gunpowder blazing
Between flint and hammer.

After representing Hugh in Strath Halladale, dreaming of the days
he had spent in the home of his elder brother at Balnakil, Rob Donn
permits him an appreciative word for his less mountainous inheritance near the Caithness plains.

This is a place as it happens
Of braes and plains,
As pleasant a place
As adorns your country.
However magnificent your dwelling
It is your way of life I envy so much—
The weeks pass pleasantly for you
As you look out on the deer forest.

Take my farewell once more
To him who pays for the dram
And the hand that provides venison
And the heart without fear—
To where Iain Mac Eachainn is
And I a while without seeing him,
My good compannion, accomplished, manly—
You were the deer's enemy.
At the moment for restraining the puppies,
For holding them and catching them,
Anyone better at giving the word
I never saw.
Our expeditions were fortunate
For hunting the hinds.
You would deploy the hunting party
And put the hounds on the job.

Take my farewell at the same time
To Donald son of Donald,
Excellent, equable companion
Whose conversation never tired,
Who with his customary manners
Would be with us at the Bard's spring,
Who would meet the friends at your board each
  month.
There would be hospitality for a space
Among the people in your company
And when they desired it,
Deep measuring of the cups.
Often my mind would be swirling
With all the topics that were raised,
And it was no ill-will for those people
That sent me away hastily.

Characteristically, the Chief's son is to be seen in this poem
handing out compliments not merely to his brother and his cousin
but in similar terms to far humbler members of the clan hierarchy.

Take my well-considered greetings
To Donald son of George—
And although I have lost his acquaintance
I would like to be with him,

55

Proclaiming as is proper
That he is a pretty, kindly man
And when he takes offence
It is as well not to oppose him.
When the wind used to change on us
And the roe were running at full speed
At the time when we let slip the leashes,
It was a loss to be without you
Ascending the cold mountains
With the excellent swift strides
Which proclaimed modestly
That your strength was not slight.[20]

This poem of 176 lines is among those that can be dated to the years before Rob Donn reached the age of thirty, like his lament for Ann Morrison and his flippant song about conjugal relations. He had not yet been presented with a theme for the first of his elegies, but already his talent had soared like a sun that would never set, illuminating his remote, archaic society and preserving its lineaments forever. The range and originality of his techniques are as remarkable as the modernity of his thought. "A man's a man for a' that," he proclaimed many years before Robert Burns was born, and in songs satirical, grave and gay he explored the nature of man as he observed it in the little tribal kingdom of the Mackays.

But presently an event occurred beyond its frontiers that was to test his insight and judgment in an altogether new manner.

REFERENCES TO CHAPTER III

1. *Rob Donn*, 260-5, verses 1, summary of verses 2 and 3, verses 4, 5, 6, 7, 8, 10, 11, 12, 14. Cf. H. Morrison's explanation of the song, which is hard to reconcile with verse 3, line 5.
2. *Ibid.*, 243-5, entire poem without refrain. Hew Morrison's explanation suggests that the boat was called the *Dragon* and that its skipper was the streaker. In fact a member of its crew was the offender, to whom this name was given.
3. *Ibid.*, 445, first stanza.
4. Reay MS. 33/24 (26).
5. *Rob Donn*, 278-9, lines 9-32. For line 10 the 1829 edition of Rob Donn's poetry gives *Fad a léigeach' o thir*, whereas the 1899 edition has *Moran mhiltein o thir*.
6. *Ibid.*, 279, lines 25-28.

56

7. *Ibid.*, 399-400, the entire poem. In the third line of the first verse *mur* is read as *mar*.
8. *Ibid.*, 401, the entire poem without its refrain.
9. *Book of Mackay*, 315.
10. *Rob Donn* 1899, 131-3.
11. *Ibid.*, 341, lines 5-8. The 1829 edition gives *toireim teannadh* for *toirein teanntadh.*
12. *Ibid.*, 156-8, the first eight stanzas.
13. *Ibid.*, 340, line 9.
14. *Ibid.*, 6, lines 5-6.
15. *Book of Mackay*, 203.
16. *Ibid.*, 330.
17. *Rob Donn*, 28-31 : Macdonald MS.
18. Bighouse MS. (b) 10.
19. *Ibid.* (b) 11.
20. *Rob Donn*, 87-92, stanzas 1, 2, the second half of stanza 3, 4, 5, 9.

CHAPTER FOUR

Distant Thunder

"THESE two Sabbaths past," wrote the minister of Durness in his diary on 23rd September 1745, "the congregation was obliged to wait longer than usual, by reason of the post, whose news I thought it duty to peruse overly before I could come in; as the peace of the nation is presently broken by a new rebellion that is on foot in favour of the Pretender's eldest son, who landed in Lochaber about the middle of last month. A company of vain men have joined him, in all probability to their own ruin. Many are the reflections that may occur to any thinking person on this unaccountable event, such as 1) what a long tract of undisturbed peace have we unthankfully enjoyed in this island? No shorter a period than thirty years, viz. since 1715. Never was this nation so long at ease on end, neither is there any in Europe that I read of can boast of the like providential privilege." Murdo Macdonald liked to enumerate his thoughts in this way. His second category considered the ingratitude that made sinful man ripe for such a visitation: the third contemplated the justice of God in inflicting such a punishment: the fourth referred with surprising compassion to those blind mortals who had resisted every attempt to turn them into Calvinists, and who were now rejecting their Protestant sovereign, "who seem to fear neither God nor the King."[1]

In the minister's diary is to be found a graphic illustration of the way in which news was disseminated throughout the Mackay country, expounded from pulpits with a biblical key to clarify the meaning of events. There can be no doubt that he preached to his parishioners in Gaelic exactly as he wrote in English in his diary, because he noted on more than one occasion that he had done so. The diary also reveals how long it took even such urgent news to reach the most distant corner of the mainland. Prince Charles landed on Eriskay on 23rd July and raised the royal standard in Glenfinnan in Lochaber on 19th August: this was the news that the Reverend Murdo was expounding to his parishioners less than

58

two hundred miles away, a whole month later, as fast as it had reached him.. While he was doing so, Edinburgh was surrendering to the Jacobites on 17th September, and five days later the Prince defeated General Cope at Prestonpans, where the Chief of Mackay's youngest son Alexander, who had joined the regular Army in 1737, was captured.[2] The victory left Prince Charles master of Scotland, though once again it was not until a month later that Murdo Macdonald was able to comment on the event.

"The rebellion in this nation is come to a greater head than was at first thought," he conceded on 17th October. "The city of Edinburgh on 17th of last month came into the hands of the enemy and the pretended King and his son the present Knight's Errant were proclaimed with great solemnity at the Cross. Some time thereafter there was a battle fought about seven miles to the east of the city, wherein the King's forces were obliged to yield themselves mostly prisoners after the slaughter of some hundreds of them. This puts the victorious mad; and accordingly they vaunt themselves as if the cause were entirely gained; but there is still a stronger possibility for their being mistaken. Lord! Thou art the great man of war, for the 'Lord of Hosts is thy name'." Macdonald assumed with complete conviction that God could not possibly have taken the side of the Roman Catholics, but was merely using them as a scourge to punish the sins of true Christians. He also noted that the Jacobites possessed no other allies. "No foreign power is yet arrived in favour of our enemies, and we are told that a considerable army of our own and Dutch forces were some time ago on their way to meet the rebels."

News generally reached the seat of the Chief first, from whence it was despatched to the far west. Lord Reay had fortunately provided in advance for the emergency by making his peace with the Earl of Sutherland, the most powerful Hanoverian in the north of Scotland. The Gordon Earls had been for centuries the most dangerous enemies of Clan Mackay, using their influence with the Crown and the administration in Edinburgh in endless intrigues designed to secure possession of the old province of Strathnaver. They had acquired its central valley of the Naver, but since the third Lord Reay had succeeded to the chiefship in his childhood he had avoided any further loss during the two previous emergencies which had ruined so many others of his position, the Revolution of 1688 and the uprising of 1715.

Since then his disputes with the house of Sutherland had revolved round the debateable lands beside which John of Mudale lived, the

Dirriemore or Rough Bounds. Only a fortnight before the Prince landed in Eriskay, Reay wrote to Sutherland: "I heartily wish that all our differences were buried in oblivion, and to that end I have made some proposals which I think are equal and honourable, and for the real interest of your Lordship's family as well as my own, and which my son George will lay before you whenever your Lordship pleases."[3] He had chosen as his advocate the son who had so recently handed his title in Strathmore to Iain Mac Eachainn after qualifying in the profession of his mother's people, the Dowells of Edinburgh.

Accordingly the two men were ready to sign their agreement before the Prince's standard was raised in Glenfinnan: "to secure our acting with mutual harmony and uniting the strength of both our families and adherants, so as to be able in any public danger to render the more considerable and effectual service to his present Majesty, King George the Second, for supporting the succession in the Protestant line of his most Illustrious house, and for securing the present happy establishment in Church and State, and for defeating the designs of his Majesty's enemies, both open and secret." Beyond the parish of Edderachillis in the west the Macleods of Assynt were believed to have Jacobite sympathies, and they had been suffering for some years from a take-over bid by the house of Sutherland which they had already attempted to resist by force before the Earl's lawyers advised him in 1738 not to try to substantiate his title in Assynt. The threat still hung over its inhabitants and may have influenced their attitude to Prince Charles as a possible saviour at a time when their security was so gravely threatened.[4]

To the east of Strath Halladale the Sinclairs were also believed to be disaffected,[5] while to the south there were the Jacobite Macdonalds and Mackenzies to reckon with.

The Chief of Mackay had shown himself so prompt and enthusiastic in support of the Hanoverian cause that only the slow speed with which intelligence travelled can account for his delay in ordering a muster of his clansmen at Tongue. It was late in October before the minister of Durness could record: "There is an order come from the Superior of the country for an universal gathering of all that are able to carry arms, that on Monday next there may be a rendezvous at Tongue, where there are to be equipped for the public service a proper number. This has made our meeting thin, as the people have need of all the time they have to prepare for this expedition. I have been a while of the day employed with the few who came in conference, prayer and reading, and closed with proper exhortations

60

in a suitableness for the present juncture of providence." In other words, he made very certain that none of his parishioners became infected with the political heresies that his presbytery was reporting from Assynt.

Lord Reay next ordered Macdonald to travel to West Moine, although he had recently paid his routine visit there, in order to put its inhabitants into an orthodox frame of mind before they joined the muster. As Rob Donn was not likely to have been away from home at this season of the year and Macdonald wrote of a muster of all capable of bearing arms, it may be assumed that he listened to the minister expounding the justice of the Hanoverian cause before setting off for Tongue with the contingent from West Moine. One can only speculate on the possible reasons why a man just over thirty years old, whose participation in the deer hunts must have trained him to be one of the most accurate marksmen in the country, was not selected for the service.

Macdonald himself was delayed in West Moine by ill-health after the departure of the recruits. "I was confined on the other side longer than I intended to stay by some indisposition of body and mind under which I laboured now for several weeks together. It is of the goodness of my God that my miseries are not as often and lasting as my sins." These, according to the confessions in his diary, generally took the form of sexual dreams.

But after his return to Durness early in November the minister suffered a different kind of defilement. "Most of last week I was taken up with attendance on a person of distinction who is seldom here, and expected that the neighbourhood here should signify their regard by much attendance. In such company I have reason to be afraid of receiving more harm than I can do of good, since I'm in far greater hazard of symbolising with them than they are ready to come my way. Lord, wash away any filth contracted in such societies." By a process of elimination these cryptic words may be taken as referring to the Chief's third son George, and they constitute the earliest, ominous description of the spendthrift man who was to die bankrupt, leaving his descendants to wreck the Mackay country by selling its remaining titles to the house of Sutherland. It is evident that he was a habitual absentee from the parish in which his father had invested him with the wadset of Strathmore. Now, whether the Chief wished to preserve his heir at Balnakil from danger, or whether the Master of Reay lacked the necessary capacity, it was George who was sent on one of his rare visits to the west to supervise further recruitment.

61

Daylight was already short and the ground boggy underfoot when the men of the Reay country travelled to Tongue. On 21st November Macdonald recorded disconsolately: "The weather (which was during the harvest and what came of the winter the best that has been since the memory of any now living) is broke ten days ago, and turned so very stormy with windy frost and snow that it bears hard upon man and beast." It was so wild in fact that "last Sabbath there was no sermon by reason of the stormy day."

On 6th December, the day on which the army of Prince Charles reached Derby, the storms abated and the minister set out courageously for West Moine which he had not visited since the muster, over a month earlier. "I set out from the other side in a fair and calm day; so I came safely here in the evening, though not without some indisposition of body and mind, yet in such circumstances as afford matter of thankfulness and complaint." As he went about, preaching and catechising in the district, Rob Donn received the doubtful benefit of some extremely intricate and tortuous explanations of God's purposes, faithfully preserved in the minister's diary. "In this drumly period wherein the Providence of God with respect to the public keeps the minds of all lovers of our own (? land) in such an anxious suspense as to the event of our national commotions, which is rendered doubtful by the seeming advantages of the enemy and the advances we are told he makes towards England, and the slow progress made by our Councils, Armies and Navies against that insurrection, I hear that many of my brethren are preaching political doctrine according to the times. I have done nothing yet this way, only was now and then giving exhortations before and after sermons, and particularly last time I was here, when the men of my parish were on their way out of the country."

While the Jacobite army began its retreat from Derby to Scotland, Macdonald travelled to Eriboll, that fertile oasis on the east side of the loch opposite the island called Corrie in English, An Còrr-Eilean in Gaelic. Here he observed on 16th December, after his first night in his new surroundings: "I discoursed the landlady for some considerable time on the state of religion in her family; the rather that at many former occasions I have been at no small pains with her husband in order to bring him under due concern for his soul, but to very little purpose hitherto if I judge according to appearance. The man being the grandchild and great-grandchild of ministers, and the woman a minister's daughter, I look upon myself as nearly allied to them, and in proportion would gladly contribute my best endeavours to their advantage. I gave her proper instructions for being useful to her husband this way, as she has made some advances in profession beyond him, and she has undertaken to follow the advices given." Macdonald's diary leaves little doubt that in addition to his sense of loyalty to the other members of his priestly caste, he was motivated by the belief that his contribution to the war effort consisted in helping to turn aside the wrath of God, manifested by the Jacobite successes, by cementing the faith of his flock.

Many young children came to his diet of catechising in Eriboll, and when he had instructed them he travelled to Muisel to perform a ceremony of marriage. Here his host and hostess could only have been Iain Mac Eachainn and his thrifty wife, on whose spiritual progress he unfortunately did not see fit to comment. He remained there for five days and during this time "I had the comfort of a visit from my wife who stayed with me till Thursday morning when, on account of her family, she was obliged to leave me." It seems likely that she was driven to make that journey in the depths of winter by concern over her husband's unusually long absence, and most remarkably, she achieved it on foot which, as he remarked, "would have defeated her many years ago." Even a century later people disappeared during winter journeys through that wild country, and their bodies were not discovered until months afterwards.

After his wife's departure the minister displayed undiminished fortitude by travelling from Muisel to attend a presbytery meeting in Tongue. "Through the Moine I was endeavouring by religious conversation to be useful to two or three that were in company. Thus we made the coarse road comfortable." He found the seat of the Chief buzzing with military activity. "There was a thrang of men in the place by reason of a second company that are going on the national expedition, who went off this day." But still Rob Donn was not of their number.

The Chief's first preoccupation had been to secure the frontiers of the Mackay country. Hugh of Bighouse manned the eastern border, posting men along Druim Holstein, a gentle ridge compared with the precipitous country of the west but a formidable enough barrier seen from the plains of Caithness. It is a tradition that the men of Strath Halladale were reinforced by inhabitants of the Naver valley, of whom Angus Mackay from Skelpick near the river-mouth suffered severely during the chill winter he spent on that inhospitable ridge.[6] There is a strong presumption that George of Strathmore's business in the west, when his behaviour gave such offence to the minister of Durness, had been to plant a detachment of soldiers in Edderachillis to watch the Assynt border. The direct route south from the seat of the Chief ran out of the Mackay country beside Ben Klibreck and thence past the eastern shore of Loch Shin at the township of Lairg, which means Pass. Here Lord Reay also sent a force of men and advised the Earl of Sutherland to do the same, for the pass led to the head of the Kyle of Sutherland beyond which lay the hostile lands of Ross-shire.

Their militia was formed into the Earl's regiment in which Hugh of Bighouse became a Lieutenant Colonel, his brother George a Captain. The swashbuckling William Mackay of Melness received a Lieutenant's commission while that devout poet John of Mudale joined the crusade as a somewhat elderly Ensign. The only surviving son of Hugh of Bighouse had reached military age by this time, and he was also given the rank of Ensign.

By the time the second company was ready to march from Tongue, the two northern potentates were faced with a call for troops to serve far beyond their own territories. President Duncan Forbes of Culloden had asked for reinforcements to be sent to the small army that General Lord Loudoun had brought north, and it was Captain George who commanded the Mackay company on its journey. Meanwhile Lieutenant William of Melness was present with the forces of Loudoun when they surprised Castle Dounie and captured the two-faced Lord Lovat. On 12th December he sent a graphic account of the adventure to the Earl of Sutherland. No doubt he acted correctly in making his report to the Colonel of his regiment, but in a society whose military affairs were still being organised on such traditional clan lines, one may suspect continuing animosity in his failure to address this account to his Chief and kinsman.[7]

As usual, it was not until a month after the event that Murdo Macdonald learned of the battle of Falkirk which the Jacobite army fought on 17th January 1746 in the course of its retreat to the north. "The withering state of my soul," he confessed on 23rd February, "keeps me from recording anything about the public, which continues embroiled by the unnatural rebellion which still rages in the bowels of our nation. There was another engagement about 17th of last month near the famous Torwood, the particular account whereof we have not yet, but are told that there was considerable slaughter on both sides." It had indeed been an inconclusive engagement. "We now hear that the enemy, after being driven from England and met with the brush above, are on their way to the north in two bodies, the one coming by Aberdeen and the other the Highland way towards Inverness: and that the King's army is pursuing them with the Duke of Cumberland on their head:

64

for which reason it is thought they may yet give some trouble. Though almost dispersed, there are new levies of men ordered to be made and march to meet them forthwith. O Lord of Hosts, arise and let thine enemies be scattered, and let them who hate thee flee before thy face." In the emergency the minister tended increasingly to equate God with the tribal Jehovah of the Old Testament Jews, and to regard him as the exclusive property of the Calvinist Elect.

Rob Donn happened to receive the latest news almost as soon as his minister did because "I was from home for the most part of this interval on the other side of my parish, going about the several parts of my function viz. marrying, baptising, preaching and meeting in conference with my people, some of whom being distinguished above others, called on me, otherwise I had not gone so soon after being so long thereupon and lately." Macdonald's English prose is of an extremely high standard, especially considering that he spent most of his life speaking in his native Gaelic tongue, and he rarely betrayed that he was writing in a foreign language by such misuse of words. It may appear from the English writings which his colleague the minister of Reay published that this was a common accomplishment, but a study of the Reverend Alexander Pope's unpublished compositions leads to the conclusion that his published prose had been carefully edited, and that he possessed nothing approaching Macdonald's facility as an English writer.[8]

Ever since the defeat of the Jacobite cause, the last forlorn stand of Prince Charlie's men in Inverness and their destruction at Culloden have evoked an admiration and sympathy that time has not dimmed. But the feelings of Hanoverians in the far north were very different at the time when the enemy appeared on their doorstep. Returning to his manse in Durness, the minister recorded on 17th March, "I saw friends to the eastward in soundness of body and tranquility of circumstances, the more to be remarked as we hear of the contrary lot of our fellow subjects and Christians who now in the neighbouring shires are greatly distressed by the outrageous barbarities of waging enemies: which, though they seem to be arguments of an expiring cause, are notwithstanding very grievous to the sufferers in the meantime. The accounts of these matters are not quite certain in regard the channel of communication is all this time stopped by the violent interceptions of the enemy, who we hear is now at Inverness, to whose bounds the Duke of Cumberland is coming with slow marches indeed by reason of the surprising desolations made by these savage plunderers as they come along."

Exaggerated rumours of enemy atrocities are a common accom-

F

paniment of wars, and they soon multiplied when General Loudoun retreated across the Kyle of Sutherland by the ferry which links the erstwhile capital of Ross-shire at Tain with that of Sutherland at Dornoch. After him came the Jacobite Duke of Perth with 1500 men and a number of boats which had been gathered in the Moray Firth. He reached Tain in a thick fog and crossed into Sutherland on 20th March despite the entrenchments which Loudoun had dug on the opposite shore. At Dornoch he captured two ships filled with supplies for the Hanoverian army, but not the much-needed treasure chest, which had been removed hastily to a man-of-war standing out at sea. A few miles to the north the Earl of Sutherland fled from Dunrobin castle by ship, taking with him all the public money of the country, and leaving his wife behind to entertain the Jacobite leaders with what zeal she was able to command. The Jacobite Earl of Cromartie was among her guests, but since his party had once again been cheated of the money they needed so desperately to maintain their army at Inverness, he sent his son Lord Macleod north into Caithness to discover what the Sinclairs there might be able to provide.[9] No wonder the minister of Durness wailed on 26th March: "The poor people here are like reeds shaken with the wind, hiding all their portable effects and at a loss what to do with themselves."

He did not know yet of the exciting events that had occurred the night before at the seat of the Chief. An armed sloop originally called the *Hazard* and renamed the *Prince Charles* had been on her way to the Jacobites with a consignment of £13,000 in French gold coins when she became engaged in a long running fight with the British naval vessel *Sheerness*. After sustaining over eight hundred shot, the *Prince Charles* fled into the most unlucky inlet she could have found on that coast, the Hanoverian headquarters at Tongue. She was observed by the Chief himself from the windows of his home, passing the Rabbit Islands followed by the *Sheerness*, which stood off in the deeper water while the *Prince Charles* ran on the shoals. Aboard her were French and Spanish officers, fifty soldiers and the crew making a total of 120 men: and all that gold. They tried to make their way south past the home of Donald Forbes at Ribigill with their precious cargo, but before they could clamber to the safety of the mountains the Sheriff Substitute courageously sallied out to intercept them with a mere handful of men while reinforcements hastened to their aid from Tongue house. Here, as luck would have it, Captain George had returned in the company of several of the officers of Lord Loudoun's regiment who had retreated with their General into Sutherland and about eighty of their men, and these rushed on the unfortunate foreigners with as many others as they could muster at such short notice. Five of the foreigners were killed defending their treasure, and the rest were taken prisoner, while one of the chests broke and another went missing.[10] Local tradition relates that it was flung in a loch, and that from time to time the cattle drinking from it would be found with a golden *louis d'or* in one of their hooves.

"By all appearance we may daily expect these devouring locusts into the heart of our country, nay to our very doors," the Reverend Murdo had predicted. Now the locusts had arrived scattering largesse and leaving him to ponder afresh upon the strange workings of providence, and to make some shrewd comments on the behaviour of the guests at Tongue and their hosts, faced with such a prize. "This ship I say is like to prove a bone of contention between some of our stranger Dons, in a sort of exile with us at present, and our own great folks who dispute the prize with them and are like to cast out about the discipline thereof: and this on account of the absence of our native officers, who being on a post of defence in the skirts of this parish, could not be got in time enough to the little skirmish." It was perhaps as well that William of Melness was not present to enter into a new financial dispute with his Chief.

The minister permitted himself the intriguing picture of "the enemy's coming upon us and snatching away the contenders with the prey while they are differing among themselves about it." But the masterful old Lord Reay solved the difficulty by placing the treasure—apart from what was missing—aboard the *Sheerness* with the prisoners, and himself escorting them to Edinburgh while his gallant guests returned to their military duties. The minister heard of this development when he visited West Moine at the end of March "partly to see those of that side in this troublesome period, wherein we are kept very uncertain as to the number of measures and our enemies, of whom we have such various accounts as keep some, nay the generality, in a state of anxious suspense. Now we hear of their designs to invade us immediately, and then that they are not to come at all: sometimes that they're within a few miles of us, and before this can be well digested we'll hear of their being in the remote parts of another country."

In fact time was fast running out for the Jacobites. After they had lost the military war-chest at Dornoch and the Sutherland funds at Dunrobin and the French gold in the *Prince Charles*, Lord Macleod failed to bring them any relief from Caithness, although he went all

67

the way to Thurso in search of it. The Prince did send him orders to cross Druim Holstein and invade the Mackay country, but only one minor Sinclair laird had joined his colours in Caithness so that he lacked adequate resources for such an expedition: and early in April all Jacobites in the far north were ordered back to Inverness because the Duke of Cumberland was at last reported to be approaching from Aberdeen.

On 13th April 1746 Murdo Macdonald noted, "All this time my family is almost in extreme want of necessaries, my own victual is spent a while ago, and what I get in borrowing is scanty and ill to draw. Such as would cannot, and such as can will not supply us: and this at a time when we dare not send to Caithness where my living mostly is." This is a surprising statement, for fertile Durness might be expected to have provided a glebe capable of supplying the minister, while the granary of Balnakil house stood nearby. But winter lasts long in those latitudes and it had arrived before the news of the uprising alerted people to anticipate such an emergency. If the minister now found himself in want, there may have been hundreds of others on the brink of starvation.

Macdonald's words must not be taken to imply that he or the people of the west necessarily depended always on the larger agricultural capacity of Caithness, for the weather often differs so greatly between east and west that there are seasons of fruitfulness in the one at the same time as scarcity in the other and *vice versa*. For instance Alexander Pope wrote from Reay in May 1774, "The price of victual is falling daily. Demands from the south are but slow, and the crop in the highlands was last year so plentiful that very little will be bought by the highland Lairds, besides Edderachillis has been so stuffed with herrings that they are full of money, and cheap to get their victual from Ross which is far better grain than our Caithness small corn."[11] In the year of the Jacobite uprising Macdonald's parish had simply been unlucky.

Over vast areas of the Highlands, however, there was worse in store for thousands of others. It was on 15th April that the Earl of Cromartie attempted to return south with his three hundred men, and was captured in Dunrobin castle with his son Lord Macleod. We may perhaps believe the report which reached Macdonald that they were taken with fifteen other officers while they "were drinking and carousing", for little other solace remained to them and the Countess of Sutherland doubtless did her best to detain them hospitably. Their men were already attempting to cross the Little Ferry below Golspie which leads to the Dornoch peninsula, and here they were set upon by Ensign John Mackay of Mudale and the Sutherland militia. It was said that after the men had been taken prisoner, the poet entered Dunrobin castle, pistol in hand, and searched for the Earl of Cromatrie until he found him hiding under a bed.[12] On the following morning the army of Prince Charles Edward was destroyed at Culloden.

While the defeated were subjected to barbarities never recorded in Scotland since Roman Catholics had been defeated by Calvinists in the civil war of Charles I a century earlier, the minister of Durness fell gravely ill. He believed he had suffered a stroke, though the symptoms appear to have been those of a severe attack of influenza. "I find myself as feeble as a child, and [with] every lith and limb fettered with pain do I move my body or any member of it; nor can I with ease cough, yawn or sneeze." He spent a week in bed "wherein I swat for two days", and was bled. While others were dying in horrible circumstances under Butcher Cumberland's reign of terror, Macdonald himself experienced some of the pains of death before recovering sufficiently to exclaim, "How good art thou O my God, that there's not a worse account of me, when my body might have been a feast for worms, and my soul already prey for devils, my house might be desolate, my wife a widow, and my children orphans, my post vacant, and my name and memory quite extinct."

Such were his reflections on the Sabbath evening of 27th April. By 1st May he was well enough to have travelled to the presbytery meeting in Tongue where the Reverend Walter Ross was moderator. On that day they put their signatures to the address in which they gave thanks to the Lord of Hosts for his mercies vouchsafed through his instrument the Duke of Cumberland. "The Ministers of the Gospel and Elders of the Presbytery of Tongue beg leave with hearts full of joy and thankfulness to Almighty God to congratulate your Royal Highness on the successful progress of his Majesty's armies under your wise and valorous conduct against the insolent and audacious attempts of foreign and domestic enemies to our happy constitution." Culloden was a battle that it would have been impossible to lose and it was the only battle the martial Duke ever won.

"Permit us further, great Sir, to observe with pleasure and joy that when this unnatural rebellious insurrection of an infatuated part of our nation called your Royal Highness to a new scheme of action here, how quick was the agreeable change of the state of the true friends to our happy constitution. When our captivity was turned we were like men that dreamed: we were happy before we knew it.

The name of the Duke of Cumberland became terrible to the rebels before they saw him, and when he came to Culloden they soon felt the dint of his victorious arms."[13] Three days later Macdonald noted that he had entered on the fifty-first year of his life, and the twenty-first year of his preaching. He was still worried by the shortage of provisions and accordingly travelled to Hope township in West Moine in search of supplies, only to discover on his return that his agent in Caithness would be able to resume deliveries that had been interrupted during the troubles. "I got supply with no difficulty and brought it home the very next day: when I found at my house an express from the gentleman above-mentioned, importing favourable accounts of matters that seemed perplexed before: also making such offers as will, in all probability, put me in case to pay what I have been all this time borrowing, and supply my need for the whole season. O who should not trust such a faithful and attentive providence?"

The Chief of Mackay had much cause to feel the same, as he enjoyed the congratulations of the Scottish capital on the part he had played in supporting the Hanoverian cause. It was in September 1746 that he delivered himself of his reflections to some unknown member of the Government concerning recent events. He was still in Edinburgh when he wrote, "As I have the right settlement of the Highlands much at heart, I beg leave to hint to you whether it would not be for the interests of the Government, and a means to establish these wild people in peace, that his Majesty should not give any of the forfeited estates in property to any subject. But all to depend on the sovereign, right factors employed with power to grant long leases, to use the people well, promote the industry and ever to plant colonies of old soldiers among them, and thereby make them taste the sweet of being free of tyrannical masters. And for promoting the scheme of erecting new parishes more speedily and with less expense to the Government, I am persuaded if there was a free collection over all the nation for that purpose it would have the desired effect and prove in time a means to civilise these people, as I have found by experience. As his Royal Highness has been our glorious deliverer by his valour and conduct, I hope by his prudent and wise direction he'll fall on proper methods to make these ignorant people useful subjects, which will make him famous to posterity, as it is easier to conquer than to civilise barbarous people."[14]

His advice is a curious mixture of sound sense, religious bigotry, and libel against the Gaelic race to which he belonged. He ought by the time he wrote it to have heard enough about Cumberland's

70

behaviour in the Highlands to have restrained him from ending, "If there's anything wherein I can be in the least useful, if his Royal Highness honours me with his commands they shall be cheerfully obeyed."[15]

It might have been expected that Rob Donn would have employed his talents in composing utterances resembling those of his minister and his Chief, that he would have stepped forward as the Hanoverian equivalent of Alasdair Mac Mhaighstir Alasdair, the passionate bard of the Jacobite cause. It was already evident that Rob Donn was no Duncan Macintyre, a simple country-lover who would cheerfully churn out indifferent Gaelic verse on such themes as his superiors desired—in addition to composing his incomparable hymns to nature. On the other hand Rob Donn was a devout Protestant, whose neighbours and relatives had just fought (and in some cases died) for a cause whose justice had been thoroughly and repeatedly explained to him. And even if the abstract issue had not appealed to him, there were such episodes as the capture of the sloop filled with French gold to celebrate. But the bard celebrated none of them. He did compose his pibroch song for Isabel to the pipe tune "Welcome to the Prince" at some time between the winter of 1745 and 1747 when Isabel married. But for the rest it may have appeared that he lacked a capacity to respond to gunfire more distant than that of his own deer forest, that his sympathies were restricted to the small circle of the smoky ceàrn.

Then, before Culloden was fought, he broke his silence with an enthusiastic address to Prince Charles, and not long afterwards he did so again with an outburst that displays a courage and an independence of mind unsurpassed in Scottish Gaelic literature.

The defeat of the Jacobites was followed by statutes which disarmed the Highlanders and proscribed their native dress. Lord Reay's advice was adopted in the Vesting Act which transferred the titles of some forty forfeited estates to the Crown, to be administered by commissioners. An Act abolishing the heritable jurisdiction of Scottish landlords applied to loyal and disloyal subjects of the King alike, as did the proscription of Highland dress and the law which made it illegal to possess a gun.

So, so King George!
What a mockery of your good faith
To make new laws
That double the bondage.
But since they are fellows without honour

It would be better to strike than spare,
And there will be fewer to support you
When the same thing happens again.

If your enemy and your friend
Receive the same punishment in Scotland,
Those who rose against you
Made the better choice;
For they have a good friend behind them
Who stood by those who trusted him,
And several who did not go to France with him
Received pensions when he left.

This was not altogether true, though Rob Donn may be forgiven if the hearsay on which he depended was faulty. The King of France certainly continued to make generous provision for the exiled court at Saint Germains, in a palace at least as magnificent as any in Britain. But Prince Charles himself regarded those who had suffered death or ruin in his cause as subjects who had merely been doing their duty, and showed little gratitude after his departure. Of the two young cousins, each as foreign as the other, who had come to Culloden to play for such high stakes, it was Cumberland who earned lasting infamy by his conduct after the victory, but it was Charles who had brought ruin to the Gaels by coming to their country in the first place. Rob Donn does not seem to have known that the Chief of Mackay had been receiving a pension of £300 a year from the Crown since 1707, nor to have appreciated what Duncan Forbes had foreseen when he predicted after the Prince's landing that the attempt would be no more than a brief fire of straw, though it would bring much evil in its aftermath. But he observed that evil with an eye unclouded by the fog of Macdonald's metaphysical logic, and he commented on it fearlessly.

O my pity for you, Scotland!
How your argument is proved
That the part you chose
Has been your ruin in every respect.
Observe the Government's meanness
Towards all who supported it
While they have given you a bait
That will tear your entrails apart.

72

The English have taken the opportunity
To leave you weakened
So that you will not be accounted
As warriors any longer.
But when you are lacking
Your weapons and your equipment,
You will receive a thorough frisking
And your punishment will be all the swifter.

I see your misery
As something unprecedented—
The best part of your hawks
Chained to a kite.
But if you are lions
Retaliate in good time,
And have your teeth ready
Before your mouths are muzzled.

There were fourteen of these stanzas, several easily to be construed as treasonable during a reign of terror in which people were being carried off to imprisonment, deportation and death.

Now, young Charles Stewart,
Every clan places its hope in you
That sought to crown you
And set the country alight.
They are like serpents in hiding
Which cast their skins last year
But are making ready their fangs
To arise on the day of your coming.

Many a man is beseeching
You to come, Charles,
To lift the yokes
From those who are oppressed,
Who say in their hearts
Though their tongues may lie,
"Godspeed till we see you
"Back in Britain and Ireland."

Many a young hero
Who is now sleeping

73

Between the braes of Strath Cluanie
And the banks of Lochaber
Would support the cause of your father's son
In your claim to the crown and the throne,
And the troops would return
To avenge the day of Culloden.

Not surprisingly, Rob Donn was summoned to Tongue to answer for his astonishing utterance. It is unlikely that even so erudite a minister as Murdo Macdonald would have been able to tell him of Egil the Skald who (according to the saga of Snorre Sturlason) once saved his life in comparable circumstances by composing what became known as his "neck verses." It cannot even be assumed that the minister would have felt charitable enough to help Rob Donn in this way even if he had been able to do so, after seeing his teachings mocked with such blasphemy. But Rob Donn was resourceful enough to think of Egil's solution for himself, and he reached Tongue with two extra stanzas in his head which, he explained, ill-disposed people had evidently suppressed in order to get him into trouble. He hastened to recite them to his accusers.

If it be the greater sinner
Whose power ought to be overthrown,
Was it not James the Seventh
Who proved steadfast in mind?
Whose honour would you impugn
If you would praise the worthless?
It was his faith in his creed
That gave strangers the kingdom.

The subtlety of the argument is matched by the skill with which Rob Donn selected his example from the safe distance of the Glorious Revolution of 1688. Discreetly he concluded by returning to the present.

We acquired a King from Hanover,
Established over us by statute.
We have a Prince opposing him
In defiance of the law.
O God who is the judge,
Who sees neither as faultless,
May he put forward
The one whose sins are the less.[16]

74

Thus Rob Donn proved his capacity for purveying Murdo Macdonald's religious clap-trap, tongue in cheek, and his gift for parody
saved him. Nor did he spare the court, which had embarrassed him,
from the whip-lash of his tongue. The poem in which he castigated
its members cannot be dated with certainty, but it is plausible to
envisage Rob Donn, dismissed with a caution, setting off to find his
friend George Macleod the piper in the inn by the ferry.

> *I will go in search of George*
> *Because I ought to be in his company*
> *Since we are brothers in music,*
> *In the language of mouth and chanter,*
> *Because he is a man of sense*
> *And it is fitting one should enquire about him;*
> *And I expect I shall encounter him*
> *In the house below the church.*
>
> *The court we had in Tongue—*
> *Long will we remember its proceedings—*
> *A judge and a clerk were there*
> *Without reason or justice in them.*
> *Forbes was there with his wiles,*
> *And Hugh and the Englishman.*
> *How evil that trio is*
> *Wherever it assembles.*[17]

Donald Forbes the sheriff substitute and Hugh of Bighouse ought
to have anticipated that unless Rob Donn's mouth was stopped he
would be certain to have the last word.

REFERENCES TO CHAPTER IV

1. Murdo Macdonald MS. diary.
2. *Book of Mackay*, 194.
3. *Ibid.*, 450, 451.
4. *John Home's Survey of Assynt*, ed. R. J. Adam, Edinburgh 1958, ix-xvii.
5. A. Lang, *The Highlands in 1750*, Edinburgh 1898.
6. *Book of Mackay*, 267.
7. Sir William Fraser, *The Sutherland Book*, Edinburgh 1892 (later cited as
   Sutherland Book), ii, 93.

8. Cf. his letter of 1763 published in *Leabhar na Feinne*, with that of 1774 published in *Scottish Gaelic Studies*, 1966, xi, 105-10.
9. *Sutherland Book*, i, 422.
10. *The London Gazette* 15th April 1746: *The Gentleman's Magazine* 1746: R. Pococke, *Tours in Scotland*, Edinburgh 1887, 129.
11. *Scottish Gaelic Studies*, 1966, xi, 108.
12. Sir William Fraser, *The Earls of Cromartie*, Edinburgh 1876, i, ccxx-ccxxi.
13. *Book of Mackay*, 453-6.
14. *Ibid.*, 456-7.
15. *Ibid.*
16. *Rob Donn*, 82-6, stanzas 2, 3, 7, 8, 9, 11, 12, 13, 15, 16.
17. *Ibid.*, 426, the entire poem. The editor of this edition follows that of the 1829 edition in offering a different explanation for Rob Donn's words, but it obviously cannot be the right one, whether or not the context chosen here is correct. Cf. an examination of the way in which Rob Donn's first editor was capable of confusing his notes in *Scottish Gaelic Studies*, 1965, x, 162-70.

CHAPTER FIVE

Early Elegies

THERE is no evidence that Rob Donn composed an elegy before the year of Culloden, though it is possible that he did so. From the year 1746, however, at least eleven elegies can be dated to the period of a poet's life in which he can be expected to reach his fullest maturity; between the ages of thirty-two and forty-nine. Two others are definitely of later date, while there are five that cannot be dated even approximately. In one of the most chiselled and serious of literary forms the illiterate rhymester, the bawdy satirist, composed the body of poetry that is generally considered to constitute his finest work.

The earliest commemorates the premature death of the Tutor of Farr's eldest son in 1746, the latest the death of the Tutor's third son in 1773, and between them they express the enduring regard that Rob Donn felt for this family, reflected also in his poems for those other brothers, George of Handa and Rupert who perished in Jamaica.[1] When the bard did not esteem a man in life, as a rule he would raise no monument to his memory though he was the Great Lord himself. On 21st March 1748 the third Lord Reay died in Tongue and Rob Donn did not utter a word.

On the other hand there were occasions when he remained silent, presumably from grief. The early death of Iain Mac Eachainn's daughter Isabel seems to have been one of these. He had depicted her in her youth, defending the rustic life of Strathmore against her sister's strictures, and more recently he had described her among the young calves in the high pastures, in the pibroch song that has given her immortality. In 1747 she was married to John Sutherland, the only son of the manager of the Durness estate, Kenneth Sutherland of Keoldale, and there could scarcely ever have been a grander wedding in the Strath.

There was every reason why Rob Donn could have expected to be invited to this wedding, except that he had lampooned the bride's mother as a mean and exacting task-mistress and had castigated her brother John Mackay, son of the improvident erstwhile tenant of

Strathan Melness, over that transaction concerning a bull. It is hard to discover any but Iain Mac Eachainn's wife Catherine who could have attempted to snub the bard by withholding an invitation despite the fact that he had been brought up in the bride's home at Muisel and lived only a short walk away at Bad na h-achlais. Iain Mac Eachainn must have been a complaisant husband, as well as a reckless one, to agree to such a slight and he paid the penalty. For Rob Donn came to the wedding without an invitation, and he brought with him a hilarious poem. In his Byronic concern to depict what lies beneath the surface of human behaviour, he was much given to removing people's trousers, literally as well as metaphorically, and now he did it again. His plot revolved round the circumstance that many guests at such weddings slept in the barns, where it would have been easy for a joker to remove a pair of trousers during the night. The refrain of the bard's song runs:

> *Did you divine or detect or hear*
> *Who on earth carried off the trousers of Rory's son?*
> *Those trousers were here when we went to sleep,*
> *And when morning came they were gone.*[2]

Every suspect was treated light-heartedly except for the mean Catherine and her father William, whose necessitous circumstances received succinct mention.

> *The breeks were trampled*
> *Amongst the straw*
> *And Hugh went dancing with*
> *The lassies.*
> *When his intoxication left him*
> *He took a bound*
> *In search of his trousers*
> *And couldn't find them.*
>
> *If you had been near him,*
> *You would have laughed*
> *Even if you had rheumatism*
> *In your hip-joints,*
> *To have seen his loins*
> *When he missed his covering,*
> *And he searching in every corner*
> *And shrugging his shoulders.*

Iain Mac Eachainn,
If you carried them off
To prevent sin
And remove temptation,
If you took them
You had no need to.
You had had your day
Before you found them.

Catherine, William's daughter,
Make some trousers for the lad
And don't take a penny
In payment for them.
Who knows but it was your father
Who took them to wear?
He needed as much
And time was when he would have done it.

After achieving his revenge with such an economy of words, Rob
Donn added another seven verses, peopling the scene in his customary manner. First he recalled the mishap of a certain John, son of
Donald, who had secured some of the missing gold from the *Hazard*,
jettisoned by the fleeing foreigners by the Kyle of Tongue. John
could not hold his tongue, but boasted of the properties he would
be able to buy, until his story reached the ears of the Chief, who
summoned him to the Bighouse and compelled him to disgorge his
loot.

The trousers whose loss
Caused friction at the wedding—
There were more mockers
Than there were patches on them.
Unless John son of Donald kept them
To make pouches for the gold,
There weren't in West Moine
Enough people to waulk them.

Rob Donn's remark makes it evident that in these early days of
trousers after the proscription of Highland dress, they were being
cut out of locally woven cloth for want of imported material.

Unless John son of Donald made
Pouches for the gold of them,

79

There weren't in West Moine
Enough people to waulk them.
As for William son of Patrick,
They would be no use to him—
They wouldn't reach
Up to his hips.

There's a man in West Moine
Called John son of George
And I wouldn't be surprised
If he walked off with them.
They were so tight
That unless he alters them
They will be more like
Cow-fetters on him.

Don't let him out on the braes
In his present condition,
For fear he will be vexed
By the bulrushes.
Don't let him leave home
For the moors or the woods
Lest the water-shrew come
And nip him.

There's not a raven or crow
Or eagle or buzzard
Or serpent of the glen
In its coils,
Nor creeping things in the plants—
Though the subject's disgusting—
That they wouldn't prefer to the nasty fellow
Rubbing against them.

This stanza and the one that follows were omitted from the first
edition of Rob Donn's poetry, published in 1829, fifty years after
his death. It was edited by the Reverend Dr Mackintosh Mackay,
grandson of Christine Brodie whom Iain Mac Eachainn's son Hugh
had courted before his departure for Jamaica. "We have to acknowledge," the minister explained in his introduction, "the blame or
merit of having suppressed a few of the bard's humerous sallies, which
seemed to us of immoral tendency, or at least unworthy of record.

To those who feel disposed to censure this suppression, we tender no apology whatever." But Rob Donn's words have survived the smugness against which he fought such a merry fight all his life.

> *If you saw any like them,*
> *They had a leather belt.*
> *There was a hole on the fly*
> *And a patch on it,*
> *And it needed repairs*
> *To the cloth of the breech*
> *Where the dun member*
> *Used to rub against it.*

Rob Donn reserved his final verse for John Sutherland, and his remarks suggest that in the horse-play which preceded a wedding here, the bridegroom ran the same risk of losing his trousers as in other times and places.

> *John, son of Kenneth,*
> *You're the one who was lucky—*
> *Though there were a lot of bad*
> *People here—*
> *When you were so adroit*
> *That you never lost a thing*
> *And so smart over the trousers*
> *You won.*

Are we to conclude that it was the bridegroom himself who had removed Hugh Mac Rory's breeks, or had Rob Donn invented the entire incident before he reached Muisel, bent on revenge?

It may be that he saw Isabel for the last time when she set off for Keoldale with her husband. The Reverend Murdo Macdonald noted on 11th May 1748: "my intercourse with heaven was yesterday interrupted by the attendance on the burial of a young woman of some figure in this parish, who died within a year of her marriage." Her corpse was carried the short distance to Balnakil to be buried in the cemetery where the remains of Rob Donn would also be laid to rest one day. On 19th May the minister recorded that John Sutherland had already joined his wife in death. "I went aside to see the husband of the lately buried young wife, who sickened only three days after his wife's burial and died about 1 o'clock yesterday." Macdonald added that he was "one of the most amiable youths and

pleasant companions."[3] It has been assumed that the pair left a
baby daughter, but according to the minister's unpublished diary
this was John Sutherland's illegitimate child.[4] Such was the tragedy
for which Rob Donn composed no elegy in the year of the Great
Lord's death.

But when Iain Mac Eachainn retired from his droving activities,
the bard made a poem comparable to the farewell to the deer forest
which he had placed in the mouth of Hugh of Bighouse at the time
when he went east to live in Strath Halladale. It is the earliest of
Rob Donn's reflections on old age and is filled with nostalgia for lost
energies and the delights of youth, and it preserves a peculiarity of
Iain Mac Eachainn's speech.

> *How solitary I am this year,*
> *And how melancholy I am on that account—a,*
> *Gleaning fields on the uplands*
> *And deer in the rough pasture instead of what was*
> *   there.*
> *Desperate is the fate that befalls the living limbs,*
> *Some of them following where thought leads them—a.*
> *My understanding has kept close to my necessity here*
> *And the fair has drawn me in desire—a.*
>
> *I awake restless, full of little starts,*
> *Wanting fresh news of each man—a.*
> *I cannot sleep on account of this,*
> *Drink or food I neither want nor ask for.*
> *I scarcely hear those who are beside me*
> *When their laughter and good humour are at their*
> *   height—a,*
> *Remembering how I was young at the fairs,*
> *Looking over my shoulder, and I an old man—a.*[5]

He had left to Hugh of Bighouse a responsibility that they had
formerly shared, and with it the social diversions that Ramsay of
Ochtertyre commented upon. Among these had been their visits to
the Campbells of Barcaldine castle, and the allusion to this family
which Rob Donn placed in the mouth of Iain Mac Eachainn bears
on the possible date of this poem. For in 1749 Hugh's eldest
daughter Janet married Barcaldine's brother Colin Campbell of
Glenure, the Red Fox of Robert Louis Stevenson's novel *Kidnapped*,
who was murdered in 1752 after his wife had borne three daughters

to him. These circumstances were to be of the utmost significance to the Mackay country, since the girls were to become the ultimate heiresses to the estate of Bighouse in Strath Halladale.[6] Rob Donn left Duncan Bàn Macintyre to compose an elegy for the Red Fox, while his own allusion to Barcaldine raises the question whether he would have introduced it so casually if the murder of Hugh's son-in-law had already taken place.

> Play your hand, Hugh, as your good sense directs you.
> Make hay while the sun shines brightly—a
> And remember that a man possesses no powers
> That a little time will not strip from him.
> Remember me on the day of Michael's fair
> In a wilderness bothy under the shadow of bushes—a.
> My spirits are as heavy as lead
> Because I am in the north while you are in the south.
>
> O you are in the great houses as you love to be
> While I am in fog and gloom,
> And you are increasing your knowledge
> Among all men, big and small.
> Now you are off to see
> Barcaldine and his wife—a
> And though my steps have become slow
> My thoughts are not more often here than there—a

This is Rob Donn at his most perfectly simple.

> Cha tric' mo smuaintean 'seo na sin—a.
>
> O I think I am there.
> I shall take firm hold of my cane
> And I shall think at the appropriate time
> That it is only a semblance of misfortune in my mind.
> I shall think I see your features,
> Your strong hand with rein and whip in it—
> And your picture is before the eyes of my mind
> Just as that hill is before my actual sight.
> In making the acquaintance of all the drovers
> I wore out many a boot and spur—a.
> I gained great fame with cattle
> For many a day before I ceased—a.

You are a friend: anything you gained is no loss
And you reap what I sowed—a
And I am pleased that your reputation is fresh
Although I am this year entirely alone—a.

Iain Mac Eachainn himself composed the verses in which he described how he had given up another of his occupations.[7] Although the poetry is undistinguished, his poem is of exceptional interest in that it preserves the authentic voice of the tacksman whose interest in poetry had inspired him to take the little rhyming herd-boy of Strathmore into his household so many years before. It also pays tribute to Rob Donn's most exceptional gift among Scottish Gaelic bards, the composition of so many of his own original airs for his songs. Iain Mac Eachainn's lines also betray a charming modesty, and at least a nodding acquaintance with the Latin tongue. But it is obviously the reference to Rob Donn that has preserved this poem alone amongst those which Iain Mac Eachainn's friends had esteemed highly.

The gardener has a small plant
That will not grow in every soil.
The son excels his father. (Filius ante patrem.)
Its foliage overspreads its roots.
If claims are made for these talents
In a certain place beyond,
My portion of poetry
Will be well paid for by Rob Donn.
There was a time when I would compose verse
Which friends would esteem highly
When they sat in the tavern.
Assuredly I would not be overlooked.
But now I have given up that art;
My appetite has deteriorated,
I will abandon that form of diversion.
Look you, I have given you pride of place.

When the light does not shine
All the land is deprived,
But when the sun breaks through
Every hill and plain rejoices.
My work has fallen to the ground;
It will perish for want of airs.

But with every judge who has a knowledge of poetry
Rob Donn will be remembered for ever.[8]

To this compliment the bard responded at Iain Mac Eachainn's
death with the earliest dateable of that series of masterpieces which
was to earn him the contemporary verdict:

> *Fhilidh chiallaich na h-Alba,*
> *Rinn na marbhrainn a b'f hearr!*
> *O Scotland's poet of good sense,*
> *Greatest of elegists!*[9]

And in those final years of his retirement Iain Mac Eachainn received
an intimation of the monument that would be erected over his grave,
in the wide-ranging elegiac utterances that human sorrow and misfortune evoked increasingly from Rob Donn.

That of 1754 was exceedingly curious. At the southern end of
Loch Eriboll where Strath Beag runs out of the Reay Forest there
is a lonely habitation called Polla. Rob Donn would pass it whenever he walked or rode straight through the hills from Strathmore
to Durness, and so he would have had frequent opportunities for
acquaintance with Ewen who lived there, before the day when he
called to find him lying ill and alone in his wretchedly poor surroundings.

> *It is a long time, a long time,*
> *A tediously long time*
> *Since the day you fell mortally ill*
> *Without a soul to bemoan your misery.*
> *If the time has gone by*
> *And you have not used it well,*
> *Though you have but a week's respite,*
> *Mend evil ways.*[10]

An interesting tradition tells that Rob Donn used to compose his
poetry aloud to himself, and that he sat by Ewen's fire as he wove
these words into shape. But the poem to which they served as a
refrain was inspired by a dramatic piece of news from the south.
On 6th March 1754 Henry Pelham, brother of the Duke of Newcastle
and Prime Minister of Great Britain, had preceded Ewen to the
grave.

> *Often enough, Death, you remind us*
> *Never to cease suing for salvation,*
> *And it is apparent to me that before you're done*

85

You carry off both the mean and the great.
Since the middle of spring
We have had ample warning
That you pass at a bound from the courts
To the corner where Ewen lies.
But if we were to believe you, Death,
The world would not beguile us
When there is not one of Adam's seed
Whom you would disdain to swoop upon.
It seems to me certain
That you search high and low.
You took Pelham from greatness
And you got Ewen from Polla.

As the short, squat figure of the bard crouched, composing over the hearthstone, he evidently forgot that Ewen behind him was not yet a corpse. He was, if the tradition speaks true, listening with increasing anger.

You come to that sort
Whom great men mourn
And you come to the people
For whom no lamentation is heard.
There is none between these extremes
Who is free from anguish,
Who has not cause for anxiety,
Between Pelham and Ewen.

They have fallen around us
As though struck by bullets.
We should be alerted by this sound
As by a trump in our ears.
You who are the least among men,
Did you hear that Ewen was ill?
You who are the greatest in these places,
Did you hear of Mr Pelham's death?
O friends of my heart,
Will not the fate of these two move us?
We are like the candle in the lanterns,
Both ends inexorably being consumed.
Where in the world was there
Anyone more lowly than your father's son,

86

While there was none higher than the other
Except the King on his throne?

The elegy (if such it can be called) consists only of these five verses, which is perhaps to be explained by the tradition that Ewen had had enough by this time and creeping out of bed, clouted Rob Donn over the back of his head. Once, the bard mentioned that the ashes of the hearth-stone had matted his hair, and it might well have occurred on this occasion since he could easily have been toppled forward as he squatted before the hearth.

This poem raises once again the question of his originality of thought.

But pallid Death, an equal visitor,
Knocks at the poor man's hut, the monarch's tower.

Had those lines been composed by Alexander Pope, they might have raised a presumption that Murdo Macdonald had translated them for the bard's benefit, but in fact they come from the fourth Ode to Sestius by Horace, translated by Branwell Brontë long after Rob Donn's death. There is no evidence that the minister's wide reading extended to Horace. On the other hand Rob Donn's compositions nowhere betray a debt to Alexander Pope comparable to the similarities between his thought and that of poets of whom he could not possibly have heard.

In 1755 he composed a more conventional type of elegy, except that once again it commemorated two men, and that it contains a peculiar verse structure adapted to its impressive air. Each of its eleven stanzas contains four groups of three lines, of which the first two are short and flow into a longer third one. The men whom he lamented were the schoolmaster of Farr and the minister of Edderachillis, and this time he commenced angrily:

'S e mo bheachd ort, a bhàis!
My curses on you, Death![11]

The structure of this elegy is linked to the question, when Rob Donn composed his lament for John Mackay the religious poet of Mudale, for in this he used a comparable form of three-line verse, two relatively short ones followed by a longer one. Nearly twenty years later he returned once more to this form in an elegy, but his usual vehicle was the eight-line stanza. Unfortunately the date of John

87

of Mudale's death is unrecorded, unless in a lost portion of Murdo Macdonald's diary: but since his father died in 1707, Mudale must have been of mature years when he played his enthusiastic part in the Forty-Five, and his death may well have occurred during the ensuing decade. Rob Donn expressed no resentment against death on this occasion, as he might have done if Mudale's end had been premature.

> *Death took from us, under our very eyes,*
> *Away from the borderlands of Strathnaver,*
> *The one man who has left none comparable behind*
> *him.*[12]

Rob Donn was careful to trace Mudale's descent back to William Mackay of Achness, the last of the Abrach chieftains who had lived in the ancestral home above Loch Naver before its valley was acquired by the Gordons in the seventeenth century, whose son was known as Neil Williamson.

> *Occasion of pride to the Abrachs,*
> *A strong hand that would not threaten,*
> *Kindly John son of Robert son of Neil.*
>
> *A resolute form that was manly,*
> *A trusty mind filled with honour,*
> *A hand that made good the speech of his mouth.*
>
> *You were a true companion*
> *And you were an example to the children,*
> *Your treatment of others and of yourself were*
> *all one.*
>
> *You were bountiful, modest,*
> *And free with your pocket,*
> *Chief of poets and abode of the needy.*

After four more such triplets, Rob Donn ended by invoking the religious poetry which would continue to exert its influence for the next century and more.

> *And if what I have said be not true*
> *Concerning the outstanding Christian,*
> *Let me leave his witness to Mudale himself.*

88

Thus Rob Donn commemorated men who had left a name and good works behind them, at the same time as he pondered on the lives of others that had been comparatively barren. And the most notable elegy that he composed in this second category concerned two bachelor brothers, sons of the tacksman of Rispond at the opposite end of Loch Eriboll from where poor Ewen lived in Polla. An old maid lived with them as their housekeeper, and all three died within the same week, though in what year is not recorded. To the barrenness of their lives was added the meanness of their characters, and whenever it was that Rob Donn composed his reflections, he seems to have taken up the same train of thought that had been interrupted at Polla.

> *These were men who caused no dissension—*
> *So far as anyone knew—*
> *Nor did they perform one act*
> *That the world calls grace:*
> *But they were conceived and born*
> *They were reared and they grew*
> *A sweep of life passed over them*
> *And in the end they died.*[13]

This chilling indictment belongs to the growing corpus of elegies that Iain Mac Eachainn must have heard, and that he may have heard, before he died in 1757 and provided Rob Donn with the theme for the most ambitious exercise in this form that he had yet attempted.[14]

> *Iain Mac Eachainn, now you have died*
> *Where shall we go to find*
> *A man to replace you in your clan*
> *In the role of gathering or spending?*
> *Certainly there is a grave danger*
> *That no old man will do it,*
> *And though he be found in the younger generation*
> *Few of us now alive will see him.*
>
> *Indeed your life did not resemble*
> *Those of men still living*
> *Who have gathered money and lands*
> *That others will scatter,*
> *Men who will be cut off*

Without a friend to mourn them,
Whom no praise will reach
Save: "look at the land they redeemed."

They are within the letter of the law
And they are sharp over debts
And they are punctilious in paying
What they owe one another.
But for the rest, it will be stowed away
Though it's hard to hoard against hospitality:
And their purses and their eyes
Are equally shut to the man in need.

To this bastard half-honour
Hundreds of them yield.
They far prefer indebtedness
To God than among men.
They will come by a loss that they cannot overtake—
It is the apex of their condemnation:
"Wherefore did you not give to the poor
"Food, drink and clothing?"

O if only I could, I would wish
To chronicle your fame
In shining letters
In order that young people should see them,
For an account of you is much needed
By those who come after you—
Just as your goods, as long as you lived,
Were to him whose wealth was scarcest.

You who have breath and ability,
If you desire a reputation that is estimable,
Now the time lies before you
And you ought to seize it.
You are in the battle of death
That took this hero to the grave from us.
Let each one of you lay hold on this example
And I give you my hand it will win renown for you.

For although there are some who ridicule
The person who is generous,

90

It is my entrenched opinion
That it is right to present this petition.
Fast enough the generations follow
That will make the oldest amongst us wise
Not to sacrifice eternity
For three score years.

Many a man without comfort
You equipped with stock by your dealings,
And foolish lads lacking sense
Obtained wisdom by listening to you.
Indeed I know of none
Save the irredeemably foolish
Whose mind is not indebted
To your goods or your good sense.

You who did not enjoy a bite of food
If you knew anyone in the world was hungry,
You who would pick out the needy
Without having heard his cry,
To you it was better that a pound should be lost
Than that an ounce should weigh upon your mind.
You threw your bread upon the waters
And your descendants shall recover it many-fold.

I see the worthy man in want
And he melancholy and weary
And he without money in his pocket
Going past the inn.
I see the poor widow weeping,
I see the beggar famished with hunger,
I see the orphan naked
And he going about in rags.

I see the musician not esteemed,
Losing his talent for lack of practice,
I see the man in need of counsel
Failing in his business and his courage.
If I took pains to enquire
What is the reason for this great lamentation,
Everyone would answer me:
"Alas, isn't Iain Mac Eachainn dead?"

91

I see this multitude of people
Objects of pity now you are not alive,
And though it is the loss that is uppermost
I see the gain to the hospitable
As it has been made manifest to me this year,
Many kindly people of whom I was unaware
Like the constellation of stars
Which appear when the sun has set.

It is usual in laudatory elegies
According to the custom of this country
To adulterate them with flattery
That swamps them.
But though I were on my oath
To Him who controls the elements for me,
I have mentioned nothing concerning this man
But what I witnessed with my own eyes.

Isobel had died nearly ten years before her father, and his complaint on his retirement that he was entirely alone raises a presumption that his thrifty wife Catherine was then dead also. His son Hugh had emigrated to Jamaica years before, but he also possessed a son John who witnessed a transaction in the year of his father's death. As for his refined daughter Mary, who preferred the urban life of the Lowlands, she married a man who earned one of Rob Donn's most vicious lampoons, in which are to be found some puns on Mary's role as a wife which his first editor could only have published because he did not understand them. The occasion for this poem was the loss of one of Iain Mac Eachainn's cows, and the accusation of Donald Mackay, Mary's husband, that Rob Donn had stolen it. Eventually the cow reappeared, with the identity marks cut from its ears. Rob Donn assumed that Donald himself had stolen the cow, removed its lug-marks, and then sought to extricate himself by accusing the bard when its disappearance was noticed.

I passed some of my days
Throughout yonder strath
Spending my life
In the home of a gentleman.
I was long in your company
And with the others,
And I did not have a glimpse of Mary,
Such was my disgust for Donald of the Lugs.

92

It is pitiful to me that my neighbour
Does not possess a nobler nature.
I thought my silence concerning him
Would earn me a reward.
Although I was so amenable
That I did not expose them,
I would rather his horns
Were short than his ears.

Since I may not now lay bare
Your deceitful design,
I will make your horns
As short as a calf's,
And when I fix crooked horns on you
I shall always expect—
Though he himself should treat me coldly—
That I shall get a reward from his wife.

The fact is that the fool married—
A tradesman—when he was blazing.
He doesn't lose an ounce of his wealth
Without losing a pound of love.
Loosely hanging ears were left
And a slender, shrivelled horn.
Mary strove awkwardly with him,
Leaving him short-eared, hornless.

Rob Donn alluded next to a quarrel between Donald and another neighbour, who was severely injured in a fight with him.

It was a good bull that was bruised
And its virility impaired.
The man with the long ploughing gear
Let that claim lapse.

Evidently Mary's husband was the sort of man of whom Rob Donn could safely prophecy in his concluding verse:

When this eary song
Is spread about the country,
The herds will pick it up
As they round up their cattle.

93

It will be on the lips of the reapers
Gleaning in every field.
There will not be a voice untuned to it
And every ear will be turned to hear.[15]

Such was the candour with which Rob Donn had depicted a tacksman's family as no other is delineated in Gaelic literature, until he closed his account with the obituary for Iain Mac Eachainn. The strictures in it could perhaps be applicable to Donald of the Lugs (and the reference to ounces and pounds is actually echoed in the elegy). They could have been provoked by Catherine if she outlived her husband, or by the behaviour of their son Hugh if he had returned to Strathmore from Jamaica by the time of his father's death. He did return, a widower with an only daughter who married one of the Tutor of Farr's sons while Hugh remarried, though not to his early love Christine Brodie.[16]

So far as Strathmore was concerned Rob Donn's forebodings, the earliest that are dateable in his poetry, were to be amply fulfilled. The light that was extinguished by Iain Mac Eachainn's death would never be rekindled, from that day until the valley into which the bard had been born became an empty wilderness. In the Mackay country as a whole, other changes had followed the Great Lord's death, and although Strathnaver had avoided the fate which befell the Jacobite lands of the Highlands, a writing was on the wall there also whose meaning Rob Donn could only guess.

REFERENCES TO CHAPTER V

1. *Rob Donn*, 11-13, 52-5: *Book of Mackay*, 331.
2. *Rob Donn*, 151-5. The entire poem is translated.
3. Macdonald MS.
4. *Book of Mackay*, 315.
5. *Rob Donn*, 101-2. The entire poem is translated.
6. *Book of Mackay*, 306.
7. *Scottish Gaelic Studies*, xi, 162-70.
8. *Rob Donn*, l-li.
9. *Ibid.*, lii, lines 23-4.
10. *Ibid.*, 46-8, where a wrong date for Pelham's death is given. The entire poem is translated, with the refrain placed first: cf. the partial translation in D. Thomson, *An Introduction to Gaelic Poetry*, 200.
11. *Rob Donn*, 1.

12. *Ibid.*, 14-15. Verses 1, 2, 3, 4, 5, 10: *Book of Mackay*, 258-9.
13. *Rob Donn*, 50, lines 9-16. Stanza translated by John MacInnes in *Scottish Studies* XII, 42. Cf. Derick Thomson's verse translation of the entire poem in *An Introduction to Gaelic Poetry*, 200-2.
14. *Rob Donn*, 32-5. The entire poem is translated. The date of Iain Mac Eachainn's death is scribbled on a scrap of paper amongst those of Hew Morrison in the National Library of Scotland, presumably from a lost portion of Macdonald's diary. An English verse translation of the elegy by Iain Crichton Smith was published in *An Gaidheal*, 1958, liii, 59-60.
15. *Rob Donn*, 138-40, first four stanzas, first half of 5, and 8. The date of Mary's marriage is unknown and the poem undateable.
16. *Book of Mackay*, 315.

CHAPTER SIX

Administrative Stresses

WHEN the third Lord Reay died in 1748 a rather singular disposition of the properties of the chiefship came into effect. The Great Lord had entailed the estate on his son in 1732 when the Master of Reay married Marion Dalrymple. After she had died, leaving him with two sons, a new arrangement was made upon the Master's re-marriage in 1741. The entire property was bequeathed to trustees upon the third Lord's death, except for the barony of Durness.[1]

There are various possible explanations for this. The Great Lord may have been concerned to protect the rights of the orphaned heirs to the chiefship from the possible claims of a step-mother and her children. He may equally have wished to safeguard the interests of his own third wife[2] and her large family. But above all it seems probable that the incapacity of the Master to manage his affairs had become apparent by the time he wished to remarry, and that his father seized the opportunity to place the administration of the estate in other hands after his death.

The consequence was that when Donald became the fourth Lord Reay in 1748 he merely continued to enjoy his barony of Durness, managed by Sutherland of Keoldale, while his half-brothers Hugh of Bighouse, George of Strathmore, and Alexander the soldier became the effective trustees of the remainder, which they conveyed to Hugh by lease to administer. It was provided that the fourth Lord's heir should live in the Chief's mansion at Tongue when he should come of age[3] and in 1757, the year of Iain Mac Eachainn's death, he was married to Marion, the third daughter of Hugh of Bighouse. But this dynastic union failed in its object, for Marion died in 1759 without having borne a child to her husband.[4]

When Rob Donn spoke in the elegy for his dead patron about those who were within the letter of the law, sharp over debts, and punctilious in paying what they owed one another, there appears a strong presumption that he was referring to Hugh of Bighouse. The bard's attitude to the Great Lord's second son reflects both his outspokenness and his ability to change his mind over the years. In earlier times he had reproved him for sharp practice during a droving expedition, then he had represented Hugh as a devoted brother and a friendly companion to the folk of the west in his great poem of farewell to the deer forest. He had placed compliments to Hugh in the south of Ian Mac Eachainn after his patron's retirement from the droving trade, yet at another time, perhaps much later,[5] he responded savagely when invited to admire a new suit that Hugh was wearing.

> *. . . There is not a button nor a button-hole in it*
> *That hasn't taken money off a poor man.*[6]

Hugh's father the Great Lord had helped to turn him into a fortune-hunter, and Rob Donn became progressively more outspoken in his dislike of the man's methods.

Inevitably these were experienced in the lands of West Moine, for they did not belong to the barony of Durness although they were a part of its parish. In these patriarchal days the happiness and prosperity of Highland communities depended greatly on the qualities of their leading men, and Durness was fortunate in the lifelong residence there of Murdo Macdonald the minister, the fourth Lord Reay and his manager Sutherland of Keoldale. According to Rob Donn, Strathmore in West Moine had been equally favoured by the presence of Iain Mac Eachainn.

There was another respect in which Rob Donn testified to the good fortune of Durness, for the last time in any part of the Mackay country. At some time between 1741 when the Master married Christine Sutherland and 1748 when she succeeded as Lady Reay, he composed a song that tells how popular she was.

> *The whole world loves*
> *The cheerful countenance of Kirsty Sutherland.*
> *There are nine delighted with her*
> *For the one who scowls at her.*[7]

Perhaps the one who scowled was the pious minister, equally vexed by her Episcopalian beliefs and by the merriment of the big house that her cheerfulness did so much to quicken. But Rob Donn also suggested that she had "met prejudice", coming as she did from Sutherland, in the poem in which he celebrated her elevation as a peeress in 1748. In the previous year she had displayed her loyalty

97

to the family into which she had married by using her influence to aid her brother-in-law George of Strathmore to become Member of Parliament for Sutherland.

Welcome to your Ladyship,
And thank you for what you did.
It would be unnatural
If I did not play my part in the event.
It is your policy towards that party
From which you have met prejudice
To increase their renown and honour,
Even at the expense of friends.

The brother who desired to enter
The Parliament of the King
Received evidence of your friendship,
A thing that did not fail to cause disappointment.
How will you be repaid
The obligation by the Chief of Mackay?
What you did then was a deed
Not to be expected of a wife.

We were happy hitherto
When we heard the beginning,
That through your intervention
They gained the day.
Through the support of those votes
Honour was added to your reputation—
A quality more distant from the village
Than other things of the court.

There is no reference whatever to the Honourable George Mackay M.P. except Rob Donn's allusion to "the brother", which would be sufficiently slighting without the earlier hint that he had been rude to Kirsty Sutherland before he received her help. Perhaps she had been provoked as deeply as the minister when Captain George visited Durness during the Forty-Five, and the Reverend Murdo commented on his insufferable behaviour: if so, she was capable of an equal spirit of forgiveness. Incidentally, the bard's word for the votes that she manipulated in such a decisive manner was the English loan-word *baran*, and it illustrates the trouble he took to inform himself about subjects that he had not been taught in a school. For it stood for

98

the "parchment barons", as they were called because they had been enfranchised by the grant of empty paper titles designed to enlist them as subservient voters. It was part of a system that succeeded finally in turning Scotland into one vast rotten borough, controlled by a single manager in the interests of the government in power.

But if Kirsty Sutherland did something on that occasion not to be expected of the Chief's wife, it was nothing to what she did next. An army deserter had fled to Durness soon after her husband had succeeded to the Chiefship, closely pursued by a detachment of troops. Rob Donn continued his panegyric:

> *I will not mention these points*
> *Without recalling others,*
> *For you did something a week ago*
> *That was more praiseworthy still—*
> *Stopping the capture*
> *Without any injury to justice,*
> *And the party that had no pretext*
> *Except the prowess they got from drink.*

The deserter's name was Kenneth Sutherland, which may have emboldened him to fling himself on the mercy of a lady of his clan.

> *The alert young man arrived*
> *With the Sutherlanders at his heels,*
> *And before a word that he'd been seized*
> *In the young Lord's garden*
> *A few in that village*
> *Who could tell a bonnet from a shoe*
> *Made the party stand on their guard*
> *While Kenneth took off to a hiding-place.*

The house at Balnakil had been built in the previous century by the second Lord Reay, who had been educated at Sorø Academy in Denmark while his father was fighting with his clan regiment in the Thirty Years' War, and it may not be fanciful to see in its architecture the influence of the Danish manor-farm. The back of the house rises above the sands of Balnakil, sacrificing the splendid panorama of cliffs beyond the bay in order to avoid the westerly winds that sweep across that coast from Cape Wrath. A court-yard enclosed by two wings faces east across the green parks of that limestone promontory. It contains no imposing central entrance with hallway and wide staircase within, only an unpretentious door set on one side of the court beyond which the stairway is so narrow that it could hardly have contained the fashionable women's dresses of the eighteenth century. The ground-floor was designed as a granary and place of provision for this far-western estate, while above there was an imposing panelled room extending along the mansion's central block. Whether by accident or design, Kenneth did not choose one of the doors leading to the ground-floor premises when he had bolted through the garden and across the court. He chose the entrance which took him to those narrow stairs. At the head of them can still be seen the little closet beside the panelled reception room into which Lady Reay pushed her clansman in his extremity. She then welcomed his pursuers as they tumbled up the stairs, ushering them into the great room beyond Kenneth's hiding-place. She ordered drink for them: she summoned the women who were working about the premises and improvised a dance.

> There was merriment there and festivity
> Amongst men and women and children,
> There were alert, eager men there
> Dancing to a tune they didn't know.
> You would hear the storms of noise
> From the boards beneath their feet,
> Every other man amongst them stumbling—
> It was a theme for Rob Donn.

> There was a lady beside the threshold
> Standing there, alert, formidable.
> I don't know the pass
> He went out by, on my life.
> But between the woman's legs,
> Without bonnet or weapons,
> Very near the fissure where he was born,
> There he made his escape.[8]

Rob Donn has used the actual English word *pass* in this stanza, which Dr Mackintosh Mackay did not exclude from the 1829 edition of his poems. Perhaps the minister did not spot the pun between a military pass and the portion of female anatomy given in a later line, or perhaps he could not bring himself to suppress such a sample of Rob Donn's art in the use of words.

Lady Reay's resourcefulness, in smuggling the deserter to safety down that narrow staircase beneath a woman's skirts, was not the only theme she provided for Rob Donn. It was about this time (as we may assume since the proscription had apparently not yet become effective in the district) that she took a kindly interest in a matter that cannot have pleased the minister. It concerned Catherine Mackay, who gave birth to an illegitimate child of uncertain parentage, and then married the bard's friend George Macleod, the lame piper, Local gossip accused a man of the name of Sutherland who was known as the *Geigean* (meaning, perhaps, the little fellow). Rob Donn placed a song in the mouth of Catherine Mackay with the refrain:

> *George Macleod fancies me*
> *And he expects I will marry him.*
> *They have spread it about this place now*
> *That George Macleod fancies me*
> *Although in a way*
> *He is a source of annoyance to me.*

The song describes how George Macleod courted her with his music while she still thought about the Geigean.

> *Don't you see how the clever Geigean abandoned me,*
> *With his fur doublet and his belted plaid?*
> *I would prefer him, equipped in his attire,*
> *To your wealth, your person and your pipes.*[9]

In another poem Rob Donn explained in some detail the parts that others had played in this scandal, nor did he assume that it was necessarily the Geigean who was the father of Catherine Mackay's child.

> *Mary the midwife was experienced:*
> *She performed the deed of mercy,*
> *Taking a Mackay, a Sutherland or a Macleod*
> *From the place she couldn't see,*
> *And although she couldn't tell*
> *How many months she was pregnant,*
> *She let him out of his prison*
> *In Katy's lower room.*

I used to see you often
In the presence of many people,
Saying you never kissed
Anyone except the piper.
But when we looked carefully
At the deed you were carrying,
Although your lips were very deceitful
Your tail told the truth.

For her Ladyship was artful
And she was responsible for the marriage.
She would lose a man out of her clan
If the boy's paternity were attributed to George.
She would bring a wether from the headland
So that the nurse could have meat from it
And a boll for bread
Of the best-winnowed part of the barley.

But others, the bard suggested, were staking their own clannish claims, while he advanced those of his own, putting forward that handsome young bachelor George of Handa, or John Mackay of Strathy as an alternative parent.

Then the wife of Donald son of Donald said,
"It is right that hundreds
"Should bring him up as a Macleod
"Since poor George is greying.
"But if he's a Sutherland
"My brother will get the first share of rearing him,
"And if he's a Mackay
"I will undertake his feeding henceforth."
Captain John of Strathy
Was waiting at the time,
But when he was to go to the Session
An excuse turned his back.
But supposing I thought the child was his,
Rather than that he should be questioned or bothered
I would hold him up for baptism
In return for that horse I received.

I've another little secret
To pass on to the laird of Island Handa.

102

He was at Balnakil
At about the time last winter.
Since the matter is uncertain,
And since the wheels may turn,
He had better be fed secretly
Until the offspring's paternity is proved.[10]

On the whole, Rob Donn's attitude is one of tolerant banter, yet he did not conceal his disapproval of the men who might have seduced Catherine Mackay, and of the girl who yielded to temptation. Lady Reay evidently came to the rescue, encouraging Catherine to marry the lame and greying piper, helping to provide for the illegitimate child, and no doubt helping to silence the censorious by her example. In the eyes of some people her help to Catherine may place her in a more attractive light even than the part she played in securing George's entry into Parliament or the deserter's escape: yet it is the only act of hers that earned the criticism of Rob Donn. His rebuke was a gentle one, such as he administered to his friend the piper also, and not to be compared with the vitriolic comments he would make about a subsequent Lady Reay. In this third poem on the subject, more in the nature of a homily, his heaviest censure fell upon the girl's unnamed seducer.

My opinion is that you will make no soldier
When you took her while she was a virgin.
You had an opportunity day and night.
You have lost your reputation although the heir is yours.

George is as wise as a scamp
In not making off with his wits about him.
He took the dead body of the hind
After she had been wounded by the hunter's son.

After more in this vein, addressed both to George Macleod and to the Geigean, Rob Donn rounded suddenly and briefly on Kirsty Sutherland.

I find it odd in the Lady of the parish
Whom I never knew to be other than upright,
When she influenced the keeper's eldest grandson
To depart from the upright standards of his forbears.[11]

103

With these words the bard moved as far as he was able into line with the teachings of the minister of Durness on the subject of sexual delinquency, though there is no surviving entry in his diary to reveal whether he expounded the case of Catherine Mackay from his pulpit. This is unfortunate, since it would have been fascinating to learn how Macdonald equated the sinful compassion of Lady Reay with her Episcopalian errors or with her convivial habits.

But as it happened, Macdonald was obsessed at this time with the errors of his own brethren in the presbytery of Tongue, and in particular with those of their senior brother the Reverend Walter Ross, who had moved from Creich in Sutherland to Tongue with his English-speaking wife in 1730. What made this dispute doubly painful to Macdonald was that Ross was his uncle, and his only relative in the Mackay country. "I have got a rude attack from one who should be my friend by the ties of nature, office and grace," he wrote on the Sabbath evening of 12th February 1749. "I would gladly overcome evil with good, but as I find myself as unjustly as virulently attacked, I think that silent forbearance in this case might be misconstrued as contempt of my libeller or an acknowledgment of the libel."

The case concerned a proposal by the ministers of the eastern parishes to abridge the celebration of holy communion, an issue that had been in dispute since 1743. By 28th May 1749 Macdonald faced the ugly prospect of a personal confrontation with his uncle. "The Sacrament of the Supper is advertised to hold in the parish of Tongue on 18th June ensuing, a piece of very great news. But the indisposition I am like to be in by reason particularly of my odds with the minister of that place makes me not a little afraid of the occasion. I look upon myself as the person injured, and so does the other on himself, and probably there are appeals to heaven on the opposite sides of this controversy." To appeal to heaven against rebellious Catholics had been uncomplicated enough: to appeal against his own uncle in his own presbytery was a very different matter.

Behind the protagonists in this controversy stood their supporters. Macdonald's was the minister who had succeeded Brodie in Edderachillis, the Reverend John Munro, "the only brother worth the name to me." The ally of Walter Ross was a minister of entirely different character named John Skeldoch; who had been placed in the parish of Farr in 1734 through the patronage of the Earl of Sutherland, since this parish comprehended the Naver valley which belonged to that earldom. While Macdonald had devoted himself so conscientiously to his religious duties on his modest stipend, Skeldoch had caused public scandal throughout the Mackay country by grabbing lands for himself and demanding servile labour from his parishioners to work it. In 1743 the presbytery was examining the complaint that the minister of Farr was "encumbered by too many tacks of land", but he continued his acquisitive enterprises until in 1747 the presbytery reported to synod "anent Mr Skeldoch's oppressing or attempting to oppress the tenants of Syre." This is the property in the upper Naver valley about a mile from Achness where the Abrach chieftains had once lived. It was many miles from the church and manse of Farr on the north coast. In 1748 Skeldoch was suspended from his religious functions, which merely left him more time for his private enterprises.[12]

Such was the supporter of the Reverend Walter Ross's proposal to abridge the communion celebrations. As Macdonald travelled east to meet them in Tongue in the beginning of June 1749, he stopped to preach in West Moine. "On the Monday I was obliged to pass over the Moine, a tedious fatiguing moss of five miles on the way, in worse weather than I had in December." The very heavens, he observed, were threatening the business of that presbytery meeting, yet he felt partly reassured by his uncle's reception of him. "I came to my friend's house, where I stayed and was entertained without any sensible grudge, yet my want of wonted communications at the occasion was, perhaps, owing to my not endeavouring at a formal reconciliation."

Skeldoch was present in defiance of his suspension, to help deal with the scandal that his parishioners were now organising their religious lives for themselves. The three ministers in Tongue ruled: "The Presbytery being well apprised that there are in the several parishes some who take upon themselves to read the Scriptures and other books in the Irish language to the people, and to solve doubts and cases of conscience at such meetings, and that some of them are without the authority or allowance of the minister of the parish . . . hereby do prohibit any to convene the people to reading or conferences, except the advice and consent of the parish minister be obtained."[13]

The uprightness of Murdo Macdonald's character is exemplified in the care he took to confine his dispute over the sacrament to Walter Ross, and to avoid taking advantage of the fact that his uncle's supporter Skeldoch was a rogue. "I have been this man's friend while it was possible for me to do so," he recorded, and others might have thought he had maintained his loyalty a little longer than

105

that.[14]   When Skeldoch died in 1753, Macdonald himself confessed:
"my struggles in Presbyteries and Synods in favour of the now
deceased Mr Skeldoch were too violent, as afterwards I found
reason to conclude from his constant persisting in those offensive
ways."   Rob Donn made his own comments in an indictment of all
ministers who abused their privileged position by indulging in
secular enterprises.

> *Join their clubs and society.*
> *You'll find most of that pack*
> *Fit for peddlers or sailors,*
> *Fit for drovers or factors,*
> *Fit for parsimonious farmers,*
> *Fit for provident stewards,*
> *And apart from the calling they took their*
> *   vows for,*
> *Fit for everything excellent.*

There are ten such stanzas, each a rapier thrust that contrasts with
the hammer-blows of so much Gaelic invective poetry.

> *You may find one of them on Sunday*
> *Will assert that Christ is our Saviour,*
> *And a week after that will declare*
> *That the only profit is in works.*
> *He will fly so high,*
> *Then he will creep so low,*
> *That being neither bird nor mouse*
> *He becomes a filthy bat.*[15]

The death of Skeldoch left a vacancy at Farr only a few months
before Murdo Macdonald's son Patrick completed his theological
studies in 1754, and obtained a tutorial post while he waited to be
called to his first charge.   Patrick was just too late to be considered:
on 23rd May the Reverend George Munro was ordained minister at
Farr, appropriately enough since he had previously served in the
Achness mission at the other end of the Naver valley.   People there
had been inclined to despise him for his youth and for what some
considered to be an unbecoming levity of manner.   On one occasion
a pious neighbour had asked him to baptise his child, and Munro
came to his home to perform this rite.   "While preparations were
making for the ordinance, Mr Munro began to play with one of the

children. He fenced with the boy with a rod which he had in his hand, and chased him round the room. The pious father was so shocked by this apparent levity, that he had almost resolved not to receive baptism at his hands. The service, however, was commenced, and before the conclusion Mr Munro so clearly and scripturally laid down the nature of the ordinance and the sum of parental obligations, that the man declared he was overwhelmed with shame that he ever allowed himself to harbour any unworthy suspicions of his visitor's ministerial zeal."[16] So Munro's nephew the Reverend Donald Sage recorded, after Munro's long and fruitful ministry at Farr was over, commemorated by the initials GM and the date 1774, painted on the canopied pulpit that was erected in his church at that date.[17] And in his indictment of unworthy ministers, Rob Donn contrasted the conduct of George Munro to theirs with biting sarcasm:

> There is a great deal of talk
> Circulating among people
> That it is the waster who is hospitable
> And that a godly man is thrifty.
> They are all willing enough
> To condemn the Reverend George:
> He is guilty of liberality—
> That is the sin which is hateful to them.[18]

Macdonald's son Patrick had evidently come to visit his home at about the time of Munro's appointment, with what expectations may be guessed from a particularly tortuous entry in his father's diary. It refers to an occasion when both of them preached in the church of their uncle Walter Ross at Tongue. "My son and I preached in the pulpit of one who might rejoice at the agreeable appearance of a nephew and grand-nephew succeeding one another and supplying his place: but was so far from his disposition as to seem rather fretful than pleased: and this was consistent with himself, who did not call either of us to his Sacrament occasion which held him the week immediately before our seeing him. But this unkind dealing was made up to us by the (? discreet) behaviour of others far less concerned, who though they were not so true to my son's interest as once pretended yet are sensible of that undesigned favour done him by occasioning a settlement for him by much preferable to that in their power to give or withhold, but which they bestowed on a person that for all the glaring appearance at first is daily falling out of character." Presumably this last allusion is to the support that George Munro was already giving to Walter Ross in the dispute over the sacrament. The earlier reference is to Patrick Macdonald's appointment as minister of Kilmore in Lorne.

By the time Patrick returned in 1754, his theological studies completed, he could report that his fifteen-year old brother Joseph was making considerable progress in his musical knowledge under their father's instruction, and already "played on the violin, with an easy flowing execution", in addition to having "made considerable progress on the bagpipe." The suppression of this instrument after the Forty-Five had evidently not been enforced in Durness, neither had the minister here adopted the same censorious attitude to it as churchmen did elsewhere. Patrick and Joseph were reared in a cultural tradition unstifled by political or religious prejudice, just as Rob Donn had been, and their contribution to it was complementary to that of the bard. It was Joseph who made the collection of piobaireachd and of Gaelic airs, of which the former was lost when he took it to India and died there. But fortunately he copied the airs for his sister before he left, and this collection his brother published after his death, the earliest printed collection of Gaelic airs ever to appear in Scotland. Patrick also published a collection of bagpipe music that included his brother Joseph's *Treatise on the Theory of the Scots Highland Bagpipe*, the earliest analysis of the structure of this music that anyone had attempted.[19]

The early death of Joseph Macdonald is one of Scotland's incalculable losses, and it raises the question whether Patrick would have collaborated in his brother's work if Joseph had lived to continue it himself. All that can be said for certain is that Patrick still sought out the company of the piper and the bard after he returned home, a minister of the Gospel, because he once did so in circumstances that Rob Donn turned into verse.

> *How ashamed I am,*
> *And how much better if I had been out,*
> *When we have no food to offer*
> *Except thin runny sowens.*
> *It is ill usage of those men,*
> *Men of letters and music,*
> *The son of the minister of our parish*
> *And the piper to the Chief.*

If you would come to visit me
When I have provisions in my house,
We would not see you coming an inch
Without going a foot to meet you.
Not an hour would pass without a tune
Between rising and going to bed,
And if it were the day of Bearachan Fair
I would kill the ram for you.[20]

Perhaps these words are sufficient to suggest that Patrick was not merely concerned to save the work of his dead brother in what he published later, but that he shared fully in the literary and musical interests of his father and Joseph.

Another charge might have been open to him in the Mackay country when the Reverend John Munro of Edderachillis died on the 15th February 1755. This was one of the two men for whom Rob Donn composed his malediction on death—*'S e mo bheachd ort, a Bhàis*—and his loss was a particularly severe blow to the minister of Durness as he set off on 30th March, the time of the equinoctial gales, to attend the presbytery meeting in Tongue. "The grand affair was that of the Sacrament of the Lord's Supper, which we differed about as to the methods of celebration: the man of greatest bulk among us being for the abridged way of beginning on the Saturday, with a manifest view of curtailing the ordinance by process of time by taking off the Monday too. But however indifferent a greater or less number of days and diets may be in the sight of God, yet as the standing practice of the Church now for above eighty years and the general inclination of the people adhering thereto comes in to cast the balance, I did in opposition to the other two brethren make a stand." When Macdonald could fall back on standing practice and general inclination, it almost appears as though he was no longer sure of the views of the Wise Counsellor who had just struck down his supporter. Discussion was adjourned once more, this time until the elders of all the parishes could be consulted, and so "in the form of a boisterous wind I came over the Moine and preached this day at the meeting house here in much weakness of body and mind, occasioned partly by the toil and weariness of the journey." Thus Rob Donn must have learnt the latest score in this game longer than a cricket match, and with as many draws, in which he appears to have taken not the slightest interest.

109

So dissension continued to rumble in the presbytery of Tongue, providing its parishioners with a seemingly endless topic for discussion, while the parish of Durness continued to enjoy the presence of its admirable minister. The family of the Chief was subject to its own peculiar stresses after the Great Lord's death, while Durness enjoyed the exceptional privilege of the fourth Lord's presence there with his remarkable wife and his amiable factor. There were further stresses between the minister and the Chief at Balnakil, whose merry and convivial habits shocked Macdonald although he made allowances for his generosity. "Were the carousing life venial in any, surely there was no man more to be indulged the freedom than he who at one merry meeting used to do more good as above than in the longest Lent of abstemiousness." Hogmanay was especially distressing to Macdonald, when the Chief used to provide drink for those who assembled on Balnakil sands below his house:

When the youngsters gather
On the shore at Christmas time
Where the young men used to go
To drink from the barrels.[21]

All in all, Rob Donn's world can be seen to have been exceptionally privileged during those years following the Forty-Five in which so many other parts of the Highlands were undergoing a brutal transformation. But in 1757 the Chief developed the illness from which he died four years later, as Macdonald recorded. "All of a sudden he gave up with company and drinking wherein much of his time and money was firmly spent. Upon this resolution of his life he turned dull and useless; discontinued his wonted frankness of disposition and gave nothing in ways of charity or generosity by which for many former years he had been famous . . . what a pity that his last days should not have been the best." Rob Donn's tribute to the fourth Lord Reay contains no such reservation, but then Strathmore did not lie in his barony of Durness and it would not have been this Chief who was responsible for the treatment the bard received after the death of Iain Mac Eachainn in that same year of 1757.

REFERENCES TO CHAPTER SIX

1. *Book of Mackay*, 457-60.
2. "whom he survived"—Macdonald MS.

3. *Book of Mackay*, 458.

4. *Ibid.*, 214.

5. The Reverend Mackintosh Mackay, editor of *Songs and Poems in the Gaelic Language by Robert Mackay*, Inverness 1829, stated on page 260: "Rann a rinn am bàrd do dhuine uasal àraidh, aig an robh uachdranachd na dùthcha 's an àm." Hew Morrison in the 1899 edition stated on page 445: "Bighouse was factor for Lord Reay," thus settling for his identity, though mistaking his position.

6. *Rob Donn*, 445, last two lines.

7. *Ibid.*, 267, second verse. The identity of Lady Reay is confused in the table of contents.

8. *Ibid.*, 106-8. The entire poem is translated.

9. *Ibid.*, 288-9, the refrain and final verse.

10. *Ibid.*, 293-5, the entire poem without its refrain.

11. *Ibid.*, 290-1, verses 1, 2, and 6.

12. D. Beaton, "Notes from the Tongue Presbytery Records," in *Old Lore Miscellany*, Wick 1914, VII, 66, 108, 164-5, 168-71.

13. *Ibid.*, 167.

14. H. Morrison, "Notices . . . from the Diary of the Rev. Murdoch Macdonald," in *Transactions of the Gaelic Society of Inverness*, 1885, xi, 308.

15. *Rob Donn*, 75-7, stanzas 3 and 7.

16. *Memorabilia Domestica*, 38-9.

17. "Tigh-Tasgaidh Shrath-Nabhair," *Gairm* 1962, 306-7.

18. *Rob Donn*, 77, stanza 8.

19. *A Collection of Bagpipe Music*, Edinburgh 1803: *Compleat Theory of the Scots Highland Bagpipe*, 1927: P. Macdonald, *A Collection of Highland Vocal Airs Never Hitherto Published*, London 1784. See also R. L. C. Lorimer, "Studies in Pibroch," in *Scottish Studies* 1962, vi, 1-30.

20. *Rob Donn*, 428, the entire poem, which is not divided into quatrains in the 1829 edition.

21. *Ibid.*, 175, verse 6 of the poem, third on this page.

CHAPTER SEVEN

Animals

THE people of the Mackay country subsisted by animal husbandry supplemented by the scanty agricultural resources which the land possessed. These were limited to certain valleys and coastal basins, and they generally supported a branch of the clan gentry, such as those of Strath Halladale and Strathy, Skerray and Melness. Parcels of them had been erected into glebes for the sustenance of ministers, who were at this time predominantly of the same order, and many of whom could, if they chose, matriculate a coat-of-arms to prove it. They had, besides, evolved to some extent into a hereditary priestly caste, such as marriage in the early Celtic Church had created in the clans of MacNab, MacTaggart, Buchanan and Mackinnon, sons of priests and abbots, occupants of the canon's house, and descendants of the founder's kin of Iona.

The ordinary folk of the clan like Rob Donn enjoyed a limited access to this agricultural land as sub-tenants, and everyone lived close to the vast open spaces which domesticated animals shared with the wild life of the province. At Isabel's wedding in Muisel the bard advised the trouserless guest not to wander too far from home where he might encounter the water-shrew, raven, crow, eagle, buzzard or snake.[1] Isabel's sister Mary had expressed a horror of the high pastures in which there were only badgers for company among the cairns.[2] Rob Donn once likened some people to skulking pole-cats,[3] and on another occasion he mentioned the woman who "made the most of what resources she had when she boiled the otter that was hanging from the cross-beams."[4] There is an appearance of Biblical metaphor when he remarked: "When the cowherds quarrel, it will be a good time for the wolf to drive the lambs from the folds."[5]

Rob Donn also described the activities of the fox-hunter whom a girl asked: "Did those dogs get a carcase for you?" And the fox-hunter replied petulantly: "Didn't you see the fox's skin, and isn't that sufficient evidence for you?"[6] He kept a whole pack of dogs

112

that evidently caused much annoyance, and interfered with his attempts at courtship if Rob Donn is to be believed.

> *The rascally smith's son*
> *Is just now setting out for Durness*
> *And the question some are asking furtively is*
> *Has anyone heard how many dogs he has with him?*
> *The girls would welcome him*
> *If he drove away that pack,*
> *For they are impudent, noisy brutes*
> *When they reveal their secrets.*

> *There are expectations in this estate*
> *On the part of lassies I won't name.*
> *Information reaches the mind*
> *Through the nostrils when they are mettlesome.*
> *Although they kept it secret from us*
> *He is expected at the approach of evening.*
> *Before they see a glimpse of him with their eyes*
> *At the fifth dog he will be recognised.*

> *Large dogs will be howling there*
> *When they are tied up at the walls.*
> *There will be a wild noise of Oov! Oov! from them*
> *When they cannot reach the servants' food.*
> *There will be a resentful Feeav! Feeav!*
> *From small snapping terriers.*
> *Women at the baking will mutter*
> *"A hundred mischiefs on them! Aren't they voracious?"*

> *His wooing will be much the worse*
> *For the uproar that follows him because of them,*
> *When those frisky lurchers come*
> *That are swifter than the huntsmen.*
> *They will be watching everywhere*
> *And wagging their tails.*
> *If anyone interferes with them they are quarrelsome*
> *And if they are struck there will be an outcry.*

> *The huntsman himself will be careful*
> *Lest one of them should be injured by mistake.*
> *The ladle will be used by him to scoop cream*
> *And rub that on their shanks.*

113

J

The wooden collars will not restrain our cattle
Listening to that uproar.
There will be a scattering of ashes and embers
And the beasts themselves licking it off them.

The poem gives a merry picture of the servants' quarters in the Chief's house at Balnakil.

People bought and sold dogs. When Rob Donn quarrelled with a neighbour over the sale of a puppy there was a written agreement to appeal to. "My money bears witness and I will show the agreement which I have in the handwriting of Rory Mann." But the illiterate bard was suspicious of the written word. "I could prove to every cowherd between Sweden and France that he never had sufficient intellect to make use of ink." He added that "the puppy was whimpering and would not leave of its own accord. I lifted my shoulder-strap and tied it round the beast." So the animal went with its new owner in spite of Rory Mann "with all your fickle lies that are as lively as the Northern Lights."[7]

Rob Donn showed a strong attachment to dogs which they evidently reciprocated, for on one occasion Donald Fraser's dog did just that. His name was Boiny and the bard rewarded him with this charming lyric.

They are all laughing at me
Because the white-starred dog follows me
But it's very hard for me to destroy him
And he will never leave me of his own accord.

I will send word to Donald Fraser
That I am shedding tears
And unless I can get more benefit from it
Let Boiny remain with him.

But before we part, Boiny,
A thousand blessings on you.
Your nature is faithful, trustworthy—
That is the mouth that hasn't told a lie.

It is no wonder I am angry.
When my name was published
In the Reverend Murdo's list,
They wrote down "dog-keeper" as my occupation.[8]

114

While the lesser folk kept dogs to help them manage their cattle, and the fox-hunter for his trade, Rob Donn had been privileged to follow the deer hounds at the great huntings in the Reay forest, whose part he described so graphically in the poem of farewell he composed for Hugh of Bighouse. He never mentioned that dogs were used to round up sheep, but then he scarcely referred to sheep at all. Apparently the bard possessed a few himself, since he said he would kill the ram for Patrick Macdonald and George Macleod if they would visit him at the appropriate time.[9] He also alleged that Lady Reay had ordered a wether from the Durness headland to be killed for the nurse who attended Catherine Mackay's illegitimate child, the implication being that the finest beasts were those that grazed on that excellent pasture.[9] In another context he sang:

> *I see yonder, tending the sheep*
> *The dark, lovable, capable lassie.*[10]

But again he was referring to those green parks of Durness. In his elegy for the misers of Rispond he remarked that "their clothes were from the one fleece,"[11] but such incidental comments were all he had to make in the days before the Cheviot sheep were introduced in such large numbers throughout his country.

It is noteworthy that Rob Donn referred to the quarrels of cowherds that gave the wolf an opportunity to drive the lambs from their folds.[12] In the Gaelic Bible "the Lord is my shepherd" was translated as "the Lord is my cowherd", though the English word "keeper" was eventually borrowed in the form of *ciobair* to describe a shepherd—too late to be of service to Rob Donn.

He had as much to say about goats as about sheep. There was the time when he compared himself to a kid in size;[13] and he possessed two goats on the occasion when the tithe-collector called at his house and discovered that the minister was visiting the bard also. The tithe-collector excused himself in Macdonald's presence, explaining that he was God's factor, and made a show of leniency.

> *I am seeing now*
> *A thing I never observed before,*
> *Hearing that the tithe-collector*
> *Is God's factor.*
>
> *When our Saviour was*
> *Down among the people*

115

> *It was the man in charge of the purse amongst them*
> *Who was the evil one of the twelve.*

> *You did a thing unusual for you—*
> *You did not count my stock of kids.*
> *It would not be worse for me to have paid—*
> *There were not more than two all told.*

> *It is certainly not good nature*
> *That made you exempt them this time,*
> *But that your sin of pride*
> *Got the better of your sin of avarice.*[14]

There is also Rob Donn's poem about David from Loch Inshard, who was thought to have been drowned in a kelp-boat that took him with his butter and cheese to Orkney, which caused his goat to bleat with pleasure.[15]

James Ramsay of Ochtertyre left a footnote on the general attitude to sheep and goats at this time which probably applied to the people of Strathnaver as much as to other Highlanders. "Their popular poetry was surely well suited to a country where little more than threescore years ago every person wished to be thought a soldier—husbandry, and even pasturage, being followed no further than necessity required. And until very lately, sheep and goats were regarded as the property of the wives, being beneath the attention of their husbands; and the lowest fellow would have thought himself dishonoured by entering a byre or assisting at a sheep-shearing."[16] Whether or not Rob Donn felt dishonoured by his menial tasks among the animals, he expressed his dislike of them periodically.

> *What torment I suffer all the year round in the barn:*
> *Do you not see how the cattle dealt with Rob Donn?*[17]

His self-pity was most eloquent when his horse died and he was reduced to doing its work himself.

> *To the gentry I am no worthy specimen*
> *But an object of commiseration indeed*
> *With a wife and children and little wealth,*
> *And having lost a horse without an heir.*
> *This year I am reduced to shifts*
> *I never adopted before and wouldn't count on,*

116

My body in pain, my back beneath a creel
And a straw rope of the harrow at my tail.

Two of his neighbours had given horses to him, one of them
George of Handa, whom he praised as a horse-handler. But Rob
Donn seems to have been unlucky with horses.

> *From George I got a white gelding*
> *And from Henny a mare in fee,*
> *But before I got much services from them*
> *I lost the two of them.*
> *My prayers will be diligent every time*
> *And in each I shall petition the Lord*
> *That the best wife be given to him*
> *And the best man to the girl.*

> *Since the day on which I lost the white horse*
> *My heart has swelled often,*
> *That it was drowned, I knew not where—*
> *It has turned me quickly grey—*
> *The haunch of your carcase in bog or meadow*
> *Being eaten by the foxes of the cairns.*
> *From his youth he was reared in George's school*
> *And high was his reputation at harrowing.*[18]

But Rob Donn probably preferred to remember the white horse
carrying his rider bravely to the fairs.

> *My pony was excellent on the street*
> *For carrying a handsome rider,*
> *And he bore witness approaching the fair*
> *That he had never been worked excessively.*

In his elegy for the two dead horses Rob Donn resorted to one of
his waggish devices, gravely reporting the comments of important
people on his misfortune.

> *The Laird of Strathy, young and old, will say*
> *And Donald Forbes will observe*
> *And the Laird of Melness will repeat—*
> *He's the one who would be active in service—*
> *"It's tragic that he didn't get when young*

117

"In exchange for a measure of gold or silver
"One that would retain his affection forever
"As the white horse of Tarbet did."[19]

A back-handed swipe at his wife Janet? A well-endowed bride could expect to possess a horse: such as the bard's daughter if she should marry the local weaver's son.

> *How fortunate my child is*
> *That George would have the shuttle for her.*
> *She would have cattle and horses and shielings;*
> *She would have good food in the pot and sowans.*[20]

An old or injured horse was shot, and one of Rob Donn's mock-heroic lampoons was composed for the man who bungled this. He was none other than Iain Tapaidh, Clever John Sutherland the poet-schoolmaster, for whom Rob Donn expressed such contempt on numerous occasions.

> *You disappointed me when you shot at the mare*
> *And didn't kill her—so we hear—*
> *With weapon to eye and fresh powder*
> *And not a scrap of lead.*
>
> *I am sad and vexed*
> *And embarrassed and dejected.*
> *Handsome youth of the curly golden locks,*
> *You shot the horse with violence.*
>
> *My lad wears a blue coat*
> *And a full powder-horn slung from his shoulder.*
> *It would have been less inept if you had spared the*
> *mare*
> *Before the sound of the shot entered her ears.*[21]

But of all domestic animals cattle took first place. They were cheque book and grocery van, milkman and status symbol. A pair of cows was the dowry that Christine Brodie had in mind when she sang that she would prefer to have the heir of Iain Mac Eachainn's son sitting on her knee.[22] Rob Donn castigated the man who broke off his engagement to marry because the dowry fell short by a single young cattle beast.

An uproar has arisen
Over the wooer who lives yonder.
He desired a spouse
And the two of them were betrothed.
I thought myself when they began
That they would agree without difficulty
But a small wretch of a stirk prevented them
From tying the knot for more than a month.

It was then the girl said:
"Won't you ask me truly
"And I will say that indeed
"His disposition was fickle.
"He was definitely as willing
"As any young man you ever heard,
"And now he has become enraged with me
"Because he didn't get the dun stirk."

So he went on his way
And it was to Syre he went first.
They sent word after him
To honour his bond
He chose to be a tailor
Rather than marry.
O that he had got the wretched stirk
Even if it were to die of the flux.[23]

At the end of each of the six stanzas in this poem Rob Donn returned to the creature which was the symbol of material gain, which some preferred "to a wife or love or children."[24] Nor were they investing in a currency that became devalued, for the price of cattle rose steadily throughout the bard's lifetime.[25]

While men drove cattle to the autumn fairs, Rob Donn considered the herding of them to be women's work. He depicted Iain Mac Eachainn's daughter Isabel tending the calves near the deer-forest; while the young cattleman at the Crieff fair dreamed of his girl in similar surroundings.[25] Yet other men besides Rob Donn had to perform the tasks of a cattleman, whether they liked it or not. In his homily to the seducer of Catherine Mackay he referred to the keeper's son "who herds calves and cattle."[26] But he never conceded that a man milked a cow. This was a feminine role in contrast to the proper activity for a man, as he described both in a poem about a couple ideally matched.

119

Concerning handsome Elizabeth
I received information yesterday
That the son of Hugh son of Norman
Was hoping to court her,
A woman as attractive as there is in Scotland
To be a dairymaid with cattle
And a man as expert as any when he takes up his
weapons
To go killing the deer.

It is confirmed in every district
That Elizabeth has no rival
In any dairymaid you can assess
Between Tongue and Stoer.
It is confirmed of her companion
Since he was educated in youth
That he was everyone's choice
As a scholar or with a gun in his fist.

Evidently he was a widower, she a widow, and both of mature age.

My opinion of your agreement
Is that it will be prosperous beyond measure.
No shortage will ever reach you
Of butter, of cheese or of meat.
This is the most prudent course
Ever embarked upon by one who has been married
That the next wife he seeks
Is neither lacking in prudence nor young.[27]

Rob Donn made few references to bulls, two of them associated with people he disliked. One of these was Iain Mac Eachainn's brother-in-law, whom the bard castigated over some transaction involving a bull: the other was Iain's son-in-law Donald of the Ears, whom he accused of having injured a good bull in one of his quarrels.[28] The bard used the same metaphor in an opposite sense when he spoke of girls who were coaxed into making unsuitable marriages: "we can be sure they will beget the qualities one would expect of them, like the bad bull that mars the herd."[29] It was still customary in the Mackay country in the twentieth century for the elderly members of the two families to meet when a marriage was proposed, in order to pool their knowledge of the forbears of the engaged couple, and to decide whether the union was likely to strengthen any undesirable strain amongst a people so closely inter-related.

Rob Donn must have heard the Ossianic tales and ballads which told how Diarmaid killed the wild boar, the legend to which Clan Campbell owes its pre-heraldic totem of the boar's head. A variant of the same story gave the emblem of the bull's head to the Macleods in the Hebrides and to the Turnbulls on the southern border of Scotland.[30] Rob Donn's farcical account of the killing of a bull is obviously intended to dress ancient heroism in the motley of modern comedy.

At the time when the bull went to be slaughtered
At the hands of the man who was in Kinloch
   and his wife
They earned the utter ridicule
Of the people of the port of Skerray as a result.

George Macleod came along
With his gun in prime order
Hoping to kill the bull with it
Since they were failing to win its submission.
John son of Hugh came
And used his powder needlessly.
He didn't get the better of the bull
Though he had often killed the deer.

Murdo son of Hugh came
With a good double-axe in his fist
In the hope that he would get the hide of the belly
When he had transformed the ox into meat.
He took a swipe—
The son of the man who was usually expert—
When he lunged at its face he stuck the blade
   into its arse.

With great vexation and pride,
When he saw the axe without a head
He threw it away from him
And it landed in the mire.
An express was sent to Edinburgh
Asking for adequate sealed despatches
To secure the execution of the ox
That Murdo had wounded abominably in the
   buttocks.[31]

121

Perhaps those who enjoy watching a bull-fight may still appreciate the humour of this tale of a bull that ran from one end of the country to the other, being hacked to pieces before it was killed. The people of Strathnaver were devout, but the Christian religion has relatively little to say about cruelty to animals, and the considerable religious literature of Rob Donn's world nothing at all. He cannot be called especially callous because he ignored the fact that animals, like humans, are sensitive to pain. Murdo Macdonald never considered the matter either in those passages of his diary that have survived: he showed the common Christian preference for sexual delinquency as a subject for censure. But a man capable of Rob Donn's originality of thought and independence of judgment might have been expected to show something more than a sentimental concern lest the carcass of his horse was being eaten by foxes. The explanation for his failure to extend the remarkable humanity of his thoughts in this direction is that in the last resort they were dominated by the primitive passions of man the hunter. It was not primarily a desire to obtain food that motivated his joy in the deer hunts, nor a scientific interest in maintaining the maximum sustainable yield of the herds, but a lust to kill that was ultimately his undoing. "My choice for deer hunting would be Craig Riabhach and in the Sàl; and dragging them down in the evening by the Piper's Cairn."[32] But Rob Donn possessed no such choice. However much it excited him to watch a stag being torn to pieces by the hounds, he was privileged to enjoy this entertainment solely as the servant of Iain Mac Eachainn taking part in one of the grand hunts. When he stole away from Strathmore to enjoy the sport on his own, he landed himself in trouble.

In his poetry however he did not only describe the delights of the chase: he also asserted what may well have been the oldest common right in the Highlands unacknowledged by the law in his time, as old perhaps as the rights of commons in the Lowlands. Centuries earlier, the same right had been eroded in England, and the legends of Robin Hood had grown up around the popular resistence to royal monopoly of the deer forests. These legends had reached as far north as Aberdeen at least as early as the first printing presses were installed there and it is significant that they were selected for publication in this novel fashion, although there is no evidence that Rob Donn ever heard of them.[33]

By his time the Reay Forest was one of the largest deer preserves in the possession of a single person. When Bishop Pococke visited the country in 1760 he remarked that the third Lord Reay "used to have a grand hunt every August. They compute a thousand red deer in that country, and that four or five hundred of them have been drove into this part by about a hundred men who drive the mountains, and they have shot sixty of them in a day."[34] At a time when Iain Mac Eachainn was still living to protect him, Rob Donn was reported for poaching by John Mackay the bailiff, son of Angus who had been a forester in Strathmore in 1734. The bard rounded on his neighbour.

> John son of Angus son of William,
> Who spilt plenty of blood,
> Why did you denounce me
> This day in front of the bar?
> In my opinion it would be better for you
> To follow the other argument
> For you were killing them
> Since the day you could walk.
>
> But if it be ungodly work
> To kill the deer in the glens
> Many a worthy member of your family
> Has fallen into grievous error.
> You are descended from men who shed blood
> And the kinsfolk of your spouse are no better,
> And if that be an unforgivable sin
> You yourself will be condemned without forgiveness.
>
> This year's distemper
> Is becoming more painful and grievous
> But if we exercise a sensible restraint
> We will get an improvement in the administration.
> The settlement will come quietly
> When Ahab is restrained
> And we shall be displaying our wounds
> In the presence of Dr Boerhaave.[35]

This was a celebrated Dutchman who died in 1738, and the manner in which his name might have become a household word in Strathnaver was sufficiently explained by the author of the anonymous observations on the Highlands in 1750. "The Mackays are said to be a better militia than any of the neighbouring clans, for which this is assigned as a reason, that several officers of this clan in the Dutch service obtained the Lord Reay's countenance to recruit in his country upon this express condition, that they should return the men after being a certain number of years in the service, and take raw men in their room."[36] The manner in which they might be conscripted is suggested by the letter which the Dowager Lady Bighouse's son-in-law Patrick Dowell wrote to her in 1751, saying that the Dutch service would be an appropriate punishment for the man who had disappointed her in her search for a herd to her cattle.[37]

There is a presumption that Rob Donn was referring to Hugh of Bighouse as Dr Boerhaave, in which case King Ahab could only have been the third Lord Reay and the poem must have been composed between 1738 and 1748. The fifth Lord Reay might also have been cast in the part of Ahab but he did not succeed until 1761 and the poem appeals to Iain Mac Eachainn, who died in 1757. During the chiefship of the fourth Lord Reay it was Bighouse himself who came nearest to fulfilling the role of Ahab, while Boerhaave could only have been Iain Mac Eachainn, which is unlikely since he is addressed separately. So Rob Donn's words evidently express his views on a relatively early warning to cease his depredations in the deer forest.

> But, Doctor Boerhaave,
> I made a poem for you that they do not understand.
> Since I have precious little money
> Your work must be tempered with kindness.
> I have expectations from your plaster
> When others are stinging me
> And the longer the cure takes
> The better it will be.
>
> Iain Mac Eachainn 'Ic Iain,
> You rescued me in the middle of my troubles.
> You would testify to my character
> Behind my back and before my face.
> With your trusty counsel
> You would challenge the lawyers.
> Your substance came to my aid
> And your advice was no less.

As for other members of the gentry, the bard had the assurance to declare, not that he was losing their favour, but that they were

losing his. He actually accused William of Melness of complicity
in his misdoings, and it does not appear unlikely that this impulsive
man would have helped himself to his Chief's deer after he had been
disappointed of his share in the Bighouse inheritance.

> *William of Melness, it seems to me*
> *That friendship does not stand on one foot.*
> *You kept well in with me*
> *Until you got me the plunder.*
> *When you saw me ensnared*
> *Under the high authority of Tongue house*
> *You grew hard of hearing*
> *And you did not help the examiner.*
> *Since my friendship has grown cold*
> *Towards the gentry of this country*
> *It is necessary for me now to seek*
> *The crooked road I didn't wish for*
> *To where clever old Donald is,*
> *Reading the catechism in Sgudaig,*
> *To see whether he will preach in these quarters*
> *The fifth petition of the Lord's prayer.*[38]

Donald Sutherland was the catechist in Tongue. Obviously Ahab
could not have been the fourth Lord Reay in Durness, and it follows
that Rob Donn was making his appeal to Hugh of Bighouse under
the flattering pseudonym of Dr Boerhaave during the last years of
the third Lord. The same may be inferred in another poem which
the bard composed about a man who was actually evicted from the
neighbourhood of the forest as a punishment for his poaching
activities.

In commenting on the misfortunes of his neighbour, Rob Donn
used the dialogue technique that he had employed in his argument
between Isabel and Mary concerning rustic life in Strathmore.
After an opening stanza in which he set the scene, he gave the first
word to counsel for the prosecution.

> *News has just reached us*
> *Which will grieve Hugh,*
> *That he is to be banished from the place*
> *That has caused him anguish.*
> *He is surrounded on all sides by the deer-forest*
> *And he is in a helpless plight*

Under penalty of death, with only a pen in his hand
That won't ignite a grain of powder.

Prosecution:
        Shall we be merciful to such a man,
        Who does not stay his hand at a threat?
        Considering all the chances we gave him—
        Though he has paid that fine twice over—
        Never would I believe a word
        From one of his anti-social nature.
        Though I were given a haunch I would not go security
        A couple of times for Hugh.

Defence:
        Hugh is useful in the deer-forest
        Though the Chief of Mackay often turns on him.
        He is stalwart with arrangements of his own
        For killing deer in the summer.
        Though you deprived him this year of deer-hunting
        You have done so in a deceitful manner,
        By treacherous tricks, putting him away from hunting
        On the twenty merklands of Maldie.

Prosecution:
        We didn't do that with cunning strategy:
        It was but a small measure compared to what he deserved,
        And it was his custom to be in every place
        Deceitfully waiting for an opportunity against them.
        Sàl and Craig na Ruaige would tell
        Of his many acts of oppression
        And every cairn there says
        That he spent a night in the vicinity.

Defence:
        Although he was long in the neighbourhood
        The cairns were not his range.
        The man who would reach the head of the strath
        Would find him in his own place.
        If Sàl and Craig na Ruaige are
        Stirring up lying stories about him,
        I'm not saying but before he dies
        Both of them will be paid back.

126

Prosecution:
> *It was not a source of indignation to us,*
> *Though he was often arresting*
> *And robbing us of the deer*
> *That always frequented our braes.*
> *Glasfeidh was announcing to me yesterday*
> *That she left her death-ransom on him*
> *And Meall a'Chleirich is convinced*
> *That he himself will not reach Kintail.*[39]

As in the dispute between Isabel and Mary, Rob Donn has given the last word to those with whom he is not in sympathy, and there is much in this unresentful, bantering poem to suggest that it may be his earliest utterance on the theme of deer-poaching. For it was a theme on which he was eventually to speak with extreme bitterness, lashing those who protected the Chief's deer forest. John Mackay the bailiff, son of Angus the forester, earned this reproof from him.

> *Within the span of a brief lifetime*
> *I would never have believed the report*
> *That was circulated by you, even if I had killed the deer.*
> *If I had support behind me*
> *Or if I had a friend at court,*
> *I should have expected you to be he.*
> *But that company has grown so disagreeable*
> *That I was not aware it had gone.*
> *I am certain that fortune aided me—*
> *Firm, all-seeing Providence,*
> *That caused scarcity and want—*
> *As the whole fanfare blasted over my head.*
>
> *Get wisdom, dear fellow.*
> *Despite deference and respect*
> *You will only live a span of years.*
> *There may be a defect now*
> *In the judgment you pronounce*
> *That will nail you in a similar predicament.*
> *You have prosecuted with rigour*
> *Respectable, worthy people*
> *Whose priming never caught fire on them,*
> *And there are no oaths concerning the mountains*
> *That will not bring down curses on your head—*
> *Great will that punishment be unless God restrains you.*

127

Part of your reputation is no lie—
It will endure longer than your body.
According to your power you were most vicious;
You prosecuted harshly
Deeds less reprehensible than your own.
There is not your like among your hundred neighbours.
The law you used so harshly
Will now be turned on yourself.
Your wisdom resembles that of Haman.
Try for a brief spell
To exercise generosity in the Sàl,
Then you will see that a mote is a blemish.[40]

By this time Rob Donn had adopted the position that the law which forbad general access to the deer forest was an unjust one, and those who enforced it were the enemies of his society. It was the corollary to his atttiude that the hero of his society was "a man as expert as any when he takes up his weapons to go killing the deer." Haman, the wicked servant in the Book of Esther, was contrasted with men such as the bard's own brother for whom he wrote:

There was blood on the front of your shirt
And it wasn't the blood of the haunch of a goat
But the blood of a stag at rutting time
And he was no robber, was Donald Dubh.
Heigh ho, my Donald Dubh,
Hunter of venison, Donald Dubh,
Not a talkative man is Donald Dubh
And he will have a reward for the chase.[41]

It was not merely what the bard did, but what he said with such eloquence that constituted the gravity of his offence, for this posed a far more real menace to his superiors than his Jacobite outbursts. In due course he was removed from Bad na h-achlais in Strathmore, and although the exact date when this occurred is unknown, it is likely to have happened between 1757 when Iain Mac Eachainn died and 1759 when the bard was conscripted, a somewhat elderly recruit, into the army. There has been disagreement between his editors concerning his destination. Dr Mackintosh Mackay stated in the 1829 edition of his poems that he was sent to Fresgill, the lonely little oasis on the eastern slope of the Moine headland. The editor of the 1899 edition, Hew Morrison, preferred another spot of the same name on the west side of the Kyle of Durness, though he gave no grounds for this correction, and apparently overlooked the fact that the bard would have enjoyed at least as tempting access to the forbidden deer here as in Strathmore. Nor would he have been living any longer in the barony of West Moine administered by Hugh of Bighouse. Fresgill on the Moine seems the more probable place of exile, and it may not be fanciful to attribute to this time and place the unusually sentimental and nostalgic little song he composed about the beloved surroundings he had left. For the view from Fresgill contains a magnificent panorama of the Reay forest in the distance beyond Loch Eriboll, the peaks of Foinaven and Arkle, the heights behind which lies the delicious little glen that Rob Donn pronounced Gleanna Gallaidh, though it is generally written Glengolly in English, following the standard Gaelic form Gleann na Goille. This was the place in which he declared that he would rather live there than in Kintail Mackay, the very seat of the Chief.

> *The view of the frontier heights*
> *Entices me yonder,*
> *And I'm thinking I will dwell*
> *In Glengolly of the trees.*
> *I don't desire your wealth*
> *And I have no need of your weapons.*
> *I wouldn't refuse your dram*
> *But I require nothing else.*
>   *Glengolly, Glengolly,*
>   *Glengolly of the trees,*
>   *Who could see it and not love it,*
>   *Glengolly of the trees?*[42]

The last verse, in which Rob Donn extolled its wealth in crops, cattle and deer, and particularly its immunity from storms, contains precisely the reflections that would have occurred to a man who had been removed from his inland valley to the barren, windswept promontory of the Moine. Here he was brought into sudden proximity with the sea, a fate that he had anticipated in the refrain of his poem appealing to Dr Boerhaave. Possibly it recalled the expedition across the Minch to Lewis that he had made in company with George of Handa.

> *It is a long time, a long time,*
> *A tediously long time*

Since I was at anchor
And seeking shelter beneath the sail.
Now if I am forced to flee
And no excuse will avail me,
Wherefore should I spare to sting you this day
As I hoist the sails?[43]

When Rob Donn was sent to Fresgill, out of reach of the deer forest, he came instead into closer contact with the life of those who sailed the seas, and he did not neglect to comment on it.

REFERENCES TO CHAPTER SEVEN

1. *Rob Donn*, 154, stanzas 8 and 9.
2. *Ibid.*, 119, final four lines.
3. *Ibid.*, 218, verse 5.
4. *Ibid.*, 321, lines 13-16.
5. *Ibid.*, 219, verse 6.
6. *Ibid.*, 136, lines 5-10: 134-5, first five stanzas.
7. *Ibid.*, 324-5, stanza 2, lines 5-8: stanza 3, lines 5-8: stanza 5, lines 1-4: stanza 6, lines 3-4.
8. *Ibid.*, 354, all 4 verses without refrain.
9. *Ibid.*, 428, line 16: 294, lines 5-10.
10. *Ibid.*, 174, opening two lines of refrain.
11. *Ibid.*, 50, line 4.
12. *Ibid.* 219, verse 6.
13. *Ibid.*, 454, lines 11-12.
14. *Ibid.*, 435, entire poem.
15. *Ibid.*, 199, second verse.
16. J. Ramsay, *Scotland and Scotsmen in the 18th Century*, ed. A. Allardyce, Edinburgh 1888, ii, 408.
17. *Rob Donn*, 237, lines 1-2: 454, line 9.
18. *Ibid.*, 340, all three stanzas. The 1829 edition contains only these stanzas, and in lines two and three of the second stanza gives:
    'S o Henni làir mur f haoidhe.
    Mus d'f huair mi ach beag d'an stà,
19. *Ibid.*, 341, stanza 4, lines 1-4: stanza 5.
20. *Ibid.*, 232, verse 3.
21. *Ibid.*, 392, the whole poem.
22. *Ibid.*, 401, concluding two lines of third verse.
23. *Ibid.*, 252-3, first three stanzas.
24. *Ibid.*, 253, lines 11-12.
25. M. Gray, *The Highland Economy 1750-1850*, Edinburgh 1957, 142-3.

26. *Rob Donn*, 181-3: 145, stanza 1: 290, refrain.
27. *Ibid.*, 221-2, stanzas 1, 2 and 4. The reference to the widower's age is in the fourth line of stanza 5.
28. *Ibid.*, 111, final stanza: 139, lines 17-20: 259, line 4.
29. *Ibid.*
30. *Early British History*, Cambridge ed. N. K. Chadwick 1959, 115. Cf. the pursuit of the sow Henwen from Cornwall to Anglesey in the tale of the Three Mighty Swineherds.
31. *Rob Donn*, 124-5, second half of stanza 1, stanzas 2, 3 and 4.
32. *Ibid.*, 146, first 4 lines.
33. G. Greig, *Last Leaves of Traditional Ballads and Ballad Airs*, ed. A. Keith, Aberdeen 1925. On pages 95-100 are samples of the Aberdonian oral traditions of Robin Hood.
34. R. Pococke, *Tours in Scotland*, 121.
35. *Rob Donn*, 141-2, first three stanzas.
36. *The Highlands in 1750*, ed. A. Lang, Edinburgh 1898, 10-11.
37. Bighouse MSS. (b) 12., S.R.O., Edinburgh.
38. *Rob Donn.*, 142-4, last four stanzas of this poem.
39. *Ibid.*, 122-3, the entire poem. The 1829 edition is followed in the penultimate line of the fourth stanza, where it gives "ag ràdh" rather than the incomprehensible "ag t-sarth."
40. *Ibid.*, 360-1, the entire poem.
41. *Ibid.*, 412, verse 1 and refrain.
42. *Ibid.*, 314-15: 141, first 8 lines.
43. *Ibid.*

CHAPTER EIGHT

Commerce and Professions

DESPITE its deep indentations, the north coast of the Mackay country lacked safe harbours and anchorages. The most easterly of the perilous little creeks and inlets used by coastal craft was Portiskerra on its promontory facing the plain of Dounreay in Caithness, still an outpost of native Gaelic speech on a language frontier that had separated the peninsula of Caithness from Strathnaver for over a millenium. It is marked also by a cleft rock beside the main road to Thurso, behind which the Mackays had rounded up cattle in a hidden gully after their raids into Caithness during the earlier centuries of strife with the Lowlanders. But old animosities between Mackays and Sinclairs had been eroded by intermarriage and commerce, and Highlanders had been attracted to the only natural harbour of the north coast at Thurso, and to the activities it had engendered.[1] Here Iain Mac Eachainn had sent his daughters to school and the Reverend Murdo Macdonald had travelled to attend the funeral of one of his brethren, after the ecclesiastical link with Thurso was severed by the erection of the presbytery of Tongue.

In the previous century a son of William Mackay of Achness, the last Abrach chieftain to reside there, had become a burgess of Thurso. His name was John Mackay and he was a younger brother of Neil Williamson, grandfather of the pious poet of Mudale. Since he had become a burgess by 1636, it may well have been he who was in Stornoway in 1635, consigning twenty barrels of herring to the ship of a Dundee merchant. The vessel called at Thurso on its way south, where Thomas Gunn added to her freight ten barrels of beef, sixteen stone of goose feathers, a hundred lamb skins, fifty calf skins, forty-three oxen and cow hides, and thirty-six ells of double white plaiding. There was a dispute at Leith before the cargo was unloaded, which led to the preservation of these details, evidence of a commerce that continued in Rob Donn's lifetime.[2]

The estate of Strath Halladale was particularly well placed to share in it, especially as the Dowager Lady Bighouse had contracted a second marriage with a Sinclair of Caithness, while her son-in-law Hugh had possessed a Sinclair mother. The manner in which the family network operated is illustrated by a letter that George Sinclair of Giese wrote to his masterful mother from Thurso on 4th December 1752, "Dear Mother, I hope you'll excuse my not coming until the end of this week, and then I will be over, God willing, health serving. What stops me is that I must see the beefs packed and put on board ere Thursday. Therefore I expect you'll send me the butter or I shall lose the opportunity of the ship . . . I have sent two small stone cans, the one with rum and the other with whiskey, six dozen apples, a tanker with honey. I wish you could return me the Gray Beards as they are borrowed. Likewise send me the Black Mug you had some time ago. I expect as the weather is good you'll not fail to send the butter. I have sent you a few potatoes . . .'[3]

The conflict between mother and son over the possession of Giese had been resolved, the latter enjoying his patrimony and dutifully serving his mother's interests in the kingdom of her first marriage. How congenial this arrangement proved to Hugh of Bighouse and his wife can only be surmised. Their own lives had been stricken with misfortunes. Both of their sons had died and earlier in 1752, the husband of their eldest daughter, the Red Fox of Glenure, had been murdered in Appin leaving only baby daughters. The Dowager Lady Bighouse continued to play an active part in the commerce of the estate until her death in 1757, in the knowledge that it would ultimately pass three times through the female line.

Of all this commerce based upon the port of Thurso Rob Donn perhaps knew little: at least, he did not comment on it. What he observed were the small craft that plied between the little harbours of Strathnaver, such as could be seen from Fresgill in the three-mile wide basin enclosed between Whiten Head and the green headland of Durness—Port nan Conn and Port Chamil, Rispond, Sango Mór, Sango Beag and Smoo. It was infinitely easier to travel between most of these townships by sea, and especially from Fresgill, where a man must otherwise scramble along steep cliffs and through a short wooded vale to reach the mouth of the river Hope. On the other hand there was the danger of the misfortune that overtook David from Loch Inshard when he loaded his cheeses aboard a kelp boat and sailed round Cape Wrath in her, only to be swept all the way to Orkney in a storm. Until the news of her safe arrival in the islands had filtered back, David was believed to have been drowned.

133

How distressing and miserable the crossing
That David made to Orkney—
There went the cheese, the kelp and himself.

Since the news of his death was confirmed
Up about the braes of Loch Inshard
The voice of the goat was merry in consequence.

Said Donald, Finlay's daughter
To the indifferent sheriff,
"Indeed I am the only person who has suffered a loss.

"If you have lost your petitioner,
"I have lost my only goodman.
"Who will mind the cattle now?"

Your neighbours were on the look-out,
Seeking news in every bay,
And such was their anxiety that they couldn't shed a tear.

But when they heard of your return
From the seas without mishap,
Then people shed tears in plenty.[4]

There are twenty of these disparaging verses, but they do not mention the type of boat in which David sailed. The editor of the 1829 edition referred to her in his Gaelic introduction to the poem as a *long*, which can be any kind of ship.[5] But since she was a kelp-boat, she may have resembled those that the Reverend John Thomson, minister of Durness, described in 1792, "About twenty of the natives of this parish are employed in navigating two sloops, the property of the tacksman of the kelp shores and salmon fishings. These sloops were built in the Bay of Durness in the years 1788 and 1789. They sail from Ruspin (Rispond) to the herring and cod fishing, in which they have hitherto been pretty successful."[6] Normally a sloop is a single-masted fore-and-aft rigged ship, but it is not clear whether those described by the minister would have been called a *Culaidh* by Rob Donn. This is the standard Gaelic word for a coble, a sea-fishing boat with a flat bottom, square stern and lug-sail. But the speech of Strathnaver was far from standard Gaelic, and the word *Culaidh* as a term for a fishing boat possessed its local meaning.

134

Rob Donn once mentioned a neighbour who acquired a new
Culaidh that he was too selfish to lend.

> *The keeper and the neighbours*
> *And the bard have been refused.*
> *Isn't the new coble beautiful*
> *With Ranald's daughter at the helm?*

> *I promised half-a-crown to you on board—*
> *I will go for a drink to Mary the midwife's.*
> *Isn't the new coble beautiful*
> *With Ranald's daughter at the helm?*[7]

Here is the evidence that Mary, who delivered Catherine Mackay's
illegitimate child, also supported herself by keeping a small inn.

One night Neil Mackay, who lived at Knapdale in Argyll, was
detained by bad weather in his coble at the Geò na Gaoithe—Windy
Creek—of Fresgill and spent the night in the bard's home. He paid
in laughter for his accommodation, as the bard described the heart-
break of the girls in other anchorages because the philandering sailor
was storm-bound at Fresgill. He also described Neil's boat in
mockery as a *birlinn*—a war galley—as he had done in the case of the
boat which took him with George of Handa across the Minch to
Lewis.

> *Said Neil Mackay,*
> *"I am going to perdition*
> *"In the Windy Creek*
> *"Beneath the black rocks.*
> *"Many a beautiful maiden*
> *"Is lamenting*
> *"Because my galley is not*
> *"Arriving at Smoo.*
> > *"Myself and my crew*
> > *"Are in great fear*
> > *"That our ropes will part*
> > *"In the long coble.*
> > *"What on earth made me*
> > *"Lie to under the rocks*
> > *"Considering there is not a place I come to*
> > *"Where I havn't a sweetheart."*

135

> *"There's many an elegant bedroom*
> *"Where I would happen to be.*
> *"When I'd be in Farlich*
> *"Not too many would see me.*
> *"Down on the machair*
> *"I'd make for Pollagluip*
> *"And when I'd be on the beach*
> *"I'd make for Pollabuic."*

Neil illustrated the adage that it is preferable to travel hopefully than to arrive.

> *"The one I can get willingly—*
> *"Small is my regard for her.*
> *"The one I know already—*
> *"A little while with her will do.*
> *"The one who lives*
> *"At Ruith na Cailce—*
> *"I must chase her*
> *"Because she runs away."*

But Rob Donn gallantly gave the last word to a girl who snubbed him.

> *"Myself, I wouldn't respond at all*
> *"To your promiscuous wooing.*
> *"Those who are keen on you*
> *"Are in danger.*
> *"Though you promised*
> *"To marry at Christmas,*
> *"By May day you might*
> *"Be back at Kilmahunack."*[8]

In identifying Neil Mackay as he did, Rob Donn recorded that although he possessed the local clan name, he did not enjoy a recognisable local pedigree.[9] His amorous propensities must have been notorious, however, for Rob Donn composed another poem in which he described Neil's opportunities when many of the young men of the district had been called away on military service.

> *There was not one of them here on May day*
> *But had the promise of a husband.*
> *The only one left of them on the night of Martinmas*
> *Is Neil Dubh, broad-beamed and flabby.*

They were sent overseas,
Red Angus, I'm sorry to say,
Hugh son of Rory and the Geigean
And smart sturdy lads they were.

As many as are unmarried
Are sorrowful, pining.
Neil Mackay can be proud of himself—
He will get all the women.

Rob Donn has named the guest at Isabel's wedding who lost his trousers and one of the men suspected of having seduced Catherine Mackay. He pictured the lassies at the gatherings on the sands of Balnakil where the open-handed Chief used to send a cask of whiskey from the big house in due season.

When the youngsters assemble
On the shore at Christmas time
Where the young men used to go
To drink from the casks,

Now gloom and scowls overwhelm them,
Without a dance-step but only keening,
Like a flock of French hens
And Neil Mackay the turkey-cock over them.

There is many a smart, fine lad
Who has been put under fire.
The most handsome and brave amongst them
Are the first to encounter danger.

In view of the tolerant cynicism with which Rob Donn depicted the girls in this predicament, it may be recalled that his poem was probably composed exactly thirty years before Mozart's *Cosi fan tutte.*

When Neil goes away from us beyond Cape Wrath
To haul the handlines with his cobles,
Many a prayer will go out,
"May good luck keep him from danger."

137

He has a sweetheart in every bay
Between Aisir and Dunnet
And when they thought they were going to be united
    in love with him,
Off he went to Kilmahunack.

Not one of all the men will come on leave
And the young girls are sad,
And although an occasional man should escape with
    his life,
It is hard on the girls waiting for them.

Neil can take the most beautiful of them
Into the bows of his coble,
And those he doesn't consider worth taking aboard,
Tom Thumb will get in with them.[10]

This was the bye-name for a certain John Macleod, and it speaks for itself.

Another kind of small fishing-boat called an *Eathar* or skiff was also used, a small craft adapted for rowing and sailing. There is a Gaelic saying: *Eathar ur is seana chreagan*—"A new skiff and old rocks." Edward Dwelly commented in his dictionary that this was "suggestive of a thousand tragedies beyond the mere literal translation. Both rock and boat are personifications; the rock is old and cunning and unscrupulous, the boat is young and simple and unsuspicious, and when the two come into collision, the boat goes down." But Rob Donn altered the saying to "*an sean eithir air seana chloich*"—"the old skiff on an old rock"—in one of his most strange and moving poems. In it he depicted not the cunning of old age, but its pathetic impotence, with an incantation of words that are not always clear in their meaning yet deeply impressive in their cumulative effect. Special circumstances must be found to explain such an uncharacteristic composition, and perhaps these consisted of his exile to Fresgill, and his loneliness and frustration when he found himself perched above those jagged cliffs of the Moine, far from his beloved dear forest.

An old seaman, an old trader
With an old wife, and they without children,
With no sign of affluence in the bundle of masts,
And bracken ash for its first load.

138

There was an old anchor without any stays in it
On an old hook at an old house.
The old cable, giving no support,
Let the old skiff on an old rock.
Three stalwarts, not one of them fortunate,
Were in dire straits and running fast
To the Rispond boat that pays no dues.
The old shrouds hang miserably on her;
Great is the problem for the pensioner
Who used to be in the ranks far away,
To be behind the leaking hulk at the helm of the
    Sheena
With no prospect of good success.
There was the old carcase of the old hulk
Which an old pirate left to the old harrow.
There was an old compass without movement in it,
An old fragment of tobacco mull;
An old dodderer on an old shore,
An old covering on each old rower's bench,
The old withered timber of the old, old man—
The very waves ashamed of you.[11]

Rob Donn's first editor explained that the *Sheena* was wrecked in a winter storm on the shore near Rispond, but it is not the details of the incident that matter so much as their influence on the bard, expressed with such a wealth of concrete imagery supported by little more than that one short adjective—in total contrast to the adjectival exuberance of his poem about the crossing of the Minch with George of Handa.

Besides the bard's descriptions of those engaged in the callings of land and sea, he made many allusions to those who followed a trade. In a region in which the horses went unshod and the few metal utensils were probably imported, it is hardly surprising that he only made the briefest of references to a smith, when he described the fox-hunter with his noisy dogs as "the rascally smith's son."[12] Yet carpenters must have been relatively numerous, and Rob Donn mentioned only the joiner who had stolen Ann Morrison from him in his youth.[13] He depicted George Morrison the miller as an opulent man, courting a girl who worked in the household of the Tutor of Farr.

139

He is well set-up on Sunday evening,
Going to the great cattle-steading
With a good blue fashionable English coat on
And a stick known as the Pony.
  Merrily Dorothy flirts with George,
  Merrily George with Dorothy.

It is the beginning of fortune for her to choose
    a professional man
Who would earn enough for her forever.
He will preserve what is left over of the meal and
    grain for her
Although Mary does not say, "it will suffice."

If you saw the lassie sitting in the shieling
She would cause great laughter,
The hero's feet like tether-blocks
Across Dorothy's groin.

He's a good clever lad with well-proved equipment
And he's not unknown to many.
Stone and mill-clapper are his weapons,
Waiting to assist with his services.
  Merrily Dorothy flirts with George,
  Merrily George with Dorothy.[14]

In Keoldale, home of Kenneth Sutherland the factor of the Durness estate, there lived a merchant whom Rob Donn lampooned with a great deal less good nature. He depicted the merchant as a turn-coat who was present on the battlefield of Culloden, where he saved himself by pretending blindness; and accused him of having acted as a double-agent. The poem emphasises his Jekyll and Hyde character by alternating between praise and disparagement.

In Keoldale yonder
There is a modest fellow
On whose brow not a frown is to be seen.

He is a worthy hospitable man
Of many parts—
Don't you know John son of Allan?

In Keoldale yonder
There is a rascal without gentility,
The old blind red fellow without honour.

Heavens, how foolish
Of you to ask whether I know
Of John son of Allan's sly eye.

Were you to see him at Dornoch
Or in Thurso
He would be standing, handsome and virile;

The merchants round the table
With the glasses in their fists
And all of them drinking with John son of Allan.

If he were merry with drinking
You could only believe he had an eye disease
As he wept with the hiccups.

Each merchant at the table
Puts a forefinger to his nose
As they make fun of John son of Allan.

He is famous, renowned
In every district of the country
And great is the respect for him in every mansion.

Many of their Ladyships
Speak in various languages,
Enquiring after John son of Allan.

There is not a noblewoman of the court
Catching a glimpse of his eye
Who wouldn't rather a dog had bitten her.

It is ill to be delivering verses
(With the skill they contain)
In praise of the crooked, bung-eyed fellow.

Ill he has deserved your good wishes
And for sure your praise will not reach him,
For he has won honour for his country.

141

> *He reviewed the troops*
> *And the new regiments,*
> *Both Charles's and the Duke's at Culloden.*
>
> *All the host there*
> *Took pity on him as a needy person*
> *Thinking that his two lumps of eyes could not see,*
>
> *Lying informer,*
> *Betraying both sides,*
> *That of Charles and the Duke at Culloden.*[15]

This is comparable with his attack on the tiend collector who came to his house when the minister was there, and gave a hypocritical impression of kindness.

The tradesman with whom, according to the evidence of his poetry, Rob Donn enjoyed a free-spoken acquaintance of the longest standing was James MacCulloch, a weaver. While he was still living in Strathmore, MacCulloch had married Barbara Miller, a common Caithness name that may indicate her origins. According to the bard's editors she became pregnant while she was in service at the mansion of Balnakil, and his account suggests that Lady Reay and Donald Forbes,t he sheriff substitute, both put pressure on MacCulloch to marry her, since he was one of her intimates. Rob Donn was not in favour of this union, and after it had been solemnised, he addressed the weaver in remarkable terms.

> *Greetings to you James!*
> *After tying the oppressive knots—*
> *Now that your wife and mother-in-law are yours—*
> *Keep the reel steady.*
> *After all the advice to refrain*
> *That reaches you from near and far,*
> *How clever you were*
> *When you won your loss.*
>
> *I am now praising you*
> *In sweet gentle songs*
> *And you dispraise me*
> *To many behind my back,*
> *And every highest judge will say*
> *Who knows our profession in the business*
> *That we in this place*
> *Are most mendacious on all sides.*

I came on purpose
To give you advice out of the strath.
There are some since your marriage
Who are doubtful of your prospects.
Put your stock in the hands of executors
When you enter the fray;
Everything will accrue to you
If things fall out well for you.

I will give you further advice
That you will find strangest of all,
That you will find most difficult to appreciate,
And that you most need.
Try to instil a belief
In your own weak nature
That there is no need for you to be jealous
Of any creature under the sun.

When sorrow lies upon you
And you cannot find relief,
And though you were weeping sadly
Until your eyes were dim,
Turn your countenance to heaven,
Praying fervently for salvation
For every guilty person who was responsible
For drawing you into the net.

Though your skill cannot make her
Achieve righteousness at one bound,
Let me see you catch her
In her peevishness so thoroughly
That she shakes her head at you
With a sudden movement as a cow does.
Do not allow her to lie or perjure herself
More than five times a day.

Do you not see the laird of Port Chamil
Rebuking you for idleness,
The gentry giving you encouragement—
Though I won't go into further detail?
Although hundreds were fucking
Your piece tethered there,
You will be responsible for the children
When it comes to paying the baptismal fees.

143

One of them is Forbes,
Who intended harm to you
When you found a means of overcoming
Every unrighteous desire he had,
When he protested
That he would see you married
So that you might be a screen
For the sinners of the big house.

And the other one of them is her Ladyship—
It's certain that she did it,
Catching you before witnesses
In your weakness by deceit—
A quick-witted, clever, influential woman
Who has given birth to and reared children.
She did your partner a good turn,
Putting the head-dress of a married woman on her head.

See how the rampant Thomas
Has got the better of many.
The rampant Norman is just as adept
At crushing corn and herbage.
See that you use an argument
Which will prove to her despite her protests
That she never kept company
With anyone more potent than you.

O bad-tempered, scolding, gluttonous hussy,
Fond of quarrelling and filthy talk . . .[16]

Even by Rob Donn's standards the candour of this poem aston-
ishes, especially in the verse in which he advises the weaver that there
is only one way in which to retain the fidelity of a nymphomaniac.
His description of the rampant Thomas and Norman is *baiteal* in
Gaelic, which means "pillar".

The doubts concerning James MacCulloch's prospects were amply
realised, and by the time at least one of his wife's children was grown
up he was moved to address her in even stronger terms.

Thank you Barbara—
You are known to be expert at the profession.
Why should I be angry with you
Since I would expect no better of you?

Since your infancy you were
The subject of the bard's censure.
More precious to you than a sermon
Was evil talk concerning others.

It is your practice to abuse
And slander anyone at all,
And to revile your mother
Especially concerning the cattle.
Though she was not married when she bore you,
You should accept her
As an example to the young
Before they learn the like of your pranks.

Your grandmother was lustful
And bore children to twelve men,
And your mother did not refuse
One single man apart from her husband.
It was your first compact
That angered the session and presbytery—
Except for Mary's match—
A hundred abominations on you all.

Your mother was illegitimate
And a great strumpet of a wench,
And she bore you a bastard
To a lout of a fellow.
Many a lamentable day
They punished her on the stool of penitence,
And you yourself got a yelping little creature
In the usual way before you were married.

Barbara, act steadily
Since you have got your own daughter married
And she is away from you and shielded
By an order she has not defied.
Your mother and your grandmother,
Margaret and yourself,
Many an evil day
Your names were called out at the presbytery.

145

L

Many bags of weaver's fees
And delicacies went to the place
Which the giddy buxom hussy
Exacted from people.
It is bony MacCulloch
Who promised to exact payment from her brood—
There's not a person who will miss
The strumpet when she dies.

The bard's sympathy for the weaver was undiminished.

I feel sorry for James
Since you came between him and the wall
With the evil of your actions,
With your disrespect and false flattery.
I compared that wicked female
With a ship that is damaged throughout,
Whose prow they keep high and dry by pumping
While the stern keeps letting it in.[17]

Men sometimes possess the gift for retaining one another's friendship despite their womenfolk, and it appears that James MacCulloch
and the bard succeeded in this notwithstanding Barbara Miller. But
the strangest part of the story was to come when the weaver's sons
grew up and began to court the bard's daughters. Rob Donn is
thought to have had thirteen children, of whom eight sons and three
daughters are on record as having reached adult years. His eldest
daughter Isabel (significant name) married in 1770, Christine his
youngest in 1773, while the date of his daughter Mary's marriage is
uncertain. Whether any of them worked as dairymaids at Balnakil
before they married remains in doubt, but it seems likely that one of
them might have found herself in the Chief's dairy when a herdsman
and the weaver's son were competing with one another for an
unidentified girl there. Whoever she was, Rob Donn offered this
advice:

O champion who is taking his course against the wind
Without any expectation on my daughter's part that you will
     ever return,
It would be better to be up with you in the Chief of Mackay's
     cattlefold
Than a champion weaver with twenty head of cattle.

146

I cannot prove, as a defect in your children,
That thieving is inherent in kinsfolk.
When each error is reprimanded over yonder
The amount of cloth and butter left over will be very
 substantial.

James MacCulloch is a man highly esteemed—
Honour is attested in his conduct since childhood.
There's not one in this township without a worry except the
 cattle—
He has wider means than obstacles to pilfering.

Some advice to you, lassie—don't settle for something
Which will be injurious to you and ultimately a mistake.
You confidently expect wealth in plenty
From what's left of the cloth, but it won't make a single
 garment.

You should see the stalwart champions we have,
Their feet operating the loom in turn
With the bobbins for the wool moving noisily backwards and
 forwards,
A boss on the outside and the reed whistling.
 He's a good fellow, red-headed, strong, swift—
 He cannot be uppermost since he didn't get her.[18]

In the end none of Rob Donn's daughters married any of the
weaver's sons, but while this remained a possibility he balanced his
high opinion of their father and the prosperity of the family against
the hazards of introducing the genetic strain of Barbara Miller into
his family. He decided that MacCulloch's son George would make a
suitable husband for his eldest daughter Isabel, while Mary would be
well able to cope with any shortcomings in a husband out of that
house.

> *How thankful I am to Isabel*
> *Although she went away yesterday without my*
> *knowing.*
> *Barbara Miller gave her encouragement*
> *And I hope she is none the worse for that.*

My lassies are without wealth
From learning the tasks of farming.
If your sons are desirous of them
Take them away for what they're worth.

I am seeing the true worth
Of these stalwarts who desired you.
Craftsmen will not be a source of vexation to you
For they will weave as much as you spin.

How fortunate my child is
That George would have the shuttle for her.
She would have cattle and horses and shielings:
She would have good food in the pot and sowans.

I will not give you long stockings—
And small is the number I have of them.
A fortune will be yours
When you marry George the weaver.

Though I myself should lose the brood that is yonder,
Indeed it would be no great hardship to me.
If I could dispose of the others
I would take one of them for Mary.

They are clever, sagacious champions
And they will steal the goats for her.
If I gave her a hammer or vice,
Mary would knock the brains out of them.[19]

In the end Mary married a Donald Mackay who had served in the
Duke of Gordon's Fencible Regiment, and she was still living with
him in Durness after her father's death.[20]

Of the learned professions, Rob Donn had most to say about the
parish ministry: about Murdo Macdonald in Durness, John Munro
in Edderachillis who died in 1755 and George Munro, the hospitable
minister of Farr. He made only a single reference to Walter Ross of
the parish of Tongue, in his poem about the streaker, and mentioned
Macdonald's wife just once in his light-hearted survey of conjugal
relations. Doubtless his meaning was clear enough at the time,
though now it is obscure.

148

The wife of the Reverend Murdo was deceiving her family.
I am sleeping and let me not be wakened.
It's his trip to Moray that caused her trouble and deprivation.
I am sleeping and let me not be wakened.[21]

Perhaps the bard's indictment of unworthy ministers was inspired principally by Skeldoch of Farr, but unfortunately he was not unique. The Reverend Dr Alexander Nicolson in Thurso possessed an estate in the parish of Reay where he "exacted arbitrary and oppressive services" from his tenants according to a deposition of 1774, obliging them to spend between thirty and forty days in each year harvesting corn and hay, cutting and bringing home his peats, without the least remuneration.[22] According to tradition, Rob Donn once encountered Nicolson after Murdo Macdonald had died and been succeeded by the Reverend John Thomson. Nicolson was reported to have asked the bard how Thomson was doing and to have received the answer, "Mr Thomson is doing what you never did or will do—he is doing his best."[23] The anecdote rings doubly true, inasmuch as Thomson came to Durness from Avoch in the Black Isle so deficient in the only language understood by most of his parishioners that he had much need to do his best, and it suggests that Rob Donn may have had Nicolson as well as Skeldoch in mind when he described ministers:[24]

> *Fit for parsimonious farmers,*
> *Fit for provident stewards,*
> *And apart from the calling they took their vows for,*
> *Fit for everything excellent.*[25]

It is curious that Rob Donn never mentioned a school teacher in Durness. On 12th February 1740 Murdo Macdonald made cryptic reference to what appears to have been the third Lord Reay's intervention in the appointment of a teacher there. "This day wherein I should have been employed in the works of retired devotion was spent in a needless meeting with the Superior and other parishioners about our school." The next allusion to this subject in what survives of his diary occurs in November 1745 when the minister noted, "Last Friday came here one Mr William Mackenzie to be our schoolmaster, to whom by the abrupt and headlong management of some persons of note in the neighbourhood I was obliged to give way before I could lay the matter with any deliberation before the wise Counsellor." However, he was able to console himself, "I have much

149

need of such a helper to ease me in so far as of the uneasy burden of teaching my children." William Mackenzie moved to the mission at Achness after George Munro had left there to become minister of Farr in 1753, and in 1769 he became minister of Tongue. Here the son of the school teacher recalled that "he was a lively, eloquent preacher of considerable talent and fervent piety, also of a fine personal appearance. He was much beloved in Achness, and no less so by the parishioners of Tongue."[26]

It was customary for young men who had been ordained for the ministry to become school teachers or tutors in private families while they awaited their first charge. Donald Sage, the author of those observations on William Mackenzie, described how his father Alexander Sage taught in Tongue until he was invited to Reay to assist the aged Alexander Pope there. Donald Sage also recorded: "My father, when schoolmaster of Tongue, met with the poet. He invited him to dinner, an invitation which was accepted. The poet was pleased with his fare and still more with his host, and at parting offered to make his entertainer the subject of a poem. This offer my father declined, aware of those high powers of satire with which his guest was endowed, and which, like a razor dipped in oil, never cut so keenly as when intermingled with compliment and praise."[27]

Perhaps Alexander Sage recalled the devastating verses that immortalised his predecessor as teacher in Tongue, John Sutherland or Iain Tapaidh. Rob Donn had referred to his troublesome brood of twins, one of whom was named Annabel, and about a century later Donald Sage revealed that her sons were still identified as "the grandsons of 'John Happay', the frequent subject of Rob Donn's withering and merciless satire."[28] No member of any trade or profession in Strathnaver received such a wide-ranging indictment from the bard as Iain Tapaidh;[29] and Donald Mackay, school teacher at Farr, was the only member of his profession to receive the kind of respectful tribute that Rob Donn could bestow with such generosity.[30]

He was not swayed by clannish loyalty, although he could give humerous expression to it. There was a surgeon named John Mackay in Armadale in 1769 who moved from there to Tongue without securing any mention in Rob Donn's verse.[31] On the other hand Dr Gordon, who had lived at Clyne in Sutherland in 1742 and thereafter emigrated to Jamaica, received an elegy when news arrived of his death in that distant island. In the circumstances it seems probable that he was an associate of the Tutor of Farr's son Rupert who also died in Jamaica, and of Iain Mac Eachainn's son Hugh who was more fortunate.

> *To the Sheriffdom of Sutherland*
> *There came distressing news from England*
> *That Doctor Gordon is dead.*
> *Knowledge of him has gone far, north and south;*
> *He was an outstanding man to speak of*
> *Though death cut him off so suddenly,*
> *A man of long continuance in the world*
> *Without its being heard that a single person disliked*
> *   him.*

In contrast with the malediction on death in his elegy for the school teacher of Farr, Rob Donn interpreted Dr Gordon's death as a reward for a virtuous life, according to the principle that those whom the gods love die young.

> *In England and in Scotland*
> *Great is the sorrow that you departed so swiftly.*
> *In the island of Jamaica*
> *People loved you even more than in the north.*
> *Though companies weep*
> *When death afflicts them so harshly,*
> *Your service did not merit*
> *To be so long from perfection above.*[32]

Very different were the verses that Rob Donn composed for Dr Donald Morrison, who attended the Chief until the day when he fell out of favour, subtle observations on the fickleness of favour and fortune.

> *A Year ago this hogmanay*
> *Sharp was the blade that could sever the affection*
> *Between Donald and the Chief*
> *Who used to be one in fellowship and affection.*
> *But whatever was on the cards*
> *He passed by us angrily yesterday,*
> *And who is more likely to be at fault*
> *Than the one who leaves the village on his own?*

> *I saw you at table*
> *The year Sheena Gordon had the tumour,*
> *And you couldn't show your face*
> *Without drawing people to you.*

But when you thought your seat
Was as firmly established as the gable of the gate,
The great stout feet slipped
On the treacherous bare flagstones, without support.

The Paths of Providence
Give us hundreds of lessons,
Making a sacrifice of some
For the instruction of their contemporaries.
But if a man suddenly falls
Through looking too hastily about him
I haven't the slightest idea
Which are more at fault, the stones or the feet.

I'm afraid myself
As I look for ground or a crevice for my heel
And I pass over the stones
That upset stable men.
But I'm hopeful despite the risk
That all my large bones will remain intact:
For although I should happen to stumble,
It isn't far from my chin to the ground.

Rob Donn referred next to Morrison's successor Dr Robert Munro, in a stanza which reveals incidentally that the Chief of fickle favour was not the amiable fourth Lord Reay but his son who became the fifth Lord, and that the hazardous pathway led to Tongue house.

The young man who's a doctor,
Who, I hear, is to succeed him,
Has learnt a lesson from two of them
To be circumspect in his ways.
But concerning the course he is following
Let me forbear from saying all I know.
But if there is substance in my advice,
This is the time when Samuel is in need of it.[33]

Ultimately Rob Donn revealed all he knew in what is possibly the most indiscreet of all his poems, but this belongs to a later context.

Since most people spoke only Gaelic while the written language of civil and religious administration was English, there was occasional need for the professional services of a notary. The notary public was

Donald Forbes, the sheriff substitute, and Rob Donn once referred to a clerk whom a woman called Briogaiseag employed to write a letter of complaint to Lord Reay. It was so ill-written that the petition proved to be unintelligible and the bard observed:

> *I certainly wouldn't entrust important business*
> *To the Lowland notary Briogaiseag used.*[34]

He was not more complimentary over "the agreement which I have in the handwriting of Rory Mann" concerning the sale of a puppy.[35] It was obviously a grave inconvenience to that society that its language was ignored for all administrative purposes.

But of all the professions, the one that recruited every section of Highland society, and especially in Strathnaver, was military service. When Rob Donn was over forty-five years old he became a soldier himself, in circumstances that remain mysterious since he never gave a reason why he should have joined the colours at such a mature age, and tradition offers no precise explanation.

REFERENCES TO CHAPTER EIGHT

1. Reay MS. 3/6, 4th Sep. 1637: *Book of Mackay*, 258.
2. *Register of the Privy Council of Scotland*, ed. P. H. Brown, Edinburgh 1905, Second series, vi, 6-8.
3. Bighouse MSS. (b) 12.
4. *Rob Donn*, 199-200, first six verses.
5. *Songs and Poems of Rob Donn*, Edinburgh 1829, 97: "Nuair a bha Daibhidh dol dachaidh leis an im agus leis a' chàise, thun a mhaighstir, f huair e air long cheilpe, bha dol an rahrad."
6. *Statistical Account*, iii, 581.
7. *Rob Donn*, 318, couplets 2 and 3 with refrain.
8. *Ibid.*, 177-80, verse 1 with refrain, verses 2, 4, and 8.
9. *A Collection of Highland Rites and Customs*, ed. J. L. Campbell, Cambridge 1975, 27-9. The ignorance of central government officials in earlier times concerning Gaelic designations has led to modern misunderstanding, e.g. in G. Donaldson, *Scotland: the shaping of a Nation*, London 1974.
10. *Rob Donn*, 174-6, verses 1, 2, 3, 6, 7, 8, 10, 11, 12 and 13.
11. *Ibid.*, 394, the entire poem.
12. *Ibid.*, 134, line 1.
13. *Ibid.*, 148-50, "An t-Saor" in the penultimate line on page 149.
14. *Ibid.*, 410-11, the first four verses with refrain.
15. *Ibid.*, 240-2, the entire poem.
16. *Ibid.*, 214-17, the entire poem to opening lines of the final verse.

17. *Ibid.*, 228-30, the entire poem omitting verse 7.
18. *Ibid.*, 386-7, the entire poem.
19. *Ibid.*, 231-3, verses 1, 3, 5, 6, 11, 12, 13.
20. *Ibid.*, xxxvi.
21. *Ibid.*, 263, opening four lines.
22. A. R. Newsome, "Records of Emigrants from England and Scotland to North Carolina, 1774-5" in *The North Carolina Historical Review*, 1934, xi, 131.
23. *Rob Donn*, xlvi.
24. Sage, *Memorabilia Domestica*, 39.
25. *Rob Donn*, 76, opening four lines.
26. Sage, *op. cit.*, 40.
27. *Ibid.*, 38.
28. *Ibid.*, 126.
29. *Rob Donn*, 112-15, 184-6, 331-8, 390-3.
30. *Ibid.*, 1-5.
31. *Book of Mackay*, 299.
32. *Rob Donn*, 59-60, stanzas 1 and 6.
33. *Ibid.*, 109-11, stanzas 1, 2, 34, 5 and 6.
34. *Ibid.*, 346, lines 15-16.
35. *Ibid.*, 32 ¼, lines 15-16.

CHAPTER NINE

Military Service

EVERY Highlander, Ramsay of Ochtertyre recalled of the age of Rob Donn, "wished to be thought a soldier", and in Strathnaver they possessed an exceptional variety of opportunities for becoming one indeed.[1]   The Dutch army in which they were able to serve for limited terms gave them a military training that evoked the comment in 1750: "The Mackays are said to be a better militia than any of the neighbouring clans, for which this is assigned as a reason."[2]   They had enjoyed this special facility ever since Hugh Mackay of Scourie had become General of the Scots Brigade in Holland and had helped to place William of Orange on the throne in 1688.   When the Great General died in 1692 his nephew Aeneas Mackay succeeded him until he died of wounds in 1697 with the rank of Brigadier General.   Hugh of Scourie's only son was killed in action in 1708, holding the rank of Major, but he in turn left two sons, one of whom reached the rank of Colonel while the other rose to be a Lieutenant General in the Dutch army before he died at Breda in 1775.[3]

The special relationship between the Mackays and their Dutch co-religionists was based as much on the Calvinist beliefs that they shared as upon long-standing military ties.   It was remarked in 1750 that "the common people of the Mackays are the most religious of all the tribes that dwell among the mountains, south or north."[4]   And an example of the behaviour that could give rise to such comment occurred when a detachment of them were stationed on garrison duty at Dunkeld after the Forty-Five.   Here they enquired where they might listen to the Word of God on the Sabbath, and were directed to the fellowship meetings held by Dugald Buchanan, the schoolmaster at Kinloch Rannoch.   It was through this encounter that Buchanan became acquainted with the spiritual songs of John Mackay of Mudale, which were said to have exercised a profound influence upon Scotland's greatest religious poet.[5]

The reputation of the Mackays both for piety and for military efficiency helped to open another field of enterprise to them.   In 1732 the English philanthropist and soldier James Oglethorpe obtained his charter establishing the colony of Georgia in America. He designed it as an asylum for oppressed Protestants from Europe and required not merely settlers, but soldiers capable of protecting the territory from the neighbouring Spaniards. Who more suitable than the Mackays for such a mission? In the year of the new colony's foundation Patrick Mackay, who had held a Hanoverian commission during the 1715 uprising, disposed of his property in Edderachillis and carried a number of its people to General Oglethorpe's settlement. His grandfather, a first cousin of General Hugh of Scourie, had fought for Charles II at Worcester and his father had commanded the garrison at Ruthven for King William in the Revolution of 1688, so Patrick was carrying an old tradition into this new hemisphere.[6] In 1734 Oglethorpe despatched Lieutenant Hugh Mackay from Georgia to the Highlands to raise a hundred men "free or servants." The objective of permanent colonisation was made explicit: "they farther allowed them to take 50 head of women and children."

Hugh Mackay became a Captain, and commander of the new fort called St Andrews, not without accusations in 1738 that he "exercised an illegal power there, such as judging in all causes, directing and ordering all things according to his will." But he held the fort against Spanish attack and Oglethorpe backed him, so perhaps he was only acting as frontiersmen must do in such a precarious predicament. In 1739 an expedition was defeated on its way to avenge a murder of Highlanders, which perhaps helped to diminish enthusiasm for any further emigration to this colony.[7] But it extended to other parts of North America. William Polson, nephew of the hospitable Reverend George Munro, minister of Farr, died there in 1755 as a Captain in the Virginia Rangers.[8]

So Rob Donn might have been alluding both to Europe and to America when he referred to the smart lads who were sent overseas, leaving Neil Mackay to take his choice of the lassies. On another occasion he spoke of those who were sent to Ireland, leaving his brother Donald Dubh in an equally fortunate position.

> *When he heard the report*
> *That the young men went to Ireland,*
> *All the best endowed girls amongst them*
> *Were paying their attentions to Donald Dubh.*

> *When we heard the rumour*
> *That the young men went away from here*

Two of them came from Cape Wrath
On the tracks of Donald Dubh.

It appears that comparatively few went soldiering in India, but it was the east that swallowed the young man whose death was Scotland's greatest loss of any in Strathnaver, Joseph Macdonald, son of the minister of Durness. The Reverend Murdo's diary contains frequent references to his anxiety over Joseph's career, for his precocious musical abilities appear to have offered him no prospects of employment. Early in 1757 the minister happened to be visiting Donald Mackay at Claiseneach in Durness, whose wife Barbara was a daughter of Kenneth Sutherland of Keoldale, and their son Captain George a servant of the East India Company. "Being in the house of the old man, father to Captain Mackay, and reading useful subjects in the usual way since he became our neighbour, again there came to the landlady a letter from Bighouse, asking her and her husband's concurrence in favour of a Caithness young sailor who wanted a recommendation to the Captain from his friends in this country, and expected thereby no small benefit to himself. This incident made me suggest to the parents that, considering their son's ability and benevolent disposition, I greatly wondered how he never called for any of his young countrymen, to whom as I understood by the hint above that he might easily lend a (?hand) by lift, and mentioned my Joseph as a proper person to be offered him as a young adventurer."

The fatal seed had been planted in the minister's mind, although it was not until 29th January 1759 that he wrote to Captain George in London, as he awaited his ship to India. Joseph was staying at this time with his brother Patrick at the manse of Kilmore. Captain George not only welcomed the opportunity to oblige his worthy minister: he also offered to defray the expenses of Joseph's expedition to India, knowing that Macdonald's stipend would not enable him to do so. But he sent this suggestion tactfully through Hugh of Bighouse to his parents at Claiseneach, and Bighouse was so preoccupied by business of his own at this time that he left George's letter in his pocket without forwarding it, and merely sent a verbal message to his parents that gave no hint of his generous offer.

When Macdonald at last heard of it, he was appalled by his apparent discourtesy, and wrote urgently to Captain George: "When I read your letter, which was sent by Bighouse enclosed to your Mamma now again in Claiseneach, I did not know of your having given any expensive recommendations to him in favour of the young

157

man, nor said he aught to Mr Mackay on the head, but that he would do his part when desired. Neither Mrs Mackay nor your Uncle Kenneth nor your humble servant could infer from such a general limit that you gave any order for money to equip the lad, to whom I did immediately send your letter then with his brother in Argyllshire. Both my sons were duly sensible of your goodness." The minister has evidently used the term "Uncle" for George's grandfather Kenneth Sutherland: he also used the term "friends" to denote relatives, a practice still common in the Mackay country.

His letter continued: "But though Joseph had body and mind for the voyage, of which I am not to this day quite sure, nay, though he were every way qualified for one of the three capacities named for a young adventurer to the eastern world, viz. that of soldier, sailor or trader, the united endeavours of my eldest son and me could not afford the lowest sum you condescended on for the boy's charges, viz. £40 sterling. For though Patrick has one of the best livings in that country as minister of Kilmore in Lorne, yet by his marriage so soon after settling there he has early given himself too much ado to assist his friends."

While Joseph waited to be killed by kindness he made a copy of the Highland airs he had collected, most of them from Strathnaver, to present to his sister. It was this copy that Patrick published after the original had been lost in India. And in the same year 1759 Robert Burns was born, who would make such excellent use of the collection that many of its airs became more widely known by Lowland names. But fatally, as it proved, Joseph did not make a copy of the piobaireachd collection that he took to India with him. "O! that I had been at more pains," he wrote to his father after his departure, "to gather these admirable remains of our ancient Highland music, before I left my native country. It would have augmented my collection of Highland music and poetry, which I have formed a system of in my voyage to India."[9] He died there in 1762.

His father had been so enthusiastic over this solution to the worrying problem of Joseph's career that he feared only lest Captain George should leave before his son was ready to accompany him. When all the arrangements were complete, the minister wrote to George: "I should now turn to your side of the affair, which was so genteelly managed that I know not how to express my gratitude. There is something so uncommonly polite in your way of bestowing the gratuity as puts me in mind of the famous Mr Pope's eulogium on a certain great man whose custom was to do good by stealth, and blush to find it fame."

These were not only the years during which Clive completed the conquests that created the Indian Empire: they were also those of the Seven Years' War of 1756 to 1763, aimed at destroying the power of Frederick the Great of Prussia. It was this conflict that gave Britain the opportunity, as Prussia's ally, of striking at the dominion of France both in India and in Canada.

At first the British government was wary of arming Highlanders in this cause, for memories of the last Jacobite uprising were not dead after ten years. When England was provided with a militia in 1757 to guard against French invasion, Scotland was refused one. Then William Pitt reversed this policy, and throughout the Seven Years' War the Highlands were turned increasingly into a recruiting-ground for the British army. The 77th Regiment of Montgomerie's Highlanders was raised, indeed, as early as 1757, and so was the 78th Regiment of Fraser's Highlanders. In the bumper year 1759 there were formed the 87th, 88th and 89th Regiments of Keith's, Campbell's and the Gordon Highlanders: together with the Argyll and Sutherland Fencible Regiments for domestic service.[10]

Even if many young men enlisted with enthusiasm, they did not always enjoy unfettered freedom of choice as the tenants at will of superiors who could also invoke traditional sanctions of honour and loyalty. Rob Donn never expressed disapproval of this, and when he told the story of two men who fled into hiding to avoid being drafted into the army, he merely exploited the comedy of the situation.[11] It can be assumed that the press gangs did not menace this remote area, as they were notorious for doing on the fringes of the Highlands, and it is evident that there would have been little point in their entering a land of such extensive recruitment.[12] Rob Donn only referred to them once, in the context of a drover who went to Crieff with cattle and was taken by an army press gang there.[13]

In 1798 a stranger to the neighbourhood named James Anderson held the lease of Keoldale, and he wrote to Captain Kenneth Mackay who was one of Lord Reay's factors, "I think they must see little who does not see this country approaching rapidly into a state of *depopulation*, and that by the very means once thought favourable, I mean the volunteer establishments. Such effect has the smattering of exercise upon the rising generation, aided by their pay, which is all converted into dissipation, that not one individual able to lift a drumstick now remains unenlisted in Durness. And I'm told the case is pretty similar in other parts of this estate, though not quite so bad."[14] It was the culmination of a trend that had continued throughout Rob Donn's lifetime.

159

In the year 1759, when Hugh of Bighouse omitted to forward Captain George Mackay's letter to his parents in Claiseneach, he certainly had much to preoccupy him. In addition to administering the estates of Bighouse and Tongue he accepted the rank of Major in the Sutherland Fencible Regiment, of which the Earl of Sutherland became Lieutenant Colonel. The fourth Lord Reay at Balnakil had taken no part in the military activities at the time of the Forty-Five and now, according to the minister, he had turned "dull and useless" since 1757 in his mortal illness. To his brother Hugh fell the responsibility of recruitment throughout the Mackay country, and it may be assumed that he was responsible for Rob Donn's term of military service as well as for his earlier eviction from Strathmore.

Charles Gordon, tacksman of Skelpick near the mouth of the Naver river, received a Captain's commission, while other Captains included John Mackay of Strathy and James Mackay, the tacksman of Skerray and Borgie's son. John Mackay who settled later in Melness became a Lieutenant, while George Mackay of the Scourie branch served as an Ensign.[15] These ranks corresponded to the numbers of men each officer brought to the Regiment from his property.

Local tradition suggests that Rob Donn was invited to join the colours as a source of entertainment to officers and men, and that he enjoyed exceptional freedom while he wore uniform.[16] He said nothing to suggest otherwise and composed some amusing songs that lend plausibility to this explanation for his presence in the army. He saw no active service and found nothing significant to say; and his only serious poem on the subject was an elegy for a young man not of his own country who had been killed in Germany. But a decade later he recalled how he had visited Dunrobin, the castle of his Colonel, and looked at the family portraits of the Earl who was to prove the last of the Gordon line.

> In this castle a little while ago,
> In the family's dining room
> I saw portraits of the five of them,
> Gallant, noble people, all of them.
> The last surviving one of them—
> Well I knew him before he died—
> I found his portrait beside me,
> Standing in his kilt and plaid.[17]

The castle of Dunrobin was enclosed, several decades after the bard's death, in a vast imitation of a Loire château by its English owner. But the portrait that he saw still hangs in it, the Earl wearing a tartan of the Black Watch sett used by the Campbells and the Sutherlands. The yellow stripe had not yet been added to this sett to compose a Gordon tartan.

Rob Donn was not a member of the contingent that visited Inveraray, where he would have been able to inspect the new castle in process of construction by that other great Hanoverian, the Chief of Clan Diarmaid. Someone wrote from there on 4th August 1760, "On Friday last arrived here in their way to the Roads, eight miles from this place, a hundred sturdy fellows of Lord Sutherland's Highlanders, commanded by Lieutenant James Mackay of Skerray; though, after a fatiguing march, they made as fine an appearance as any troops I ever beheld, and though they are but a young corps, there is scarce a regiment in his Majesty's service better disciplined."[18]

Rob Donn only mentioned in passing that he was sent to Aberdeen, Dundee and Edinburgh, while it was Inverness that provided him with the theme for his two-edged flattery. Her name was Sally Grant, and the refrain of one of his songs in her praise runs.

> *He who dances, he who sports,*
> *He who leaps and he who runs,*
> *He who listens, he who talks*
> *Are pining all for Sally.*

As usual this is no solitary miller's daughter, courted by some lonely swain, but the central figure of a lively company—this time a military one.

> *I have passed through lands far and wide*
> *Where I have seen girls and women.*
> *Between Tongue and Aberdeen*
> *There were none to compare with Sally.*

> *In Edinburgh and in Dundee*
> *And everywhere I've put my feet*
> *I saw none like her,*
> *Sally, the lass of my heart.*

> *Good her hearing, good her sight,*
> *Delicious her taste and all her talk.*

161

M

Lucky the man who approaches near
To the groves of Sally.

Good without and good within,
Pleasant in speech and in appearance,
Pleasant when seated at the head of the company,
Notable in her birth and in her nurture.

The one who wants her and won't get her
And the one who won't try for want of nerve,
I didn't know how to make
A choice between the two of them.

The stalwart captain of Grenadiers
Who leaps the highest and runs the swiftest,
There's no place where she sits
But he'd be beside her.

If they were to put her picture on the flag
Of the Earl of Sutherland's regiment
We would die to keep it there
Though the power of the Pope came against us.[19]

    This was by no means the kind of poetry that had edified the pious schoolmaster of Kinloch Rannoch when soldiers from the Mackay country had been sent to Dunkeld after the Forty-Five: not, perhaps, the sort of verse that Hugh of Bighouse expected from the regimental bard. But evidently he was powerfully moved by Sally's charms, although he depicted her as the property of the officers, and entirely respectable in addition. He composed another song about her that contained the recurrent refrain, *A ribhinn aluinn aoibhinn og*—You lovely comely young lady.

Before I set eyes on you
I heard of your renown
You lovely comely young lady—
That you were like a goddess
And that people worshipped you
You lovely comely young lady.
I didn't think that mere boasting
But proper to relate,
For when the music began

And they told me of it
I could well believe it
As she moved in the dance,
You lovely comely young lady.

It is probable that Hugh of Bighouse had been promoted Lieutenant Colonel by the time this poem was composed, and that it was he, not the Earl, who was referred to in the following verse.

The reason why Sally shows
No favour to the Colonel
Is fear lest others should be hostile to him
For as long as he lives.
She's a creature so elegant
And a creature so beautiful—
Heavens, what a shame it would be
If a girl who is willing
To be wooed by the world
Should be wedded to one man.

Concerning the Major, George
Has been speaking discreetly,
Repeatedly disclosing
That he is already married.
But when the ale goes round
At the mess tables
They drink heartily
A toast to the lady.
Each one of the others,
Except for Sally, is grateful to him.

I sat in a maze,
As though awoken from a trance,
And I saw those three
With my eyes and with insight.
According to my perception,
Judging by her expression,
Sally was wishing
The Major was a widower:
George was delighted
That she was disconsolate.

163

There is not a man
In the battalion who knows you
Who doesn't dream of you,
Whether single or married.
But when Charles pursues you—
The youngest of the Majors—
Though he has a name for harshness
In King George's army,
His disposition is transformed
Out of affection for you.[20]

With his sense of humour that so often bordered on the outrageous, Rob Donn addressed a stanza to his wife Janet after he had
returned home, using the same refrain that he had addressed to
Sally Grant.

See that I get a coat
Or a tattered jacket of a coat,
You lovely comely young lady,
Lest the fish should be
Mangling the bait on me
You lovely comely young lady;
Considering there were so many lovely girls
And Sally chief amongst them
Who would give me a hand—
And some of them would give me a kiss—
Though now I am
A thrall in Janet's house,
You lovely comely young lady.[21]

During the period that Rob Donn spent in the Sutherland
Fencibles between 1759 and 1763 he did compose some of his most
impressive poetry, but this had nothing whatever to do with his life
in the army.

REFERENCES TO CHAPTER NINE

1. Ramsay, *Scotland and Scotsmen in the 18th Century*, ii, 408.
2. *The Highlands in 1750*, Edinburgh 1898, 10.
3. H. Mackay, *Memoirs of the War Carried on in Scotland and Ireland 1689-
   1691*, Edinburgh 1833: *Papers Illustrating the History of the Scots Brigade
   in the Service of the United Netherlands*, ed. J. Ferguson, Edinburgh 1899.

4. *The Highlands in 1750*, 9.
5. *Dain Spiordail*, introduction.
6. *The Book of Mackay*, 292-4: J. P. Maclean, *An Historical Account of the Settlements of Scotch Highlanders in America Prior to the Peace of 1783*, Cleveland 1900, 149-68.
7. *Madlean, op. cit.*, 146-69.
8. *Book of Mackay*, 295: *Maclean, op. cit.*, 103.
9. Macdonald, *A Collection of Highland Vocal Airs*, 1.
10. *Sutherland Book*, i, 450-1.
11. *Rob Donn*, 423.
12. M. I. Adam, "The Highland Emigration of 1770," in *The Scottish Historical Review*, 1919, xvi, 280-93.
13. *Rob Donn*, 227, lines 3-6.
14. Reay MS. 74. Rispond, 28th December 1798.
15. *Book of Mackay*, 204, 293, 306, 313, 320, 323.
16. *Rob Donn*, xxvii-xxviii.
17. *Ibid.*, 36-7, third stanza.
18. *Caledonian Mercury*, 13th August 1760.
19. *Rob Donn*, 283-4, the entire poem.
20. *Ibid.*, 280-2, the first five stanzas. For stanza 3 line 5 the 1829 edition has "*E bhi cheana posd*," which is here preferred.
21. *Ibid.*, 436, the entire poem.

CHAPTER TEN

Sweeping Change

IN June 1760 Richard Pococke, Protestant Bishop of Ossory in Ireland, visited Strathnaver in the course of a tour of Scotland. The son of an English churchman, he had already won celebrity with the publication of a narrative of his journeys through the near East and his passion for antiquities had filled him with determination, many years earlier, to make an expedition to the Orkney islands. It is a matter of deep regret that he should have postponed his visit until after Iain Mac Eachainn had died in 1757 and Rob Donn had left the Mackay country in 1759, since he is the one man who might otherwise have placed the bard on record during his lifetime. But at least he was able to sketch his impressions of Rob Donn's world.

He rode into it through the Rough Bounds beside Ben Klibreck during one of those dismal summers that not infrequently afflict the north of Scotland. "Here it was like the month of November; we saw a breach that was made by a spring like a flood, gushing out at the side of a mountain. We came to another rivulet and sat down in a sheltered place half a mile beyond some shielings or huts, to which they come in the summer with their cattle."[1]

Here the bishop encountered the Rob Donns of a later generation as his party were eating their meal. "Some boys came near with their cattle, and afterwards two others; we invited them to take share, and when we were going away, they said their mother was coming with some refreshments, and immediately she appeared at a good distance; she carried a piggin of cream, and her maid followed her with a small tub covered, which was warm whey. She drank to us, and we took it round and tasted the whey."[1] It is possible that they came from Mudale, since Pococke's party continued north-west past there until they arrived close to the tremendous panorama of the Reay forest, the deep cleft of Gleann na Goille, the peaks of Foinaven and Arkle beyond.

Pococke wound his way down Strathmore until he reached the broch called Dornadilla, which had stood there for upwards of two

166

thousand years. He made drawings of it that show how much more of its structure then remained intact, and left an exact description of the monument whose origins were still surrounded by mystery at the time when Rob Donn played there as a child. "The hill we crossed to Strathmore is a foot of Ben Hope. Under the foot of this mountain we travelled, which is a fine natural slope with perpendicular rocks over it resembling ruined buildings. This continues on all under the mountain itself with a sort of terrace on it, from which the mountain rises most beautifully, being divided by several pyramidal risings with little hillocks between them to the number of above twenty, in which little cascades of water fall down after rain in a very beautiful manner. And before we came to this part we saw a sheet of water falling down into a hollow about a hundred feet, and 'tis said falls fifty more out of sight. All the cascades after the morning showers appeared very beautiful."[2] The bishop was as enthusiastic as Isabel Mackay had been when she defended these surroundings to her sister Mary twenty years before.

The party rode by Muisel, where Iain Mac Eachainn would surely have invited the bishop to dismount, had he been living there still, past the Merkin woods and Bad na h-achlais where Rob Donn had so recently been compelled to abandon his home, and west towards the great sea loch. "Over that Loch Eriboll we ferried, and Lord Reay's horses met me, and I rode three miles to Durness, Lord Reay's house, which is situated at the south-east of Durness bay, where there is a fine strand bounded to the north by Farout head."[2]

Pococke remained at Balnakil from Wednesday until the following Monday and the minister spent much time in his company, commenting in his diary: "he seems to be curious, ingenious and judicious, and I hope our country may not be the worse of his visit, which has probably rubbed off prejudices *hinc inde*."[3] Pococke did not mention Macdonald in person, but said of Durness: "The people are in general extremely hospitable, charitable, civil, polite and sensible. In the north-west part I met with the greatest hospitality and politeness in Lord Reay's family."[4] This, unfortunately, is all he had to say of that broad-minded Episcopalian, Lady Reay, or of her husband in the final period of his illness.

But he made interesting observations about the ordinary folk whose doings fill so much of Rob Donn's light verse. "The people live here very hardy, principally on milk, curds, whey, and a little oatmeal, especially when they are at the shielings in the mountains, that is, the cabins or huts in which they live when they go to the mountains with their cattle during the months of June, July and

167

August. Their best food is oat or barley cakes. A porridge made of oatmeal, cale, and sometimes a piece of salt meat in it, is the top fare. Except that by the sea they have plenty of fish in summer, and yet they will hardly be at the pains of catching it but in very fine weather. They are mostly well-bodied men of great activity, and go the Highland trot with wonderful expedition."[5] Only the lines in which Rob Donn described himself as a thrall in Janet's house reveal that he too indulged in fishing.

Pococke did not enter the Reay forest, but he did the next best thing when he paid a visit to the wilderness of the Cape Wrath peninsula: and this would have taken him past Keoldale and the hospitality of Kenneth Sutherland. "We passed by a little stream where we found a fawn of the red deer about a week old, that had been killed by an eagle; probably two of them shared the prey, for there were two great holes on one side of it. The herd moved it from the place and covered it with heath, in order to come and take it for the use of his house, and they say it is excellent food."[6] The observant bishop noticed the herd who was employed to tend the sheep and horses here; the deer hunts that were held on the Cape Wrath peninsula: and when he resumed his journey eastwards he inspected the Chief's salmon weir at the mouth of the river Hope. What amazed him most was to learn that goats killed and ate adders, and particularly that they made a most curious noise as they did so. In fact there was a Gaelic saying on this subject:

> *The goat's trick with the serpent.*
> *Eating away, and still complaining.*[7]

Donald Forbes came all the way to Hope to meet Pococke, "who conducted me six miles to his house over the Moine, a morassy country, impassable except to their little bog horses. Coming to the bay of Tongue, we had a more pleasant country in view, in which there are many fine spots of ground, and especially Lord Reay's estate of Tongue." As they descended towards the kyle, the Sheriff-Substitute showed the bishop where the *Hazard* with her French gold had been driven into its treacherous waters past the Rabbit Islands, and from Pococke's report of his words it is evident that the part which Forbes played had lost nothing in his recital of it.

"We passed a cairn of circular stones and in a mile and a half came to Tongue, a seat of Lord Reay's, calling by the way on Mr Ross the Minister, who came with us to that place, where the late Lord Reay had made a handsome terrace and bowling green between the house and the bay, and a kitchen garden behind the house planted with all kinds of fruit except peaches, apricots and plums. Cherries and apples are planted against the walls; and in the middle of the kitchen garden is a pillar entirely covered with dials. The Master of Reay, the Lord's eldest son, usually lives here." Evidently he was not at home when Pococke paid his visit. His wife Marion, daughter of Hugh of Bighouse, had died during the previous year, and the Master did not re-marry until October 1760. It is therefore likely that he was away in June, visiting the family of his second bride, who was a daughter of John Fairly of that Ilk in Ayrshire. Pococke ended the account of his inspection of Tongue house: "There are large plantations of witchelm, ash, sycamore, and some quicken or mountain ash." Alas, those woods on the slope above the house were largely destroyed in a storm during the present century and have not been replanted, though externally the mansion remains as Pococke saw it.

Continuing eastwards, he called at the home of John Mackay of Skerray and Borgie, whose younger brother James was to create a a favourable impression at Inveraray in August when he arrived there with his contingent of the Sutherland Fencibles. This was the branch from which Iain Mac Eachainn had sprung, its most conspicuous memorial, the little cemetery by the shore at the west end of Torrisdale bay, containing the family's elegant gravestones. "We stopped at the house of Captain Mackay, a half-pay officer of Holland, and met his brother there, who was actually in that service. We were entertained with cake and a glass of Malaga, and came on to Farr bay, to which some fine rocks extend in perpendicular veins of a black slaty stone, and whitish granite with some mixture of very pale red. This bay near a mile over consists of soft sand on which we rid, not without some apprehensions to a stranger, though all was safe." In fact it was the Torrisdale sands, not those of Farr bay (which lies beyond) over which the bishop rode, and evidently he was too apprehensive to notice the gigantic erratic block with curious ring markings on its top, or the fifty-foot raised beach dotted with hut circles, although he must have passed close by them.

"We came round the hill to Farr church, where on a stone about three foot wide and six high a short cross is cut in a circle in bas relief, and many ornaments of lines round about it so as to cover that side, which the common people imagine to be inscriptions. Hear the sea at some distance." This beautifully carved cross still stands beside the former parish church, facing west, and attests the antiquity of this sacred site, for it is probably a preaching cross of around the year 800. But it possesses no inscriptions, only its intricate but weathered interlace.

It is not clear whether the enterprising bishop clambered over the Farr headland to visit the former castle of the Mackay chiefs called Borve, destroyed by the Gordons in 1554. "In a strong situation is the ruined castle of Farr, the ancient residence of Lord Reay's family, who were called Lairds of Farr, being made peers in the time of Charles the First, when the Lord I have mentioned mortgaged all this eastern part of the estate, which was afterwards sold to the Earl of Sutherland."[8] In fact they had not been mere Lairds of Farr but lords of all Strathnaver. Perhaps it was the Reverend George Munro who gave Pococke the facts as he set them down.

The Reverend George is a bountiful man,
Dispensing food and drink.[9]

So Rob Donn attested on more than one occasion, and the bishop experienced as much. "We here dined with Mr Munro the minister, who heard of our coming."

Eastwards from Farr the contours of the country gradually alter, and although there was a weary climb for the horses between each valley, the gradient became progressively gentler, until Pococke reached the oasis of the Mackays of Strathy, a basin of flat green pasture behind its little bay. "We came to a most charming vale between the bogs called Strathy bay or Avon Strathy. It belongs to Captain Mackay, now in the Sutherland regiment, and Laird of Strathy, being an appendage from the Lairds of Farr before they were ennobled. Here is a good house and offices, and I was received with great politeness by Lady Strathy. This is a fine country situated between the foil of black bogs that hang over it, but between the house and the sea there are beautiful hills which have fine down on their summits. We set out on the 2nd, and came about four miles over another course of bogs, under which is a yellow freestone, and crossed the Avon Halladale, which rises to the south out of the Paps of Ben Griam, and passed by Bighouse, another appendage of the house of Reay that descended to the present Lord's half-brother by his marriage of the sole heiress." William of Melness would have questioned that statement had he been given the opportunity. "This is a beautiful vale of considerable extent."[10] But Hugh of Bighouse was likewise away on military service, and evidently the heiress did not entertain Pococke as Lady Strathy had done. So he passed out of the Mackay country on his long-awaited pilgrimage to Orkney.

170

The society that Bishop Pococke observed with such approval was one that had endured for a very long time, and that Rob Donn (to judge by his utterances) might have expected to continue indefinitely. But in fact it was on the point of crumbling slowly into dissolution. It has been customary to explain the process of disintegration in economic terms, and to a degree this is valid, but the immediate cause of change was the disappearance of the men who were the pillars of that society. Strathmore was never again the same after the death of Iain Mac Eachainn, neither was Durness after the death of its resident Chief, the fourth Lord Reay, and his manager Kenneth Sutherland.

The minister of Durness noted the portents of this change with a gloom fed by a variety of entirely accidental happenings. On Friday, 2nd January 1761 he sustained an accident. "After a solitary walk through Lord Reay's parks, I came to a house in the neighbourhood to keep a tryst with a few companions, and just near the place of meeting my foot slipped, and I fell on my right side with the full weight of my body, when a knife and fork in the side pocket of my breeches bruised the upper part of my thigh, which I scarcely felt at the time, nor was I much sensible of any hurt till I came home." There his condition worsened.

"In bed I couldn't lie on my right side. Yesterday the bloody hue did spread considerably beyond the first dimensions, and so it continues to do till this hour of 4 p.m. Yet I was enabled to go and come from the place of public worship, where I was refreshed as often before by the agreeable work of my good Master, and this notwithstanding the boisterously stormy day, that obliged me to extend my voice several degrees above the ordinary pitch." Conscientious and courageous as ever, the minister was rewarded with a rapid recovery. But on that Sunday he poured some extremely tetchy reflections into his diary.

"The foolish solemnity with which New Years begin and sort of expediency, if not necessity, of my witnessing the merry meetings of such occasions, particularly with our great folks, these diversions I say stand in the way of holy retirement, which God knows I would choose to be employed in at the return of the seasons. I have frequently felt and remarked the blunting influence of worldly jollity." So far as the two greatest houses in Durness were concerned, his next observation was to prove prophetic. "I have observed some who, since the beginning of last year, have been in their own apprehension and that of others at the lowest passes of pining sickness, and next miraculously restored to health as merry and wanton as if they

171

had never been so rebuked and chastened by God's hand. This I noticed with hearty regret and becoming sorrow. Lord, what shall come of them at the next visitation of the kind? No reflection do they seem to have of their own remarkable deliverance nor of the death which now has arrested so many of their acquaintances in their silent grave, that were in sound health when they themselves were so manifestly threatened with that King of Terrors. And how many are thoughtless this day of their latter end, upon whom it will come before the next revolution of the year?" One may picture the minister, his nerves inflamed by his injured thigh, booming out this warning above the noise of the wind that beat upon the church, to a congregation reduced to a mood of repentance by their recent dissipations, and well aware that the two pillars of their little society, Lord Reay and Kenneth Sutherland, were the present targets of the King of Terrors.

Two months later the minister was presented with a different source of displeasure. "I was called away," he wrote on 4th March, "to marry a couple in our great house for whom our grandees take a concern beyond the merit especially of the man, who was an obstinate offender as a fornicator but took sanctuary in the army and so became a fugitive from discipline, winter was a twelvemonth. From it he came on furlough within these few weeks and is now married, which could not be refused him. But I thought myself bound to show my dislike at least in negative way, by not countenancing him as ordinarily done to one in the character of bridgeroom. I left the cavalcade soon after buckling the parties and spent the night much more agreeably than it was possible for the merry meeting to afford." None of Rob Donn's poems can be equated with this incident.

But there were happenings to report, far more ominous than the perennial ills of drunkenness, fornication and levity in the face of death. While Hugh of Bighouse was away with the Sutherland Fencibles, and the Chief and his factor in Durness in a state of declining health, the Master of Reay in Tongue began to interfere in the running of the estate as though he had already inherited his father's title and thus terminated the responsibilities of its trustees. He too criticised his father as others did, calling him "an easy facile man, and altogether ignorant of business."[11] But this did not entitle the Master to take the steps on which he now embarked, and unfortunately the season, when he did so, was one of those wild springs which periodically threaten the husbandry of the north coast of Scotland, the worst possible time to disturb its anxious tenantry.

172

Macdonald observed: "This young heir then taking upon himself the disposal of farms without obtaining the leave of those trustees, and the majority of them opposing his scheme of settlement so very near the term, these things I say have put the people in the utmost disorder: and this not without their own fault who, thinking the new superior to have the powers assumed, flocked to him in the most confused way of supplanting and counterplotting one another, offering grand sums beyond their ability."

While all this was going on, the Master's second wife Elizabeth Fairly gave birth to a seven-month old child which died almost immediately, while Kenneth Sutherland, the man most competent to protect the interests of the inhabitants of the barony of Durness, was dying. Macdonald noted on 13th May: "Sabbath last in the afternoon I went to see a man of some figure in the place who is ailing and pining away for some considerable time past, and finds by smarting experience that a man's life or the comfort of it consisteth not in abundance of the things which he possesseth." Macdonald did not allude to the years that he and Sutherland had spent as neighbours united by a love of music and by concern for the welfare of their flock. His deep concern was Sutherland's apparently frivolous attitude to his approaching end.

"The man had been professing religion for many years; but I own my surprise that a person advanced in age, languishing so long under the weighty hand of God, should not be more concerned about the state and affairs of another world." But Kenneth Sutherland was not intimidated by the minister's fierce old Testament Jehovah, though he had the politeness to remain silent on the subject, turning the conversation in other directions until Macdonald ultimately goaded the dying man into speaking his mind. "I had nothing but indolence and silence on the affairs of eternity, while there is the greatest noise and stir about the perishing part of man." This was the more surprising to Macdonald (one might well wonder why) because Sutherland had lost his only son as long ago as 1748 "and all that he has like to be left to the base-born daughter of that son." With well-meaning persistence the minister continued to pester Sutherland until, only a few days before his death "he said with an air of dislike of my suggestions that he looked on himself as prepared for death many years past."

The end came on 30th May 1761, and on the following day, which was a Sunday, the sixty-five year old minister sat down to reflect on the neighbour with whom he had shared the rule of their parish in the sacred and secular fields for over forty years. "He was the man

173

of greatest substance and room in the place next to the Superior. There were many good things in him. Of natural sense he had a good share. He was a person of solid and even temper, capable enough of friendships: and though not rich, yet not very poor, in good works obliging, in some instances to myself and some of mine. In return to his favours I was at all times ready to do and say for his benefit, to which effect Providence opened doors by which I was not behind with him even on the worldly side of affairs." His appreciation of Kenneth Sutherland made him regret all the more that he had not been able to save this man from the weighty hand of God. "Let me be pained and tortured in body agreeably to Thy Will, but O Lord, let me not sit under such a cloud as I have seen this man do."

While Macdonald contemplated the tortures that are agreeable to the divine will, Rob Donn was moved by the news of Kenneth Sutherland's death to an utterance very different from his songs to Sally Grant. He reviewed the benefits which his society owed to Sutherland's long stewardship, and he recognised that its termination would bring the thunder-clouds to his parish.

> It is your death, Kenneth Sutherland,
> That has made these places exceedingly overcast,
> And has occasioned lamentation and sorrow
> In every woman and man possessing knowledge.[12]

But this elegy was soon to be eclipsed by a greater and gloomier one, when that simple-minded, generous man the fourth Lord Reay joined his factor in death.

In the interval the minister's spirits were lifted briefly in August by the unexpected arrival of his son Patrick, revisiting his parents for the first time since he had begun his duties at Kilmore, and presenting them with a first sight of their grandchildren. He remained for little over a week and left on 18th August. "Just as he was going off, came in the very alarming news of Lord Reay's death. He expired this morning about 9 o'clock." Macdonald left a description of the Chief's last days. "In many months past his legs were running with uncommon suppurations which about a fortnight ago were dried up, upon which he contracted a kind of fever, which in a few days greatly reduced him: from which, as he recovered, came on a flux that helped to bring him low. He turned however at last so well as to be up and walk daily, not only within but without doors. Nay, even yesterday he travelled through some room of the house. In the afternoon I saw him, talked with him. But his breath was short, and

174

his breath so heaving that I knew he had not long to live, but did not think his end was so very near." A week later his corpse was interred in the family vault at Tongue, but it was not until the end of 1761 that Rob Donn composed his exceptionally long and impressive tribute to the only one of the four men who reigned as Chief during his lifetime whom he commemorated in this way.

> *This is the most melancholy Christmas*
> *I ever set eyes upon.*
> *The want of our Chief is brought home to us*
> *At the time when the New Year is approaching,*
> *The apex of society and of entertainment,*
> *Of the men of poetry and of music,*
> *Lying in the church of Kintail*
> *In the lowest room underground.*
>
> *Many a grievous blow*
> *Death has inflicted upon us*
> *At the expense of branches of your family,*
> *Without sparing the uppermost.*
> *But never went so much mercy*
> *Beneath the sod in my day*
> *As was placed in the tomb*
> *With Lord Donald, Chief of Mackay.*

Rob Donn referred to the simplicity of his Chief's character without describing it as a weakness.

> *Your nature was more utterly winning*
> *Than a bard can express.*
> *Your peerage did not swell your pride*
> *And friendship did not diminish your regard.*
> *A knowledge of your worth should be proclaimed*
> *Throughout the entire world.*
> *Your forgiveness was ready*
> *For the man who deceived you the day before.*
>
> *Frequently your deeds proclaimed*
> *That there was no pettiness in your disposition.*
> *You gave head to the idleness*
> *That characterised the castle folk.*

175

Conferring a favour on your part
Would bring as much joy to your countenance
As avaricious men experience
When they are adding a penny to five shillings.

You were the one who learned in time
From the practices and ways of men
That extravagance and hoarding
Were ephemeral and without use:
And as much wealth as you left
Was divided among others after you.
But you were assessing your liberality
As an asset that accrued to yourself.

When the time of Martin's Fair came
And the assessment of your rents,
Your eyes would be on each paper
That the clerk had prepared.
Well you knew the worthy man
And the person who happened to be in want,
And your pen would be ready
To cancel their arrears.

If you had been avaricious by nature,
What a pile you might have made
From the rent owing to you,
And with your pension in addition.
When you received that heap,
More dear to you by far
Was the likeness of God in the face of a poor
     happy man
Then the likeness of the King on a gold coin.

Rob Donn had evidently discovered by this time that the Chiefs of Mackay were in receipt of a government pension, whether or not he had known it when he composed his inflammatory verses in the aftermath of the Forty-Five. After attributing to Lord Reay the same compassion and generosity that he had praised in Kenneth Sutherland, he devoted the middle section of his elegy to the lessons their examples taught. He had frequently proclaimed the merits of good works before this time in defiance of the strict Calvinist doctrine of free grace and justification by faith alone. But he now went

176

a step further. He made a direct assault on the extreme position which Christianity holds in contrast to other major religions, in the emphasis that it places on sins of the flesh. Rob Donn had enjoyed ample instances of this as delinquents were hailed before kirk sessions for punishment in this world as well as threats of their fate in the next, and placed upon stools of penitence while their misdoings were expounded to a shocked and fascinated audience. Not even in his comments on the Jacobite cause or the hunting of deer did he exhibit a more perilous independence of mind than upon this theme. For the others opposed him to merely human authority: in this he confronted Macdonald's Jehovah.

> *Look at the story in the Bible*
> *To the end, from the beginning,*
> *And you will find the evils that are not of the body*
> *To be the really serious sins*
> *And the failings that are mean streaks*
> *In worthy Christians.*
> *But the carnal sin*
> *Need never be in that category.*

Not for Rob Donn the obsession with celibacy or the terror of sexual dreams. In the final section of his lament he held up the fourth Lord Reay as an example to his successors, with a note of acerbity that suggests he was well aware of the recent behaviour of the fifth Lord, before he had even succeeded to the chiefship.

> *For your love was not of the same kind*
> *As that of some people who are now living,*
> *Whom public sycophancy flatters*
> *Whether they act justly or unjustly,*
> *For fear of their vindictive natures*
> *Since they are malicious in retribution:*
> *Or in the hope of receiving from their hands*
> *Good that they would not do of their own wills.*
>
> *Love of God and of your neighbour*
> *Is the substance of all the commandments.*
> *People without pity will say*
> *That they are like that by nature;*
> *But those who are rich without charity*
> *To those who come to them in need,*

177

N

The scriptures cut them off
From the people who are in communion with God
*   himself.*

There were outstanding men among your forbears
In reputation and intellect and wisdom,
Who conducted themselves as kings
In the paths of their ability.
Not one of them was your equal
In kindness to those in need,
And it is easier to wish than to feel confident
That better will come after you.

It is often that the poets of mankind
Reach the truth most concretely,
But few amongst us
Can take your place at this time.
However, since I am not a true prophet,
The person I would most like to succeed you
Is a man of talents who will excel you
Who would give the lie to my poem.

This praise of mine will not exalt you
And now you have no need of it.
Your virtues are abundantly scattered
And you are not impoverished by having them
*   proclaimed.*
But when I recite this sad poem
To the great men who come after you,
Unless the like be related of them,
Not slight the shame upon them.[13]

   The description of the fourth Lord Reay's last illness in an unpublished portion of Macdonald's diary bears on the most startling lines in Rob Donn's elegy, those in which he questions the relative gravity of carnal sin. For the symptoms described by the minister are more probably those of syphilis than of any other disease. Furthermore, the condition of his two sons by his first marriage suggests that he may have contracted this disease before they were conceived. The elder had been described by the minister as the "deformed" Master of Reay before he succeeded as the fifth Lord. His behaviour was erratic and he was short-lived. From two marriages he begot only three living daughters, two of whom never married while the marriage of the third was barren. His younger son was a lifelong idiot, although this was subsequently explained as the consequence of a head injury that he had sustained in childhood while visiting his Dalrymple relatives at North Berwick.[14]

For once the strictures of Rob Donn upon the fifth Lord are more oblique than those which Murdo Macdonald confided to his diary. But the balance was redressed in the comments each had to make about his wife Elizabeth Fairly from Ayrshire. The year 1762 opened stormily, with frost that continued into April, "the effects whereof are already felt beyond ordinary by the loss of cattle." In the following month Macdonald was inspecting the casting of his peats when he received a request from the Reverend George Munro in Farr, asking him to attend a presbytery meeting in Tongue. "On my arrival at Port Chamil, west side of Loch Eriboll, I found an express with a letter." The minister had made this journey often over the years, sometimes the arduous trek over the Moine, at others the hazardous trip by sea round Whiten Head. Now he was elderly and too weary to travel further.

"In the letter there was, by order of the grandees there, a boat to be sent for me next day, but finding myself greatly the worse for my walk to Port Chamil, I returned the express who was to be at Tongue in such time as might hinder the offered boat from setting out. In expectation whereof, I went the next day to Island Chorrie, to which place notwithstanding all my precautions, the boat came at night with a feather bed and blankets for my accommodation at sea from Lady Reay, together with a second letter from the minister of Farr, earnestly pressing me to come over all impediments to the presbytery's seat, by the positive orders of said Lady in absence of her Lord. However surprising and disconcerting this new command was, finding the sea so very mild on the morning of Wednesday, I came off early and before 12 o'clock we arrived at Tongue."[15]

Reflecting on the peremptory manners of the new Lady Reay and the eccentric actions of her husband, Macdonald shared the blame impartially between them. "The young grandees there are a mysterious couple. None that I know have more need of being advised and none asks for or takes less of it. They seem to fancy themselves to all monitor, and accordingly enter as it were independently on a variety of schemes, in all of which they are as often thwarted. As to the young Peer, such as are best acquainted with him will not easily be disappointed except in his pursuit of salutory and wise measures, which is not like to surprise them in haste: and

179

the Lady's concurrence with or acquaintance in such baffled matters from time to time is unaccountable, since her passive conduct must proceed from ignorance of her own affairs and situation, or from a similarity of sentiments and temper with those of her husband, neither of which suppositions can be easily reconciled with the rest of her, as I scarcely observed things so good about her as would reasonably give a better prospect than yet answers."

Rob Donn expressed his attitude less tortuously, in one of his most savage poems. When Kirsty Sutherland at Balnakil had helped to find a husband for a girl who had borne an illegitimate child, he had remarked mildly: "I find it odd that the Lady of the parish, whom I never knew to be anything but upright," should have acted in this manner.[16] Very different was his reaction when the new Lady Reay induced a young man to marry a member of her staff who was pregnant, and sent orders to Rob Donn not to comment on the affair. On this occasion there was no banter in his response.

> Though I did not fall into line
> When you thought I would row your oar,
> Do not conclude nor fear
> That there is any weakening in my skill or handiwork.
> Alas for him to whom it happens in this world
> To have received this evil morsel to digest,
> To show respect for the one who is at fault,
> And to silence the words of the man who reprimands
>   him.
>
> With sharp command and counsel
> There was placed in my mouth a gag like a skewer.
> Concerning the incident to be spoken of,
> Which did not resemble a love-affair so much as a
>   hunt,
> Indeed I am sorry for the pair of them,
> Who can never find satisfaction without subterfuge.
> But so far as concerns your happiness—
> Heavens, I don't expect to hear what I should like to.
>
> The noble name which gave many
> Into the possession of the greedy and acquisitive.
> Which induced gentle young women
> To go off with disreputable examples of the opposite
>   sex

Without any word of their coming back—
All the qualities we can expect
They are sure to beget,
Like the herds that a bad bull mars.

Never had the bard addressed his superiors in such terms as he now flung at the fifth Lord's wife.

It is not your favour, nor fear of you
That would weigh with me in being so long in
journeying
To give due obedience
To the greatest and highest in the land.
Were it not for that, I would be expounding
That what brought you possessions is not good sense:
That there is a degradation in haughtiness
Since it found a dwelling-place in your breast.

Degradation in haughtiness—*irios' 's an ardan*—is a phrase containing the same punning paradox as, for instance, sinister dexterity.

O Pride, it is my opinion of you
That there is a dangerous contentiousness in your
composition:
So many plausible aspects
By which you have chosen to manifest your evil ways.
As long as respectable people
Reject you from their dwelling-places
You will be certain of making captive
Poor senseless minds.[17]

Later Rob Donn could abandon the cudgel for the rapier, when Elizabeth, Lady Reay was left a young widow and suffered an illness that her doctor could not diagnose. It occurred after Dr Donald Morrison had fallen from favour and been succeeded by Dr Robert Munro, when the bard had hinted darkly, "let me forbear from saying all I know." Eventually he said it all.

How excellent is the business that brought Munro
For a while to the country.
Coming before the slightest payment
He brought about a complete cure

To a most noble lady who was in hard plight
Although she was patient in suffering it.
Over a number of years her pain increased
And she had no means of alleviating it.

When he diagnosed her malady
And that there was no expectation of her dying,
He gave her a prescription of drugs
According to the nature of her condition.
I would wager he will not count the loss
And that he did not demand a penny in payment.
Without anything from a market to apply,
Robert himself acted as the plaster.

Robert himself did surprisingly well
When he applied the friendship—
Long illness, quick cure—
And without requiring a penny in payment.
Let him be given the credit he deserved
For restoring her to health
On the bed of sickness by night watches
Without a ray of light on them.

Although she might not like it to be related
How the pain came upon her,
Her heart was rising in her breast
And she herself was not the one to deny him.
It certainly delights me, the way it happened:
It gives the lie to an old saying—
By small degrees comes sickness
And in great waves comes health.[18]

Here Rob Donn has in fact reversed the Gaelic saying: "*Muin air mhuin thig an easlàinte, ach uidh air n-uidh thig an t-slàinte.*" But in addition he has achieved an obscene pun on the word *muin* in the phrase "in great waves comes health."

One final blow remained to shatter Rob Donn's world as he had left it when he departed on his military service. In 1763 Murdo Macdonald followed his aged uncle the Reverend Walter Ross to the grave, without having won the long battle against him over the sacrament. Rob Donn sought to raise a fitting monument to the man who had spent his life, his piety and every gift with which he had been endowed in the service of the Mackay country, and in the opinion of many this is the bard's finest utterance.

> It is your death, Master Murdo,
> That has darkened these places,
> And although your elegy has been delayed
> There is eloquent reason for the silence.
> If Christianity were perfected,
> Your renown would not pass into oblivion
> Nor the efficacy of your deeds,
> But your example would be wholly preserved.
> What has grieved me in spirit
> And those who loved and followed you
> Is the magnitude of your labour before you left us
> And the scantiness of its traces that remain after you.
> Some profitable lessons will flow
> From the fringes of your grace,
> That fools did not heed
> By listening to your teaching.

In the stanza that follows, quoted earlier, Rob Donn asked who deserved praise more than the minister, and who owed it more than the bard. Then he attempted a delineation of Macdonald's character.

> Your gifts were wonderful,
> Mingled with grace
> In a person that was lovely,
> Filled with intelligence—
> The understanding capacious in its breadth,
> The will that was quick to forgive
> And the whole mind so noble
> Throughout all your life.
> Your advice kept company always
> With your help and assistance
> For those who accepted righteousness
> As you yourself guided.
> You made the reluctant willing
> And the ignorant wise,
> And the absolute joy of your life
> Was in imparting more light to them.

183

You were gentle to those in need,
You were generous with reasonable people,
You were shrewd of aspect, hard
As stone toward the miscreant,
You were bountiful in giving,
You were a diligent preacher,
You gave timely advice
And even your hostility turned to love in the end.
It is a terrible audacity to deny in fear
That the High King has means
From which to replenish what we have lost,
But it is the favour of Providence and wonderful it is,
Indeed it is near a miracle,
That this gap in our midst should be filled
In accordance with the earnest desire of the people.

Few, I find, are the enquiries
About what you said and what you did
And concerning the renown you earned
Since the day we lost you;
But great clamour and bustle
About debts and inheritance
Left by wealthy people like fetters
Upon the children who succeed them.
And it is a thing I have frequently observed,
Despite the fearfulness of impermanence,
That the ambitions of men
Turn them away from enlightenment.
But there are no chances nor changes
In these ways of fate I witness
That do not caution me with the memory
Of a former lesson from your lips.

Attentive, careful, alert,
Thoughtful, eloquent, active
In your private affairs
Without ever being slothful,
You spent your time diligently
For the good of mankind
And you did not advocate wretchedness
Or any other thing.
When pleasing virtues

184

Perish for want of practice,
Men of your mould are objects of envy,
And not wealth nor honours;
As you departed from life with its bitterness
Having fought the hardest battles
For the kingdom of fruitfulness,
To enjoy the eternal reward.

Among the succeeding stanzas is the one in which Rob Donn praised the minister's singing voice and his interest in poetry, and it is thought that the final stanza contains a hope that Macdonald's son Patrick would succeed him in Durness.

Your substance was spent
In assisting people
And as long as you were in the world
You would not consent to payment.
The most pleasing feature of these transactions
Was that not a word was said of them.
Justice will not be done to the fame of them
But with the alteration of death.
Woeful is the punishment we deserve
For the sins we have committed.
Our pillars of support are constantly cut off
And our kindred rendered desolate
With no strong leader to consult
Who will repair our losses.
Some are in anguish day and night
Lest your heir should not succeed you.[19]

But it was the Reverend John Thomson from Avoch on the Black Isle who came to Durness in Macdonald's place, despite his defective Gaelic, for which he made handsome amends when he encouraged his daughter to make a written text of Rob Donn's poetry in his manse from the bard's dictation. Long afterwards, in 1792, he showed his concern further by writing for the *Old Statistical Account*, "The celebrated bard, Robert Donn, was of this parish. His songs are well known, and discover uncommon force of genius. It is a pity that they have not been printed, to secure them from mutilation, corruption and oblivion."[20] It is an equal pity that none of the Mackay gentry whom Rob Donn has immortalised should have shown a concern for the most eloquent voice ever heard in their

185

country, equal to that of the stranger with little Gaelic who had arrived in their midst towards the end of the bard's lifetime. It was not only to the Reverend Dr Nicolson that Rob Donn might have said, "Mr Thomson is doing what you never did nor will do—he is doing his best."

REFERENCES TO CHAPTER TEN

1. Pococke, *Tours in Scotland*, 118.
2. *Ibid.*, 123-4.
3. *Ibid.*, 128, n. 1.
4. *Ibid.*, 128.
5. *Ibid.*, 127.
6. *Ibid.*, 124-5.
7. *Ibid.*, 126: A. Nicolson, *Gaelic Proverbs*, ed. M. MacInnes, Glasgow 1951, 295.
8. Pococke, *op. cit.*, 129-131.
9. *Rob Donn*, 455, first two lines of quatrain on the minister.
10. Pococke, *op. cit.*, 132.
11. *Book of Mackay*, 203.
12. *Rob Donn*, 28, opening lines.
13. *Ibid.*, 6-10, stanzas 1-6, 7, 9, 13-17.
14. *Book of Mackay*, 216.
15. H. Morrison, "Ministers of the Presbytery of Tongue 1726-63", in *Transactions of the Gaelic Society of Inverness*, 1885, xi, 307-8.
16. *Rob Donn*, 291, lines 9-10.
17. *Ibid.*, 258-9, stanzas 1-3, 5-6.
18. *Ibid.*, 374-5, entire poem: Nicolson, *op. cit.*, 375, v.
19. *Ibid.*, 20-5, stanzas 1, 3-6, 10.
20. *Statistical Account*, iii, 582.

CHAPTER ELEVEN

Disintegration

THE genetic hazards inherent in the hereditary system had come to roost in the Mackay country. When the fifth Lord Reay died in 1768, leaving only three young daughters, he was succeeded as Chief by his idiot brother. The sixth Lord was cared for by his cousins the Mackays of Skerray while the administration of the estate reverted to his uncles Hugh of Bighouse, George, formerly of Strathmore and now laird of the estate of Skibo that he had inherited from his mother's family, and Alexander, by now a General. Since the sixth Lord was incapable of marriage, Hugh of Bighouse was heir, but both of his sons were long dead, so the chiefship was bound to pass next to George of Skibo and his sons. It was an ominous prospect, for the Honourable George Mackay had spent little of his adult life in Strathnaver, and that little had failed to win him favourable opinions either from the minister of Durness or from Rob Donn.

Hugh of Bighouse made a last effort to remedy this situation. Left a widower in March 1769, he remarried on 14th April 1770 to a daughter of Alexander Mackenzie of Lentran.[1] Should Hugh beget another son, he could not inherit Bighouse, since this estate must pass to the descendants of the heiress who had been his first wife; but he would become heir to the chiefship. By the end of the summer Hugh of Bighouse had fallen ill, and travelled to Bath with his wife, where they were joined by Lieutenant Colonel Alexander Campbell of the house of Barcaldine into which his eldest daughter had married. On 3rd November 1770 Campbell wrote to Barcaldine: "Poor Colonel Mackay's last sickness and his death disconcerted me a good deal, as there was no person that had the least knowledge of him here, or nearer than Edinburgh. I took all the care of him while alive that could be taken, and have put his affairs here in order. Mrs Mackay wants his body to be sent north. How far his friends would like this I know not. I have therefore put it into a leaden coffin and lodged it in a vault in one of the churches till General Mackay comes, whom I hourly expect."[2]

187

The dynast who had been so fortunate in his early marriage had failed in the end to bequeath either of the two largest Mackay estates to sons of his own, and Bighouse fell into the lap of the eligible bachelor who had remained single until Louisa Campbell, daughter of the Red Fox of Glenure, became its heiress—George Mackay of Handa. But he inherited a property encumbered by the claims of others, Hugh's widow, his daughter who had married William Baillie of Rosehall, Glenure's younger daughter Colina, and of that veteran claimant, William Mackay of Melness. Alexander Campbell commented on the complexities of the situation in his letter to Barcaldine. "I believe Ellan Handa gets the estate of Bighouse, Mr Baillie's eldest son two thousand pounds, Colina and Mr Baillie's younger children five hundred pounds each . . . I fear the widow will not come in for the share she ought considering the sacrifice she made, and the care she took of him."[3]

While the tenantry of Strath Halladale waited to discover how their new master proposed to satisfy all these claims out of the resources he had inherited, those of the Reay country faced the prospect that George of Skibo was now Tutor to the sixth Lord, and his heir in addition. It was not merely that he was "choleric and hasty in his temper", as Donald Sage was later to recall. "He was also improvident and extravagant, while his wife, the grand-daughter of Kenneth, Lord Duffus, was not more careful. To be, during the nonage of the proprietor of a large estate, what was usually called the 'Tutor' was in those days tantamount to being the actual owner. Yet, with all these advantages, George Mackay of Skibo died a bankrupt. At his death everything went to the hammer, and so completely stripped was his family that his children were conveyed from the castle of Skibo in cruppers on the backs of ponies."[4] This is to anticipate, but Sage's words throw light on the feelings with which the Mackays faced that dark winter of 1770.

They might have expected Rob Donn to compose a fourth elegy for Hugh of Bighouse in the sequence of laments he had uttered for Kenneth Sutherland, the fourth Lord Reay and Murdo Macdonald, but the bard reserved his last statement in this series for another whose death was ultimately to cause a more profound upheaval throughout the north of Scotland than any of the others. In 1766 the Earl of Sutherland, who had been Colonel of his Regiment, had died in Bath within a short space of Mary Maxwell his wife, leaving only a baby daughter to succeed him. The Sutherland property of the Naver valley was in much the same predicament as Bighouse to the east of it and the Reay country of western Strathnaver.

Indeed, its prospects were in some respects more alarming than those of either of the others. For the succession to the Sutherland earldom became the subject of costly litigation that was not concluded by a decision of the House of Lords until 1771. The circumstances in which the Gordon family had obtained it early in the sixteenth century gave rise to a Sutherland claim for its recovery, while a later charter which stipulated that it should never be alienated from the surname of Gordon enticed a collateral descendant of the male line to make a rival claim.[5] When the baby Elizabeth was finally pronounced Countess of Sutherland in her own right, the estate was burdened with the expenses of this lawsuit, those of a Countess who had never visited her patrimony and did not do so until she was an adult, and with all the baneful consequences that have flowed, throughout the world, from absentee landownership. The Sutherland estate did not, it is true, possess as many widows and daughters to support as either Bighouse or the Mackay chiefship. But the style in which the baby Countess and her Lowland guardian Lady Alva, her grandmother, were maintained, helped to redress the balance.

Such were the circumstances in which Rob Donn composed his elegy for the last of the Gordon earls sometime after March 1771. "It is easier to wish than to feel confident that better will come after you," he had said at the death of the fourth Lord Reay, and what is so surprising is that he should have felt any greater confidence ten years later.[6] The opening of his poem is, indeed, as dark as any he composed.

> *I was born in the winter*
> *Among the lowering mountains;*
> *And my first sight of the world*
> *Snow, and wind about my ears.*
> *Since I grew up looking upon*
> *A land of ice, a northerly land,*
> *I declined early*
> *And my veins chilled.*
>
> *I made an end of composing poetry*
> *Because my talent was forsaking me;*
> *But my nature would not allow me*
> *To remain silent on this theme—*
> *The head of the family of Dunrobin*
> *Lying in the abbey at Edinburgh*
> *Without one word from a poet*
> *Being composed for him in his own country.*

Rob Donn recalled the portrait of him that he had seen hanging in Dunrobin castle when he had served in the army, and continued:

> There was another portrait honourably
> Hanging to the right of me.
> I am not surprised
> That people are sorrowful in Sutherland
> Since they lost the couple
> Who were harmonious, magnificent, handsome,
> Earl William the Colonel
> And his young spouse Mary Maxwell.

After devoting five stanzas to the merits of the dead Earl and his forbears, Rob Donn pronounced his optimistic benediction upon the little girl who had been named by the House of Lords as the true heiress.

> I was likening the chieftains
> To a good oven that was useful
> After its fire was put out,
> And when only an ember remained.
> O I am confident yet
> That in a little time from now
> That spark Betty will
> Blaze into a joyous fire.

> When you were an infant
> And when you were lacking years,
> Fortune and favour began
> To restrain your enemies.
> Your guardians were skilful
> And the aid of Providence followed them.
> Your opponents lost their expectations—
> You kept your lands and your titles.

> I will conclude this song,
> For it is a matter too lofty for my intellect,
> With one prayer for this little girl,
> That she should remain living as a sole memorial.
> I am confident in Providence
> And O God, may I see and hear
> Of your marriage to a worthy man
> Who will continue the customs of your forbears.[7]

It is one of the most notorious facts of Highland history that Rob Donn's prophecy was to receive a grizzly fulfilment. After the Countess Elizabeth had married the Marquess of Stafford (later created first Duke of Sutherland) that spark did blaze into a fire, spread throughout the Mackay country by the ground-officers of Patrick Sellar. The extent of the Countess Elizabeth's responsibility for what occurred remains a subject of controversy, aggravated by the suppression for over a hundred and fifty years of the evidence in the Dunrobin muniments.[8]

Rob Donn may be forgiven for failing to foresee events that did not occur until over thirty years after his death; but he also neglected to comment on others that followed immediately upon the change of administration in the three great estates of Strathnaver. No explanation is to be found other than the one he gave in what he himself described as his last major statement, after he had made an end of composing poetry. His talents, he confessed, were forsaking him, and he found the theme he had chosen somewhat beyond his understanding. The bard who had once been so confident, fearless and penetrating in his judgments was by now over fifty-seven years old: older than Shakespeare when he died, older than many more long-lived poets after they had ceased to compose anything worth saying. Rob Donn did compose some later dateable verses—for instance, the elegy for a son of the Tutor of Farr in 1773[9]—but we may take his word for it that he remained silent on the most urgent theme of his last years because he himself had decided to silence the tongue which the highest in the land had been unable to hold in check.

Rob Donn was living close to Balnakil at the time when the fifth Lord died in 1768. Iain Mac Eachainn's son Colonel Hugh, having returned from Jamaica with this unaccountable military rank and a sufficient fortune, became tenant of the Chief's mansion there in 1770 and is reputed to have taken the bard into his employment. There is sufficient negative evidence to suggest that here in the parish of Durness people experienced relatively little of the turmoil that was spreading farther afield. But the bard knew that Elizabeth had been pronounced Countess of Sutherland in March 1771, and he must have learned of the consequences when the lawyers and factors of an absentee infant moved into her estates to make them profitable to her and to themselves.

The exodus that followed was part of a wider movement of emigration throughout the Highlands and islands, due to a variety of causes that have been examined exhaustively, and the one that provided such a sudden impetus in the far north also afflicted other

Gaelic societies, as Boswell and Johnson discovered when they visited the Hebrides in 1773. It will suffice here to relate the experiences of the society that Rob Donn knew, and the opinions that he himself is likely to have heard.

In June 1772 the *Scots Magazine* commented on the "poor people from Sutherland" who arrived in Edinburgh on their way to Greenock to embark for America.[10] That August the *Adventure* put into Loch Eriboll to take on board two hundred passengers and carry them to South Carolina.[11] In the following year the brig *Nancy* carried hundreds of emigrants from Dornoch to New York,[12] while the *Hector* sailed from Loch Broom[13] and the *Bachelor* from Thurso, both filled predominantly with inhabitants of Sutherland.[14] Captain James Sutherland, general commissioner of the estate, singled out George Mackay, son of the pious poet of Mudale, as one of the ringleaders among those who were robbing the Countess of her tenantry. "I do not hear," he reported in February 1772, "of any embarking in this scheme but the subtenants of those who have large highland tacks, except George Mackay at Mudale (at the head of Loch Naver) and a young lad of the name of Macpherson."[15]

But the most revealing evidence of any who tried to assist the poorer emigrants is that of an improving Lowland farmer called James Hogg who had taken a lease of the farm of Sandside in the parish of Reay, and who decided in 1773 to emigrate to Carolina where his brother was a merchant, He expressed little partiality for his Gaelic neighbours, whom he described as "extremely addicted to theft and pilfering, the constant attendants of slavery and poverty." When Hogg stated his intention of leaving, local people clamoured to accompany him, and he arranged for over two hundred and fifty souls to sail with him in the *Bachelor* from Thurso. "I rejoice," he wrote, "in being an instrument in the hand of Providence to punish oppression, which is by far too general; and I am glad to understand that already some of these haughty landlords now find it necessary to court and caress these same poor people, whom they lately despised, and treated as slaves or beasts of burden."[16]

It might have been assumed that, living as he did in the parish of Reay, Hogg referred principally to George Mackay of Island Handa and Bighouse. But fortunately he preserved a list of the principal heads of families, and although it is incomplete, its evidence is suggestive. Eleven of them belonged to Reay, one to Halkirk in Caithness, four to the parish of Tongue, and no less than eighteen to parishes of the Sutherland earldom, including that of Farr.[17] Furthermore, a misfortune that befell the *Bachelor* soon after she had sailed served to preserve the authentic voices of many of her passengers, relating the circumstances in which they had abandoned their native land. For the government had grown anxious over the massive exodus of its peoples, and therefore instructed the customs officials of the kingdom to take statements from the emigrants at their departure, explaining the reasons for their step. In many cases the particulars that reached London were meagre, giving rise to a suspicion that officials were reluctant to write down all the details to which they listened concerning the behaviour of Highland landlords. But the *Bachelor* was wrecked off Shetland, and the Lerwick authorities chronicled what they were told with reckless efficiency. The evidence of the *Bachelor* emigrants would have given them a unique celebrity had not every Scottish historian who has since written on this subject suppressed it entirely.[18] In 1934 it was published verbatim in the United States, and thirty years later not a single copy of it was to be found in any Scottish library.[19] Rob Donn has not been left alone in his silence.

Here is to be found the evidence of John Catanach, the fifty-year old farmer with four children who had lived on the estate of the Reverend Alexander Nicolson at Shebster near to Reay, who deposed "that beside the rise of rents and scarcity of bread, the landlord exacted arbitrary and oppressive services, such as obliging the declarant to labour his ground, cart, win, lead and stack his peats, mow, win and lead his hay, and cut his corn and lead it in the yard, which took up about 30 or 40 days of his servants and horses each year, without the least acknowledgment for it, and without victuals, save the men that mowed the hay got their dinner only." George Morgan, aged thirty-seven stated that he had left Nicolson's estate with his wife and two children for the same reasons, and they were supported by Donald Macdonald, who added a complaint to be found in many other testimonies, "of the advanced price of corn, owing in a great measure to the consumption of it in distilling."[20] Unlike John Skeldoch of Farr, Nicolson does not appear to have been disciplined by the church courts, but probably this was merely because he was doing nothing illegal.

On the neighbouring estate of Bighouse George Mackay from Handa had many legacies to find, as well as the expenses of a family that rose in number to twenty-one children though three of these died in infancy. Four emigrants from Strath Halladale described the means by which George of Handa overcame these encumbrances. Twenty-six year old William Mackay from Craigie stated: "the rent of his possession was raised to double at the same time that the price of cattle was reduced one half, and even lower as he was obliged to sell them to the factor at what price he pleased." He also complained "that the services were oppressive, being unlimited and arbitrary, at the pleasure of the factor, and when by reason of sickness the declarant could not perform them he was charged at the rate of one shilling per day."

Another William Mackay, who was thirty-seven years old and departed with his wife, four children and a servant, deposed that his rent had been raised from £30 to £80 Scots and confirmed that the value of his cattle had sunk to at least one half.[21] Since he spoke of the encouraging reports that he had received from his brother and sister in Carolina, he could very well be the William Mackay of whom James Hogg wrote in the following year, "The first time I saw him, to the best of my memory, was in the house of Mr Pope, minister of Reay; when talking of the emigration which was then the sole topic of conversation all over that part of Scotland, the said Mackay told us that those who had emigrated the former year from his county, viz. Strathnavern, had written such favourable accounts of Carolina, setting forth the richness of the county, the cheapness of living and the certain prospect of bettering their fortunes etc. etc., and advising all their friends to follow them, that half the people of his county, he believed, would emigrate if they were able."[22]

The testimonies of the two William Mackays were supported by forty year old William Sutherland, who stated "that from his farm, which paid 60 merks Scots, he was obliged to find two horses and two servants from the middle of July to the end of harvest solely at his own expense, besides ploughing, cutting turf, making middens, mixing dung and leading it out in seed time, and besides cutting, winning, leading and stacking ten fathoms of peats yearly, all done without so much as a bit of bread or a drink to his servants." The fourth testimony is not quite so dismal as this, nor the evidence of William Macleod, who had lived on the property of George of Handa and Bighouse in the parish of Edderachillis.[23]

James Hogg remarked in 1774 that the effect of this emigration was to compel landlords "to court and caress these same poor people, whom they lately despised." Certainly George of Bighouse may have been one of those who did so, for Alexander Pope wrote to Hogg after the *Bachelor* had sailed: "Mr Mackay of Bighouse is the only good master in these parts. He has given down part of the rents of the land and gives long rents and his people are quite happy."[24]

Perhaps the same might have been said of the barony of Durness, from where no heads of families were listed among the passengers in the *Bachelor*, nor testimonies taken in Lerwick. Alexander Pope had heard a rumour that Iain Mac Eachainn's son at Balnakil intended to join the emigrants. "The Colonel, of Durness, goes again for Jamaica. Stocks are low with him and he thinks Jamaica will be some better."[25] But Colonel Hugh was still in Durness to attend the funeral of Rob Donn four years later and there is no evidence that he went abroad in the interval.

Hogg listed four heads of families from the parish of Tongue, but the reports from here were relatively mild, especially considering that the choleric and extravagant George of Skibo was now Tutor of the estate. How often the Tutor came to live in the mansion of the Chief is uncertain: Pope wrote in 1774, "Mr Mackay of Skibo comes this week to Tongue and is to stay all summer, but his lady is impatient to be at Edinburgh. It is thought Mr Mackay will not incline to go there."[26] The comments from Tongue have a mini-metropolitan air. Aeneas Mackay, who was twenty years old, had "been taught to read, write and cypher, and goes to Carolina in hopes of being employed either as a teacher or as a clerk." Hugh Munro was a twenty-six year old shoemaker, who "goes to Carolina upon assurance that tradesmen of all kinds will find large encouragement." He was only one of three shoemakers from this parish, one of whom came from Borgie and took with him his wife, a servant girl and a servant boy.

Even those who made complaints against the administrators of Lord Reay's estate appear to have suffered less than the tenantry of eastern Strathnaver. Alexander Morrison said that "the rents of his possession were nearly doubled, the price of cattle low, and little being raised in that country, what they bought was excessive dear, beside the tenants were in various ways oppressed by Lord Reay's factors." Aeneas Macleod had likewise had his rent less than doubled, from 28 shillings to 38 shillings a year, "but thereafter when the price of cattle was reduced, one half the rent was neverthe-less still kept up. Moreover, being near the house of Tongue, he was harrassed and oppressed with arbitrary services daily called for without wages or maintenance." Another emigrant from Lord Reay's property in the parish of Eddreachillis stated that his rent had been raised from 21 to 30 shillings, but those were the only three who complained against it in Lerwick.[27]

Very different was the story from the lands of the Sutherland earldom. From them came most of the people in James Hogg's list of passengers and the most damning accusations recorded by the officials of Shetland. Hector Macdonald, who was emigrating from Rogart with his three sons and two grandsons at the age of seventy-five, stated that his rent had been raised from £1-7-0 to £4, besides making the usual complaint of "oppressive services exacted by the factor, being obliged to work with his people and cattle for forty days and more each year, without a bit of bread." Hugh Matheson from Kildonan mentioned that his rent had likewise been more than doubled; and that "the price of cattle has been of late so low, and that of bread so high, that the factor who was also a drover would give no more than a boll of meal for a cow . . . and obliged the tenants to give him their cattle at his own price."

The particular evil of greedy and unscrupulous factors on the make, moving into the lands of the absentee, infant Countess, makes an early appearance in the words of those who were attempting their timely escape from it. John Ross, a forty-seven year old widower from the parish of Farr said, "The evil is the greater that the estate being parcelled out to different factors and tacksmen, these must oppress the subtenants in order to raise a profit to themselves, particularly on the article of cattle, which they never fail to take at their own prices, lately 20 shillings or 20 merks, and seldom or never higher than 30 shillings, though the same cattle have been sold in the country from 50 to 55 shillings." On the other hand, William Mackay was able to report favourably on the conduct of the man who had held a Captain's commission in the Sutherland Fencibles, although the low value of cattle, high price of bread, and favourable reports from America had persuaded him to join the emigrants. "The land he possessed was a wadset of the family of Sutherland to Mr Charles Gordon of Skelpick, lying in the height of the country of Strathnaver: the rents were not raised."[28]

The hardships of emigrants were not over when they set sail, least of all, those of the *Bachelor*. Her original complement had been 234 emigrants in addition to 32 sucking babies, the family of James Hogg and the crew. By the time they were marooned, eleven of these had died, leaving a total of 255. Certain of them sought in Shetland to make James Hogg liable for their relief, since it was he who had received their passage money in addition to a commission, and who had chartered their ship. He disclosed that he had been paid "the sum of £731 for passage money and provisions, and £15 9/- for his trouble in finding the ship and executing the contract foresaid." He was able to show that his commission of 1/6d a head was reasonable compared to that charged by George Mackay of Mudale in similar circumstances. "Forgive me to put them in mind that

196

their acquaintance who hired a ship for their friends in Sutherland and Strathnaver in 1772 took 5/- per head, besides his expenses of meeting with them and of two jaunts to Edinburgh, and it is affirmed, had other considerable profits too." But this did not solve the problem of liability when the *Bachelor* was wrecked. Hogg argued that the emigrants should seek redress from her owner, but it is not known whether they received any, nor whether any of them accompanied Hogg when he sailed to Carolina in 1774.[29]

The perils of the sea passage were impressed on people in a manner more frightening still when news trickled back across the Atlantic of the fate of those who had sailed in the *Nancy* from Dornoch. The *Scots Magazine* reported from New York: "The poor Highlanders from Sutherland, who arrived here in the brig *Nancy*, have been treated with unparalleled barbarity. Near a hundred of them have fallen victims to the avarice and inhumanity of the captain. It is impossible to express the cruelty they met with while on board. Of above fifty children at the breast, and not more than four years of age, all died but one, and many of the mothers. Seven women, who were delivered on board, all died but one, with all the children." The captain had provided tainted water "that was of itself sufficient, in all human probability, to have destroyed their lives, with black musty meal, hardly fit for swine to eat, and this to be eaten raw. In short, it seems wonderful that any of them escaped with life." In order to evade prosecution, the captain had left port secretly during the night.[30]

But even a comparatively uneventful crossing of the Atlantic under sail in the conditions endured by the average emigrant was a daunting ordeal. One of the most moving eye-witness descriptions of such a journey was written by Janet Schaw from Edinburgh, when she paid a visit to North Carolina in 1774 in the *Jamaica Packet*. She was a stateroom passenger, like Allan and Flora Macdonald when they emigrated from Skye in the previous year, and like James Hogg in the *Bachelor*. But she took a humane interest in the sufferings of the steerage folk which provoked her into scribbling some angry comments in her journal, During a storm at sea she reflected: "but what rest remained for the iron-hearted, who forced age and infancy into such distress?"[31]

For age and infancy continued to forsake a beloved land, facing the terror of known dangers in search of an uncertain future. Even old Alexander Pope wished he might emigrate, and asked Hogg to make arrangements for his son James to do so, although neither of them eventually left the parish of Reay. "Heartily would I also bid farewell to all Caithness and Strathnavern and all their gentry and commons."[32]

"*Bha'n t-subsect aig Rob Donn,*" as the bard had exclaimed on another occasion many years earlier—it was a theme for Rob Donn.[33] But now he had laid aside his trumpet: to be picked up by Donald Matheson, the religious poet of Kildonan. Rob Donn was reputed to have remarked that there was more piety in Matheson's poetry than in his own, and Matheson's description of the new order in the Sutherland earldom is certainly stuffed with biblical references, but it contains more than a greater piety.

> *I am seeing the shadow*
> *Of things that happened long ago,*
> *When the people of Israel were*
> *In distress in Egypt.*
> *He took them with a strong hand*
> *Away from Pharoah himself,*
> *And He divided the sea for them*
> *When Pharoah hastened after them.*

> *I am seeing hardships*
> *Now on every hand,*
> *Families who were respectable*
> *With their heads brought low,*
> *Servants in the role of landlords*
> *And young children as heirs,*
> *The land full of distress—*
> *O God, who can endure it?*

Donald Matheson has expressed exactly the complaint of so many of the emigrants, that in place of the old kindly relationship between Chief and clansmen on which this tribal society was based, a new order of absentee landlordism had arrived under which they enjoyed little more legal protection than a Russian serf. But Matheson expounded this as the unfolding of God's purpose to bring his chosen people through the Red Sea to a Promised Land.

> *The landlords are enslaving*
> *People at this time,*
> *Oppressing and evicting them*
> *To the land that will bring our children good.*

198

O praise be forever
To Him of highest glory
Who opened a way out there
And prepared sustenance for them.

Go, he urged his countrymen, for God himself had come to the rescue of the Calvinist Elect, and the land He had set aside for them was more truly their own than the one they would be leaving.

I am seeing again
The truth triumphant,
The door being opened
When they were hard pressed;
And if it were the children of the Covenant
Who wished to go in,
He would open wide the heavens
Lest they should be slow in entering.

And though they might go to Carolina
Or to any land under the sun,
They would not be able to meet
Save in their own land.
They are the heirs of the promises
And theirs the abundance accordingly,
And although they should encounter dangers,
Assistance in their want will reach them.

Matheson ended with a reassurance which suggests that he was well aware of the dangers of the Atlantic crossing.

My expectation for the kinsfolk
Now far from us
Is that God will deliver them
From the power of wind and ocean;
And although Providence may not accord with our
*   wishes*
For the worthy folk of the northern Highlands,
Their share of letters will arrive
To testify to their excellences.[34]

The *Edinburgh Evening Courant* stated in September 1773 that fifteen hundred had gone to America from Sutherland during the two preceding years, taking with them an amount larger than a year's

199

rent for the whole county.[35]   Little wonder that the Commissioner complained, "Ken Scobie has money to buy the emigrants' cattle, which enables them to put their dreams about America in execution, yet he has not money to pay the Countess her rent."[36]   As the number of emigrants continued to increase up to the war of American independence in 1775, so did the value of cattle continue to rise.[37] But there was a decline in the droving trade[38] which enabled factors on the spot to line their own pockets at the same time as they made it harder for tenants to raise the money for their passage, by cheating them over the price of their one source of wealth.   The extent to which they did this is amply testified by those who sailed in the *Bachelor*.

The report in the *Edinburgh Evening Courant* contains the only allusion during these years to the affluence of emigrants from Sutherland.   The *Scots Magazine*, by contrast, had made the sole reference to the poverty of Sutherland emigrants during the previous year, and it is particularly interesting because it contains such an early allegation that small holdings were being converted into large farms in the manner of the nineteenth century clearances.   "The cause of this emigration they assign to be, want of the means of livelihood at home, through the opulent graziers ingrossing the farms, and turning them into pasture.   Several contributions have been made for these poor people in towns through which they passed."[39] The press comment of the day reflected a diversity of experience with a fidelity that gave little satisfaction to the administrators of the Sutherland estate.   "Our emigrants made very false report in regard to the cause of their leaving the country." one of them scolded.[40]

Generally it was the large parties of them that attracted attention, but a few solitary figures can be seen making their way to the ships, and there must have been many more who left their native land unrecorded.   For instance, when John Mackay went to Loch Broom in 1773 to join the *Hector*, it was discovered that he did not possess the price of his fare.   The other passengers raised it for him, which he was able to repay them in entertainment during the long voyage since he was a piper.[41]   Another John Mackay, who sailed in the *Lovely Nelly* from Rogart in Sutherland, described himself as a 'ballad seller,' and deposed that he was crossing the Atlantic "to prosecute his calling."[42]

When Ebenezer Munro of Lexington fired what he claimed to be the first shot in the American war of independence on 19th April 1775, the situation was altered dramatically.   While further emigration was brought to a halt, those who had settled—in many cases quite recently—in their new homeland were torn by conflicting loyalties. Alexander Mackay, a member for Cumberland county in the Provincial Congress of North Carolina, was appointed in August one of the committee of eleven members instructed to "confer with the Gentlemen who have lately arrived from the Highlands in Scotland", urging these to join the patriot cause. But the Mackays had never been Jacobites: they were the heirs of a long tradition of military service under the Hanoverian regime: and some of the emigrants were half-pay officers with a duty of allegiance to the British crown. Several of them were among those who joined the royal standard raised by General Macdonald at Cross Creek in February 1776. The American patriots adopted the most effective means of neutralising the threat from this source by keeping officers from the Highlands locked up during the period of conflict. At the same time the Provincial Congress ordered a proclamation to be issued in Gaelic for the comfort of their wives, assuring them that they "warred not with those helpless females, but sympathised with them in their sorrow."[43]

While emigration was curtailed by the American war of independence, it created a boom in military recruitment. The 71st Regiment of Fraser's Highlanders was raised in the year that the war began, and before it was lost no less than seven more Highland regiments were formed besides two Fencible regiments and the 84th Royal Highland Emigrants. Rob Donn's son John enlisted in the 73rd Regiment of Lord Macleod's Highlanders, raised in 1777, but it was to India that he sailed in the company of one Donald Mackay, immortalised by his father as one of the relatively small number of people who worked on the land for a wage. He was said to have joined the colours to escape from charges of "criminal correspondence" with five different girls, brought before the kirk session.

> *When autumn came,*
> *Who worked at the harvest?*
> *Who did the binding*
> *Or the stooking of the sheaves?*
> *Who put the ropes*
> *Aright on the stacks*
> *But the rascally buck,*
> *If he got his pay?*[44]

Rob Donn's daughter Mary married another Donald Mackay who served in the Duke of Gordon's Fencibles, raised in 1778, to which George of Handa and Bighouse contributed a company of men.[45]

The bard's son John was killed in India at the battle of Arnee in 1782, and forty years later General Stewart of Garth commemorated him in the book he had been commissioned to write about the services of the Highland regiments. "I take this opportunity of commemorating the fall of John Donn Mackay, a corporal in Macleod's Highlanders, son to Robert Donn the bard, whose singular talent for the beautiful and extemporaneous composition of Gaelic poetry was held in such esteem. This son of the bard had frequently revived the spirits of his countrymen, when drooping in a long march, by singing the humerous and lively productions of his father. He was killed by a cannon-shot, and buried with military honours by his comrades the same evening."[46] Thus India claimed not only Joseph Macdonald, but also the only one of Rob Donn's children reported to have inherited his bardic gift. No more than a solitary couplet of John Donn's composition survives, a reminder to his companions of the games of shinty that they had played on the sands of Balnakil.[47]

But Rob Donn did not live to hear how his songs were sung in India. He did not live to see George of Skibo die a bankrupt before he could inherit the Chiefship from the idiot sixth Lord Reay, nor Skibo's degenerate grandson fritter what remained of a clan's patrimony and his own and then sell their acres to the house of Sutherland. For Rob Donn died in 1778 and his remains were laid to rest in the churchyard of Balnakil.[48]

His wife had died during the previous year, and a neighbour recalled the bard's ominous words when he attended another funeral in November. "There is my co-age committed to earth, aged sixty-three, and before this time next year I shall be laid down here too."[49] A plain slab covers the grave in which he was buried near the south side of the church, the following August. It bears the inscription ROB DONN.

REFERENCES TO CHAPTER ELEVEN

1. *Book of Mackay*, 306.
2. Bighouse MS. (a) 101. Cf. his letter of 27 October 1770 in *Transactions of the Gaelic Society of Inverness*, 1904, xxiv, 48-9.
3. *Ibid.*
4. *Memorabliia Domestica*, 34-5.
5. D. Dalrymple, *The Additional Case of Elizabeth . . .*, 1771; *Brief For the Counsels of Sir Robert Gordon, Bart.*, 1771; *Sutherland Book*.
6. *Rob Donn*, 10, lines 13-14.

7. *Ibid.*, 36-9, stanzas 1, 2, 5, 11, 12, 13.
8. E. Richards, *The Leviathan of Wealth*, London 1973, 10-11, 169-95. Even this distinguished scholar did not enjoy access to the Dunrobin manuscripts. An attempt to assess the part of the Countess appears in *History is my Witness*, ed. G. Menzies, London 1976, 38-66.
9. *Rob Donn*, 52-5.
10. *Scots Magazine*, xxxiv, 395.
11. *Ibid.*, xxxiv, 515.
12. *Ibid.*, xxxvi, 157-8.
13. G. Patterson, *A History of the County of Pictou*, Montreal 1877, 80, 456 J. P. Maclean, *An Historical Account of the Settlements of Scotch Highlanders in America Prior to the Peace of 1783*, Cleveland 1900, 236-7. C. W. Dunn, *Highland Settler*, Toronto 1953, 55.
14. W. K. Boyd, *Some Eighteenth Century Tracts . . .*, Raleigh N.C. 1927, 421-4.
15. *John Home's Survey of Assynt*, ed. R. J. Adam. Edinburgh. 1958, xxiv.
16. Boyd, *op. cit.*
17. I. Grimble, "Emigration in the time of Rob Donn, 1714-1778' in *Scottish Studies*, Edinburgh 1963, vii, 143.
18. M. Gray, *The Highland Economy* 1750-1850, Edinburgh 1957: *John Home's Survey*: H. Hamilton, *An Economic History of Scotland in the Eighteenth Century*, Oxford 1963.
19. Newsome, *op. cit.*, xi, 131, 132, 135.
20. *Ibid.*
21. *Ibid.*, 134, 137. In the latter deposition the name is given as "Wm. McRay." But the Lerwick clerk has also written "George McRay of Bighouse" so it may be assumed that both names should read "Mackay."
22. *John Home's Survey of Assynt*. xxiv.
23. Newsome, *op. cit.*, 131, James Sinclair's testimony on page 136, page 137, where the parish is written "Adrachoolish."
24. "The Rev. Alexander Pope's Letter to James Hogg, 1774," *Scottish* in *Gaelic Studies*, 1966, xi, 106.
25. *Ibid.*, 108.
26. *Ibid.*
27. Newsome, *op. cit.*, 135-8.
28. *Ibid.*, 130-6.
29. *Scottish Studies*, 1963, vii, 146.
30. *Scots Magazine*. xxxvi 157-8
31. J. Schaw, *Journal of a Lady of Quality 1774-1776*, Yale 1939, 49.
32. *Scottish Gaelic Studies*. xi, 106.
33. *Rob Donn*, 108, line 4. But the line, as quoted in the text, is taken from the 1829 edition, which is preferred.
34. Rose, *Baird na Gaidhealtachd mu Thuath*, 271-3, stanzas, 2, 3, 11, 4, 5, 12.
35. *Edinburgh Evening Courant*, 1 September 1773, 59-60. In "The Highland Emigration of 1770" in *Scottish Historical Review*, 1919, xvi, 282, Margaret Adam gives a further example of the affluence of Sutherland emigrants, evidently through misreading the *Scots Magazine*, xxxiv, 515, which relates in this respect to the Hebrides. Miss Adam's further studies, "The Cause of the Highland Emigrations of 1783-1803" in *Scottish Historical Review* 1920, xvii, 73-89 and "Eighteenth Century Highland Landlords and the Poverty Problem," in *ibid.*, 1922, xix, 1-20, 161-79 are noteworthy specimens of

confident dogmatism unrestrained by any concern for the primary sources·
Duane Meyer in *The Highland Scots of North Carolina*, Chapel Hill 1961,
is among those who have exposed her inaccuracies. The scholars who have
quoted her uncritically make an embarrassing list.

36. *John Home's Survey*, xxx.
37. M. Gray, *The Highland Economy 1750-1850*, Edinburgh. 1957. 142.
38. A. R. B. Haldane, *The Drove Roads of Scotland*, Edinburgh 1952.
39. *Scots Magazine*, xxiv, 395.
40. *John Home's Survey*, xxiv.
41. Maclean, *op. cit.*, 236.
42. Public Record Office, London. T/47/12, f 88 verso. Records of emigrants.
43. Maclean, *op. cit.*, 117-18, 127, 141-3.
44. *Rob Donn*, 409, third stanza of poem.
45. *Ibid.*, xxxvi. Book of Mackay, 332.
46. D. Stewart, *Sketches of the Character, Manners and Present State of the
Highlanders of Scotland* . . ., Edinburgh 1822, ii, 137.
47. A. Gunn, "Unpublished Literary Remains of the Reay Country" in *Transactions of the Gaelic Society of Inverness*, xxiv, 11.
48. *Rob Donn*, xlvii.
49. *Ibid.*, xlviii-xlix.

CHAPTER TWELVE

Post Mortem

IT seems likely that a spell of exceptionally warm August weather
may have made it necessary to hold Rob Donn's funeral on the very
day after his death, before mourners could arrive from any distance.
But the news reached George Morrison at Ardbeg in the parish of
Edderachillis in time to enable him to compose an elegy of fifteen
stanzas by the evening of the burial,[1] and his words bring us face to
face with the grief that filled Strathnaver on that day.

> *O you were the man of ablest mind*
> *Beyond question of this generation.*
> *Considering the opportunities open to you,*
> *Where has greater excellence been heard of?*
> *Amongst your outstanding talents*
> *You were endowed with the bardic gift—*
> *A mouth that composed and sang*
> *Poetry most beautifully.*
>
> *Poverty did not seduce you*
> *To turn aside from the light,*
> *And fear did not restrain you from speaking*
> *When the truth was your concern.*
> *No other man excelled you*
> *In praising the meritorious:*
> *But when you dispraised,*
> *That was when the wicked trembled.*
>
> *Sorrow and yearning have descended on us*
> *Now you have gone from us to the grave,*
> *You who were so sure of aim and wise;*
> *Great was your worth throughout the land.*
> *Because nature was so bountiful to you*
> *With her gifts of understanding and intelligence,*
> *Teachers and rulers received*
> *Guidance from your judgments.*

205

O Scotland's poet of good sense,
Greatest of elegists,
The treasures of your mind may be read
In every song of yours that is sung.
I cannot say in your praise
Half of what you have merited,
Since you cannot be raised from the grave
To give me better guidance.

It would be my wish that the means
Followed to preserve the memory of you
Would be to have your songs written
And set down in print.
Then, when they are read,
Excellent and incisive as they are,
Competent judges would
Pay you your due in worthy tributes.

We owe it to the ministry that the compositions of Rob Donn were written down in time to save them in what may amount to their entirety—to the daughter of the Reverend John Thomson in Durness, to the Reverend Aeneas Macleod in Rogart, and to the Reverend Donald Sage in a smaller degree. One or another of the Mackay gentry might have been expected to lend a hand, and none more so than the Tutor's son George of Handa and Bighouse, or Iain Mac Eachainn's son Colonel Hugh in Durness. It is easier to understand the indifference of George of Skibo and his brother General Alexander, successive Tutors to the idiot sixth Lord Reay, since they had rarely appeared as central figures in Rob Donn's world.

When the gentry of the sheriffdom
Gathered together with their retinue,
Part of their desire and their joy
Was to have you as one of their number.
A modicum of your good sense
Would displace the music of strings for them—
Although now you lie low
In the mould's house of forgetfulness.[2]

George Morrison's elegy makes no allusion to an aspect of Rob Donn's art that Stewart of Garth was to mention decades later, his talent for extemporaneous composition. Hew Morrison embroidered this tradition in the 1899 edition of the bard's poems. "He did not work at poetry. He did not even revise what he produced. His poems stand now as they came forth from him in the moment of inspiration."[3] Rob Donn was remembered for the speed and wit of his repartee, and many of his verses may well have been composed on the spur of the moment. Possibly he fostered the belief that his large-scale utterances flowed from him with comparable facility, just as Michelangelo tried to create an impression that his masterpieces sprang from effortless inspiration, by suppressing his working drawings.

It would have been relatively easy for Rob Donn to do this, had he wished to, since he was unable to use tell-tale ink and paper. But his greatest compositions are his elegies, one of the most chiselled forms of poetry, and although his possess the fluency so characteristic of his genius, they rarely betray the slap-dash quality of extempore utterance. On the contrary, they reveal the concentration of mind necessary to overcome the disadvantage of illiteracy in such an exercise.

> *Considering the opportunities open to you,*
> *Where has greater excellence been heard of?*

Many have speculated on what Rob Donn's achievement might have been, had he been literate in a society that could have given full rein to his talents. With his gift for dialogue and his eye for a dramatic situation he might have been another Euripides among the Greeks, for he possessed the same irreverence for conventional beliefs combined with a strong moral sense, an equal preoccupation with what lies beneath the surface of human relations. His voice is perhaps the most modern and relevant today of all that still echo from the eighteenth century Highlands, and this might appear to place him in the company of Strindberg amongst modern dramatists. But while Rob Donn could shock his audience, both for fun and in the interests of truth, he was a well-balanced extrovert who looked into people's hearts to explore what was good there, as well as what was evil or diseased.

Rob Donn's countrymen were well aware that there lived among them a man who was something more than a simple village bard, singing of homely joys and sorrows. Iain Mac Eachainn expressed this in the lines:

> *With every judge who has a knowledge of poetry*
> *Rob Donn will be remembered forever.*[4]

George Morrison said in his elegy:

> *If your learning could be measured*
> *By your store of sense,*
> *In my opinion you were another one*
> *With a wit as sharp as Pope's.*[5]

The Reverend Donald Sage was to carry comparison much farther: "Even Burns himself, high as his claims are, must yield to Rob Donn."[6] In fact neither need yield to the other, though it is right to compare these ornaments of Scotland's two literary cultures. Living earlier than Robert Burns, it was Rob Donn who was able to contribute to one of the most valuable influences on the Lowland bard, and not the other way round. For Rob Donn was the vital force amongst the various influences that led Joseph Macdonald to make his collection of Highland airs, most of them from Strathnaver, which his brother Patrick published in time for Burns to turn them to such rich account.

Robert Burns was able to do this because he was not illiterate like Rob Donn, but a sophisticated man of letters with the resources of one of the most cultivated capitals in Europe at his disposal. His choice of the Ayrshire dialect of the Scots tongue as the vehicle for his finest poetry was an optional one, since he was a fluent writer in English. Rob Donn possessed no such alternatives: he did not even possess the means of ensuring that the broad dialect of Gaelic which he spoke would be properly written down, so as to save his compositions from mutilation. The Reverend Donald Sage, who understood that dialect, wrote that when Rob Donn's poetry was first published in 1829, "the editor was anxious to give Rob Donn universal publicity in the Highlands by correcting his Gaelic; but being unfortunately no poet himself he, in his attempts to improve the poet's Gaelic, has strangled his poetry."[7] It is as though the poetry of Robert Burns had appeared for the first time in print, corrected into English.

But the achievement of the two poets is identical. Each produced a body of literature of such a quality that they will remain until the end of time as sheet-anchors against the erosion that was already lapping and licking at their two languages in the eighteenth century. Some may give the palm to Burns because he possessed a choice and exercised it as he did. Others may admire Rob Donn although he had no such option to tempt him, for the integrity with which he exploited his more limited assets. As for the relative reputations of the two poets, these are not based on their relative merits, but simply upon the fact that the poetry of Burns was intelligible to men of letters in Scotland's capital while that of Rob Donn was not. It has given Robert Burns a long advantage in the esteem he has enjoyed throughout the world, yet paradoxically it may be Rob Donn who will pass him at the winning-post. For the poetry of Burns was widely intelligible because its language is so nearly related to English, and this has made its abandonment in favour of English all the easier. But Gaelic belongs to a totally different family of languages, and it seems likely that people will still be speaking it long after the one in which Burns wrote is as dead as Chaucer's.

Meanwhile, Rob Donn remains the last and greatest of those who were in a position to interpret and illuminate the traditional, tribal way of life of Gaelic Scotland before it was destroyed. His picture bears scant resemblance to those of the Lowland writers who have ignored his testimony and that of other people whose circumstances they have described with such assurance. One thing the bard evidently could not bring himself to do. He left no comment on the disintegration of his society that he witnessed during his last years, and we can only guess at the reasons for his silence.

But the corpus of poetry that he did bequeath to posterity entitles him to the highest place amongst the illiterate peasant poets of Europe. "He stood alone," wrote Donald Sage. "His poetry is history—a history of everyone and everything with which he at any time came into contact in the country in which he lived. His descriptions do not merely let us know what these things or persons were, but as things that are."[8]

In that vanished world the figure of Rob Donn still stands, telling us of things that are.

REFERENCES TO CHAPTER TWELVE

1. *Rob Donn*, li, George Morrison's elegy, last two lines of stanza 1.
2. *Ibid.*, li-liii, stanzas 2, 3, 5, 6, 7, 11.
3. *Ibid.*, xxxviii.
4. *Ibid.*, li, last two lines of stanza 2.
5. *Ibid.*, liv, last four lines of penultimate stanza.
6. *Memorabilia Domestica*, 37.
7. *Ibid.*, 38.
8. *Ibid.*, 37.

Q

Appendix

IS TROM LEAM AN AIRIGH

This early masterpiece displays the originality of the Bard's lyrical gift. It is translated in its entirety on pages 17-18.

Is trom leam an àirigh 's a' ghàir seo a th'innt',
Gun a' phàirtinn a dh'fhàg mi bhith 'n dràsd air mo chinn:
Anna chaol-mhalach chìoch-chorrach shlìob-cheannach chruinn,
Is Iseabail a' bheòil mhilis, mhànranach bhinn.
Heich! mar a bhà, air mo chinn,
A dh'fhàg mi cho cràiteach 's nach stàth dhomh bhith 'g inns'.

Shiubhail mis' a' bhuaile 's a suas feadh nan craobh,
'S gach àit' anns am b'àbhaist bhith pàgadh mo ghaoil;
Nuair chunnaic mi 'm fear bàn ud 's e mànran r'a mhnaoi,
B'fheàrr leam nach tiginn idir làimh riu, no 'n gaoith.
'Se mar a bhà, air mo chinn,
A dh'fhàg mi cho cràiteach 's nach stàth dhomh bhith 'g inns'.

On chualas gun gluaiseadh tu uam leis an t-Saor
Tha mo shuain air a buaireadh le bruadraichean gaoil;
De 'n chàirdeas a bhà siud chan fhàir mi bhith saor,
Gun bhàrnaigeadh làimh riut tha 'n gràdh dhomh 'na mhaor,
Air gach tràth, 's mi ann an strì,
A' feuchainn r'a àicheadh 's e fàs rium mar chraoibh.

Ach Anna bhuidh' Ni'n Dòmhnaill, nam b'eòl duit mo nì,
'Se do ghràdh gun bhith pàight' leag a-bhàn uam mo chlì;
Tha e dhomh á t'fhianais cho gnìomhach 's nuair chì,
Diogalladh, 's a' smùsach, gur ciùrrtach mo chrìdh.
Nis, ma thà mi ga do dhìth
Gum b'fheàirrde mi pàg uait mus fàgainn an tìr.

Ach labhair i gu fàiteagach, àilgheasach rium:
"Chan fhàir thu bhith làimh rium do chàradh mo chinn;
Tha sianar gam iarraidh o bhliadhna do thìm,
'S cha b'àraidh le càch thu, thoirt bàrr os an cinn.
Ha, ha, hà! an d'fhàs thu gu tinn,
'N e 'n gaol a bheir bàs ort? Gum pàigh thu d'a chinn!"

Ach cionnas bheir mi fuath dhuit, ged dh'fhuaraich thu rium?
Nuair 's feargaich mo sheanchas mu t'ainm air do chùl,
Thig t'ìomhaigh le h-annsachd 'na shamhladh 'nam ùidh,
Saoilidh mi an sin gun dèan an gaol sin an tùrn,
'S theid air a ràth gu h-às-ùr,
Is fàsaidh e 'n tràth sin cho-àrda ri tùr.

BRIOGAIS MHIC RUAIRIDH

*The most celebrated of Rob Donn's bawdy satires was composed in
1747 for the wedding of Iseabail Nic Aoidh. The whole poem is
given in English on pages 78-81.*

An d'fhidir no 'n d'fhairich no 'n cuala sibh
Cò idir thug briogais Mhic Ruairidh leis?
Bha 'bhriogais ud againn an àm dol a chadal
'S nuair thàinig a' mhadainn cha d'fhuaireadh i.

Chaidh 'bhriogais a stàmpadh am meadhon na connlaich,
'S chaidh Hùistein a dhanns leis na gruagaichibh,
'S nuair dh'fhàg a chuid misg e gun tug e 'n sin briosgadh
A dh'iarraidh na briogais, 's cha d'fhuair e i.

Nam bitheadh tu làimh ris gun deanadh tu gàire,
Ged a bhiodh siataig sa' chruachan agad,
Na faiceadh tu dhronnag nuair dh'ionndrain e 'pheallag,
'S e coimhead 's gach callaid 's a' suaithteachan.

Iain Mhic Eachainn, mas tusa thug leat i,
Chur grabadh air peacadh 's air buaireadh leath',
Mas tù a thug leat i cha ruigeadh tu leas e,
Chaidh t'uair-sa seachad mun d'fhuair thu i.

Chaitrìona Ni'n Uilleim, dean briogais do'n ghille,
'S na cumadh siud sgilinn a thuarasdal;
Ciod am fios nach e t'athair thug leis i g'a caitheamh—
Bha feum air a leithid 's bha uair dhe sin.

Briogais a' chonais chaidh chall air a' bhanais,
Bu liutha fear fanaid na fuaigheil oirr';
Mur do ghlèidh Iain Mac Dhòmhnaill gu pocan do'n òr i
Cha robh an Us-mhoine na luaidheadh i.

Mur do ghlèidh Iain Mac Dhòmhnaill gu pocan do'n or i
Cha robh an Us-mhòine na ghluaiseadh i.
Mu Uilleam Mac Phàdraig, cha deanadh i stàth dha,
Cha ruigeadh i 'n àird air a' chruachan dha.

Tha duine 'n Us-mhòine d'an ainm Iain Mac Sheòrais,
'S gur iongantas dhòmhsa ma ghluais e i;
Bha i cho cumhang, mur cuir e i 'm mudhadh,
Nach dean i nas mutha na buarach dha.

Na leigibh ri bràigh e 'm feadh 's a bhios e mar thà e
Air eagal gun sàraich an luachair e;
Na leigibh o bhail' e do mhòinteach nan coileach
Mun tig an labhallan 's gum buail i e.

(Chan eil fitheach no feannag no iolair no clamhan,
No nathair a' ghlinne 'na cuachanan
No smàgach an luisean, ged 's gràineil an cuspair,
Nach b'fheàrr leo na musaidh do shuaitheadh riu.)

Nam faiceadh sibh 'leithid, bha bann oirr' do leathar,
Bha toll air a speathar 's bha tuathag air,
'S bha feum aic' air cobhair mu bhrèidean a gobhail
Far am biodh (am ball odhar) a' suathadh rith'.

Ach Iain Mhic Choinnich 'sann ort a bha 'n sonas,
Ged 's mòr a bha dhonadas sluaigh an seo,
Nuair bha thu cho sgiobalt 's nach do chaill thu dad idir
'S gur tapaidh a' bhriogais a bhuannaich thu!

MARBHRANN DO MHAIGHSTIR MURCHADH MACDHOMHNAILL

*The elegy, composed after the death of the Reverend Murdo Mac-
donald in 1763, contains ten sixteen line stanzas, of which the
following are translated in the text:
Stanza 1, page 183; stanza 2, lines 5-8, page 35; stanza 3, page 183;
stanza 4, lines 1-8, page 37; stanzas 4, 5, and first eight lines of 6,
page 184; stanza 6, lines 9-16, page 185; stanza 8, lines 1-8, page 36;
stanza 10, page 185.*

'Se do bhàs, Mhaighstir Murchadh,
Rinn na h-àitean seo dhorchadh,
'S ged chaidh dàil ann do mharbhrann
    Labhraidh balbhachd ri cèill.
Nam biodh a' Chrìosdaidheachd iomlan
Cha rachadh dì-chuimhn' air t'iomradh,
No do ghnìomharan iomlaid,
    Ach leantadh t'iomchan-s' gu lèir.
Gur h-e chràdh mi 'nam mheanmnadh,
'S do luchd gràidh agus leanmhainn,
Meud do shaothrach mus d'fhalbh thu,
    'S lugh'd a luirg ás do dhèidh:
Bheir cuid leasanan buadhach
O bhruaich fasanan t'uaghach,
Nach tug daiseachan suarach
    As na chual' iad uait fèin.

Fìor mhasgall chionn pàighidh,
No stad gealtach le gàbhadh,
Bhrìgh mo bheachd-s' ann an dànaibh
    'S mi nach dèanadh, 's nach d'rinn;
Ach nam biodh comain no stàth dhuit
Ann a t'alladh chur os àird duit
Cò na mis' do 'm bu chàra
    'S cò a b'fheàrr na thu thoill?
'Bhuidheann mholtach-s' a dh'fhàg sinn,
Ged nach urr' iad a chlàistinn,
'S còir bhith 'g aithris am pàirtean
    Gun fhàbhor 's gun fhoill,
Oir 's buain' a' chuimhne bheir bàrda
Air deagh bhuadhannaibh nàduir
Na 'n stoc cruinn sin a dh'fhàg iad
    Is còmhstri chàirdean ga roinn.

Bha do ghibhtean-sa làidir
Air am measgadh le gràsan
Anns a' phearsa bha àlainn
    Lomlàn de'n a' chèill;
An tuigs' bu luchdmhoir' gu gleidheadh,
An toil a b'èasgaidh gu maitheadh,
'S na h-uile h-aigneadh cho flathail
    Fad do bheatha gu lèir;
Bhiodh do chomhairl' an còmhnaidh
Le do chobhair 's do chòmhnadh
Do luchd-gabhail na còrach
    Rèir 's mar sheòladh tu fèin;
Dheanadh tu 'n t-aindeonach deònach,
Is an t-aineolach eòlach,
'S b'e fìor shonas do bheòshlaint
    Bhith tabhairt còrr dhoibh do lèirs'.

Bha thu caomh ri fear feumnach,
Bha thu saor ri fear reusant',
Bha thu aodannach, geurach,
    Mar chloich, ri eucoireach, cruaidh;
Bu tu 'n tabhairteach maoineach,
Bu tu 'n labhairteach saothrach,
Bu tu 'n comhairleach tìmeil
    'S crìoch a' ghaoil ann ad fhuath.
Tha e 'na ladarnas gàbhaidh
Bhith le h-eagal ag àicheadh
Nach eil stoc aig an Ard-rìgh
    Nì an àird na chaidh uainn,
Ach 's fàbhor Freasdail, 's is iongnadh,
No 'n nì as faisge do mhìorbhail,
Am beàrn seo th'againn a lìonadh
    Gu blas miannach an t-sluaigh.

Leam is beag na tha dh'fhaighneachd
Mu na thubhairt 's na rinn thu,
'S mu'n a' chliù sin a thoill thu
    O'n là chaill sinn thu fèin;
Ach mòran tartar is straighlich
Airson fèich agus oighreachd
Fàgaidh beartaich mar *fhine* e
    Air an cloinn ás an dèidh.

214

'Se 'n nì as minig a chì mi,
Dh'aindeoin diombuanachd tìme,
Gu bheil gionaich' nan daoine
    Tarraing claonadh 'nan cèill;
Ach chan eil iomairt no *motion*
Anns na freasdail seo dhòmhsa
Nach toir leasan 'nam chòmhdhail
    Le seann nòt o do bheul.

Toigheach, faicilleach, fiamhach,
Smuainteach, focalach, gnìomhach
Ann do ghnothachaibh dìomhair
    Gun bhith dìomhain aon uair,
Chaith thu t'aimsir gu saothrach
Airson sonas nan daoine,
'S cha b'e truaillidheachd shaoghalt
    No aon nì chur suas.
Nuair tha nitheana taitneach
Dol am mudh' a chion cleachdaimh,
B'e chùis f'harmaid fear t'fhasain
    'S cha b'e beartas is uaills',
A' dol o'n bheatha bu sheirbhe
Tre na cathan bu ghairbhe
Dh'ionnsaigh Flaitheas na foirfeachd
    Gu buan shealbhachadh duais.

Gu bheil cealgaireachd chràbhaidh
Air a dearbhadh gu gàbhaidh
Tha 'na gairistinn r'a clàistinn
    Is ro chràiteach r'a luaidh;
Nuair a thuit thu le bàs uainn,
Mar gum briseadh iad bràighdean,
Dhùisg na h-uilc sin a b'àbhaist
    A bhith an nàdur an t-sluaigh.
Gu bheil cath aig an Ard-rìgh
Gu bhith gabhail nam pàirtean
Anns na chruthaich e gràsan
    Thug air adhart gach buaidh;
Rinn siud sinne nar fàsaich
Anns an talamh-s' an tràth seo,
Seo a' bharail th'aig pàirt diubh
    Tric ga leughadh air t'uaigh.

215

An duine thigeadh a suas riut
Ann an guth 's ann an cluasan
Chan fhacas riamh is cha chualas
   Is 'se mo smuaintean nach cluinn;
Ged bu bheartach do chràbhadh
Bha do mheas air gach tàlann,
'S tu a thuigeadh na dàinte
   'S am fear a dheanadh na ruinn;
Chuid a b'àirde sa' bhuaidh sin
Tha 'ad air stad dheth o'n uair sin,
Ach na daiseachan suarach
   Tha mun cuairt duinn a' seinn;
Nuair a cheilear a' ghrian orr'
Sin nuair ghoireas na biastan:
Caillich-oidhch' agus strianaich
   An coilltibh fiadhaich 's an glinn.

'S eòl domh daoine san aimsir-s'
Dh'fhàs 'nan cuideachd glè ainmeil,
Tigh'nn air nitheanaibh talmhaidh
   Ann an gearrbhaireachd gheur,
Ach nuair thogar o'n làr iad
Gus na nithibh as àirde
'Sann a chluinneas tu pàirt diubh
   Mar na pàisdean gun chèill.
Fhuair mi car ann do rianaibh-s',
Le do ghibhtean bu fialaidh,
Nach do dhearc mi, mas fìor dhomh,
   An aon neach riamh ach thu fèin:
Càil gach cuideachd a lìonadh
Leis na theireadh tu dìomhan,
'S crìoch do sheanchais gun fhiaradh
   Tigh'nn gu diadhaidheachd threun.

Bha do chuid air a sgaoileadh
Gu bhith cuideachadh dhaoine,
'S fhad 's a bha thu san t-saoghal
   'S tu nach faodadh bhith pàight;
Chuid bu taitnich' 'nan iomchainn
Chan eil facal mu'n timcheall,

216

Cha bhi ceartas mu'n iomradh
Ach le 'n imrich 'nam bàs.
'S truagh am peanas a thoill sinn
Thaobh nan ciontan a rinn sinn
Bhith sìor ghearradh ar gaibhlean
'S ar cuid theaghlaichean fàs;
Gun cheann làidir gu fhoighneachd
Cò nì 'n àirde na chaill sinn;
Cuid dan cràdh là is oidhche
Nach tig t'oighre nad àit'.

Index

Aberdeen, 64, 122, 161
Aberdeenshire, 3
Achness, 26, 88, 105-6, 150
Achovarisaid, 46
Airth, 24
Aisir, 138
Alva, Lady, 189
Anderson, James, 159
Angus of the Alasdairs, 15
Anne, Queen, 1
Appin, 133
Argyll, 22, 158
Argyll and Sutherland Fencibles, 159
Arkle, 1-2, 129, 166
Armadale, 150
Assynt, 1, 3, 33, 46, 49, 60-1, 63
Avoch, 149, 185
Ayrshire, 169

Bad na h-chlais, 19, 78, 128, 167
Badcall, 46-8
Badilhavish, 40
Baillie, William, of Rosehall, 188
Balnakil, 5, 36, 39, 51-2, 54, 61, 68, 81, 99, 103, 110, 114, 137, 142, 146, 160, 167, 180, 191, 195, 202
Bannockburn, 29
Barbour, John, 29
Barcaldine, 82-3
Bath, 187-8
Bharraich, castle, 5
Bighouse, Dowager Lady, See Ross
Bighouse, Mackays of, 4
Black Isle, 149, 185
Boerhaave, Dr, 123-5, 129
Borve, castle, 5, 170
Borgie, 195
Boswell, James, 28, 192
Breda, 155
Briogaiseag, 153
Brodie, Mrs Barbara, 46
Brodie, Christine, 46-9, 80, 94, 118
Brodie, The Reverend George, 33, 46, 104

Brontë, Branwell, 87
Bruce, The Reverend Robert, 24-5
Buchanans, 112
Buchanan, Dugald, 155
Burns, Robert, 56, 158, 208-9

Caithness, 3-4, 6, 11, 26, 33-4, 39, 44, 53-4, 63, 66-8, 70, 132, 142, 157, 192, 198
Calvin, John, 25
Campbell, Colonel Alexander, 187-8
Campbell, Colin, of Glenure, 82, 133, 188
Campbell, Colina, 188
Campbell, Louisa, Mrs Mackay of Bighouse, 188
Campbell of Barcaldine, 82, 187
Campbell, clan, 121
Campbell's Highlanders, 159
Canada, 159
Cape Wrath, 1, 3, 7, 9, 53, 99, 133, 137, 157, 168
Carolina, 192-5, 197, 199
Catanach, John, 193
Charles I, 69, 170
Charles II, 156
Charles Edward, Prince, 30, 58-60, 62, 65, 68-9, 71-4, 142
Chaucer, Geoffrey, 29, 209
Claiseneach, 157, 160
Clive of India, 159
Clyne, 150
Cope, General, John, 59
Creich, 104
Crieff, 14, 26, 119, 159
Cromartie, Earl of, 66, 68, 69
Cromwell, Oliver, 4
Culloden, 65, 69-71, 74, 77, 140
Cumberland, "Butcher", 64-5, 68-72, 142

Dante, 47
Dalrymple, Marion, Lady Reay, 36-7, 52, 96, 178-9

218

220

Murdo, son of Hugh, 121
Murray, John, carpenter, 16-17

Naver, loch, 3, 25, 88, 192
Naver, river, 8, 25, 32, 160
Naver valley, 9, 39, 49, 59, 63,
   104-6, 188
Netherlands, 6-7, 155, 169
New York, 192, 197
Nicolson, The Reverend Alexander,
   149, 186, 193

Oglethorpe, General James, 156
Orkney, 3, 24, 40, 116, 133-4, 166,
   170
Ossian, 23-5, 27, 121

Papa Stronsay, 24
Papa Westray, 24
Patrick, Saint, 23-4
Pelham, Henry, 85
Pentland firth, 40
Perth, Duke of, 66
Perthshire, 14
Peterhead, 40
Petrarch, 16, 18
Pitt, William, 159
Pococke, Richard, bishop of Meath,
   122, 166-71
Polla, 85-6, 89
Pollagluip, 136
Polson, Captain William, 156
Pope, The Reverend Alexander,
   22-24, 32, 65, 68, 150
Pope, Alexander, 31-2, 37, 87, 158,
   194-5, 197-8, 208
Port Chamil, 133, 143, 179
Portskerra, 132
Port nan Con, 133
Prestonpans, battle, 59
Pronsy, 52
Prussia, 159

Rabbit islands, 66, 168
Ramsay, James, of Ochtertyre, 14,
   82, 116, 155
Ranald's daughter, 135
Reay, 22, 32, 65, 68, 149-50, 192-4
Reay forest, 2, 5, 8, 85, 115, 122,
   129, 166, 168
Reay, Donald Mackay, first Lord,
   4, 6-8, 52, 99
Reay, John Mackay, second Lord,
   4-5, 99
Reay, George Mackay, third Lord,
   2-3, 5-8, 33, 59-61, 64, 67, 70-2, 77,
   79, 96-7, 110, 124-5, 149

Reay, Donald Mackay, fourth Lord,
   5, 36-7, 51-2, 54, 61, 96-8, 110, 122,
   124, 160, 167-8, 171-2, 174-9, 188-9
Reay, George Mackay, fifth Lord,
   52, 96, 124, 151-2, 169, 172-3,
   177-80, 187, 191
Reay, Hugh Mackay, sixth Lord
   159, 179, 187-8, 202, 206
Rhenevie, 32-3
Rispond, 9, 39, 89, 115, 133-4, 139
Rispond misers, 89, 115
Robin Hood, 122
Rogart, 196, 200, 206
Ross, John, emigrant, 196
Ross, Katharine, Lady Bighouse,
   6-7, 53, 124, 133
Ross, The Reverend Walter, 44-5, 69,
   104-5, 107-9, 148, 168, 182
Rossal, 9
Ross-shire, 5, 64, 66, 68

Sage, The Reverend Alexander, 6,
   150
Sage, The Reverend Donald, 107,
   150, 188, 206, 208-9
Sal, 11, 14, 26, 40, 122, 128
St Andrews, 32
St Andrews, U.S.A., 156
Sandside, 192
Sandwood, 4, 7, 49
Sango Beg and Sango Mor, 133
Schaw, Janet, 197
Scobie, Kenneth
Scott, Sir Walter, 39
Scourie, 2, 4-5, 7, 46, 49
Scrabster, 44
Shakespeare, William, 191
Shebster, 193
Shetland, 193, 196
Shin, loch, 64
Sinclair, George of Giese, 133
Sinclair, Janet, of Ulbster,, Lady
   Reay, 5-7
Sinclair, Robert of Giese, 6, 53, 133
Skeldoch, The Reverend John,
   104-6, 149, 193
Skelpick, 63
Skerray, 8, 45, 112, 121
Skye, 27-8, 30, 41
Sleat, 24, 72
Smoo, 39, 133, 135
Snorre Sturlason, 74
Soro Academy, 99
Stafford, Marquess of, 191
Stevenson, Robert Louis, 82
Stewart, General David, of Garth,
   202, 206
Stoer, 50, 120

Stornoway, 49, 132
Strathan Melness, 9
Strath Beg, 2, 85
Strath Halladale, 4, 6, 8, 27, 53-4, 60, 63, 82-3, 112, 133, 170, 188, 193-4
Strathmore, 2, 4, 7-9, 11, 19, 24-6, 42, 60-1, 77, 84-5, 94, 97, 110, 122, 125, 128-9, 142, 160, 171
Strathnaver, 3-4, 6, 16, 25, 30, 33, 39, 49, 59, 88, 94, 116, 122-3, 132-4, 155, 157, 170, 187-8, 191, 194-5, 197-8, 205
Strathy, 4, 8, 112, 171
Sutherland, 3, 22, 25-6, 33, 45, 49, 52, 64, 66-7, 69, 97, 104, 151, 192, 195-7, 199-200
Sutherland, Barbara, of Keoldale, 157
Sutherland, Christine, Lady Reay, 52, 97-101, 103, 115, 142, 144, 167, 180
Sutherland, Donald, catechist, 125
Sutherland, Captain James, 192, 200
Sutherland, earls of, 59-61, 64, 66, 68, 104, 170
Sutherland, Elizabeth, countess of, 189-91, 196, 200
Sutherland, the Geigean, 101-3, 137
Sutherland, John, (Iain Tapaidh), 41-2, 45, 118, 150
Sutherland, John, of Keoldale, 77, 81-2, 173
Sutherland, Kenneth, of Keoldale, 52-3, 77, 96, 140, 157-8, 168, 171-4, 176, 188
Sutherland, Kenneth, deserter, 99-101
Sutherland, William, earl of, 160-2, 188-90

Sutherland, William, emigrant, 194, Sutherland Fencibles, 160, 164, 170 172
Swordly, 7
Syre, 9, 105, 119

Tain, 66
Thomson, James, poet, 28, 30-1
Thomson, The Reverend John, 134, 149, 185-6, 206
Tongue, 4-8, 22, 24, 27, 33-4, 39-41, 43-5, 53, 60-4, 66-7, 69, 74-5, 77, 79, 96, 104-5, 107, 109-10, 120, 125, 132-3, 148, 150, 152, 160-1, 168-9, 172, 175, 179, 192, 195
Torrisdale, 8, 169
Torwood, 64
Thurso, 11-12, 33, 39-40, 44, 68, 132, 141, 149, 192
Twickenham, 31-2

Uist, south, 27
Union, treaty of, 2
Uriah, 27, 41
Urradale, 24

Vikings, 3, 24
Virginia, 156

West Moine, 7-8, 16, 32, 34, 36, 39, 61-2, 67, 70, 79-80, 97, 105, 129
Whiten head, 39-40, 133, 179
William II and III, 2, 4, 155-6
William, son of Patrick, 80
Williamsons, 15, 26
Worcester, 156
Wordsworth, William, 28

223